Modern and Postmodern Cutting Edge Films

Modern and Postmodern Cutting Edge Films

Edited by

Anthony D. Hughes
with Miranda J. Hughes

Cambridge Scholars Publishing

Modern and Postmodern Cutting Edge Films,
Edited by Anthony D. Hughes with Miranda J. Hughes

This book first published 2008 by

Cambridge Scholars Publishing

15 Angerton Gardens, Newcastle, NE5 2JA, UK

British Library Cataloguing in Publication Data
A catalogue record for this book is available from the British Library

ISBN (10): 1-84718-513-4, ISBN (13): 9781847185136

In memory of
Jocelyn R. Hughes
1934-1991

TABLE OF CONTENTS

LIST OF ILLUSTRATIONS

ACKNOWLEDGEMENTS

I wish to thank Dr. Michael Degnan, Dean & Director, The Center for Excellence in Teaching, Hilbert College, and Dr. Thea Harrington, Chairperson, English & Communication Arts Department, Hilbert College, for their ongoing support in the completion of this project. I also wish to thank the Hilbert College Faculty Development Committee for its funding assistance. Thanks also go Hilbert's IT Department and, in particular, Robert Pawlewski, for his excellent technical assistance and Josephine Sewastynwicz for her typing assistance. Many thanks also go to all my wonderful colleagues and contributors. It was truly a pleasure to work with each of them, and I am very proud of their highly professional, original, and scholarly work. I also wish to thank SONY Pictures, D.C. Comics, and Paramount Pictures for their generosity in providing still shots for this manuscript. Moreover, I would like to thank my dear sister, Dr. Miranda Hughes, whose assistance with the editing process was invaluable. Lastly, I wish to make an extra special thank you to Amanda Millar, my editor at Cambridge Scholars Publishing, for all her professional advice, patience, and support. Ms. Millar is the epitome of an Editor's Editor.

مـ

INTRODUCTION

ANTHONY D. HUGHES

Modern and Postmodern Cutting Edge Films closely examines a wide variety of major filmic texts that established permanent, iconic shifts in modern and postmodern US culture and filmic practices. These films and their visionary, trend-setting *auteurs* each introduced new manners of seeing that were imitated by later directors and absorbed by popular culture itself. The primary rationale for this collection is simple: it is new and different. No anthology explores the concept of the cutting edge film across such a wide variety of *genres* and with such a diversity of theoretical approaches and subject matter. All the contributors bring unique voices and multi-disciplinary perspectives to their respective chapters. This book will interest scholars from many disciplines, in particular, filmic, political, historical, feminist, and *genre* studies. Contributors have minimized theoretical terminology so lay readers can enjoy and understand the text. This text is user friendly and accessible to readers who possess familiarity with basic film analysis and theory. It can be used as a text in both graduate and upper-level undergraduate film classes. *Modern and Postmodern Cutting Edge Films* will be invaluable to instructors of film theory and history for many years to come. Indeed, we feel that this anthology is itself a cutting edge text of film scholarship.

Several essays in this collection examine the idea of fashion and clothing as expressive of not only character and *mise-en-scene* (that is, everything that goes into composing a scene in a film) but of ideology itself. For example, Lisa Nelson's essay, *Black Leather, and White Fantasy: or, the Semiotics of Racial Danger in 1950s America* (Stanley Kramer, 1953), discusses Marlon Brando's infamous black leather jacket. This jacket became so ubiquitous in mainstream Hollywood filmmaking and popular culture that iconic mutations of the prototype are still seen over half a century later in films such as the Wachowski brothers' *The Matrix* (1999). Although some essays such as Nelson's specifically examine a single iconic article of clothing, other essays define the notion of "fashionable" more broadly. For example, other fashion statements that films may "wear" include stylish, new visual "looks", such as the musical *genre*'s postmodern, makeover in Baz Luhrmann's *Moulin Rouge!*(2001) or the Sci-fi *genre*'s political makeover in Steven Spielberg's remake of *The War of the Worlds* (2005). Other discussions, such as Hughes's *Fashionable* Femmes Fatales*: Cutting the Edges of Customary Morality in Paul Verhoeven's Basic Instinct* (1992), deploy the notion of "the fashionable" (what's morally hot and what's not) to track the evolution of mythic figures such as the *femme fatale* from her early silent film incarnations to her postmodern rampages. As the *femme fatale's* character and clothing evolve (or perhaps, devolve), so do her powers to challenge and ultimately, subvert the customary morality. Conversely, as her doomed male lovers "devolve" from impeccably pressed military uniforms to ragged raincoats, so too do their classical their powers wane, hand in hand with their re-romanticized, anti-heroic positions within popular culture.

Several essays in this collection examine gender as a social construct— for which cutting edge films are both mirror and catalyst. Gender-benders foreshadow and short-circuit subterranean shifts in the representation of masculine and feminine subjectivities in mainstream culture. Barbara Tilley's *What Is Woman? Transsexual Love in Different for Girls*; Stephen Brauer's "*Men Is What We Are": Fight Club, Style, and the Authentic Masculine*, and Douglas Howard's '*Batman Begins: Insanity and the Cutting Edge of Heroism*' are three key essays that examine the representation of gender in postmodern cinema from a variety of fascinating perspectives. The endless breakdown and reconfiguration of gender models via the cutting edge film is one of the major threads traced throughout this collection.

This collection focuses primarily on films from The Modern and Postmodern Periods, (1950-1980 and 1980-present, respectively), but each chapter includes meticulous research and a thorough historical grounding, fluidly moving through major film periods when necessary. Essayists examine the myriad ways in which filmic fashion delineates character, theme, and heralds later film movements. In most cases, by definition, cutting edge films foreshadow reconfigurations of customary morality and future film styles and attitudes; however, this collection also examines films that cut too deeply, too soon, and are therefore, initially highly unfashionable and controversial. For example, although Verhoeven's *Basic Instinct* clearly shifted the *femme fatale* film from its Classical to its Postmodern stage, its graphic depiction of Lesbian love and the female body were controversial and vehemently protested against by Gay Rights groups and certain conservative U.S. groups when it first hit the theatres. Although all these essays examine the fashionable or unfashionable as a specific set of visual signifiers that ultimately establish new filmic looks and fashionable modes of seeing, other essays discuss specific film *genres* as cutting edge forms, which move, for example, the Sci-fi or Musical *genres* into their next evolutionary stages. Consequently, some essays examine specific films as groundbreaking works that set new standards for visual design, editing, computer generated imagery (CGI), and other special effects.

Lastly, contributors explore the phenomenological nature of the cutting edge film. What does it mean to be a first-time viewer of such films? Do cutting edge films always tend to shock, surprise, and challenge the customary morality? Do they always demand and create new "meaning/s" and manners of seeing? For example, D. W. Griffith and other silent film *auteurs'* experiments with *montage* editing has evolved in remarkable ways. We now live light-years from The Silent Period in arguably a post/post modern age in which rapid-fire montage is "the new cool" and has become the primary filmic fashion that mainstream Hollywood films must wear to be "hip" and maintain a suspension of disbelief. Clearly, an entire new generation of filmgoers only tolerate films that exhibit perhaps a minimum of fifty to one-hundred shots per minute (SPM). Such radical shifts in audience expectations and modes of seeing have profound effects on what one sees and expects from the worlds both inside and outside the local I-MAX theatre. Filmgoers today are "wired" very differently from those of even five years ago.

In light of these technological advances, this collection also considers the epistemic nature of film phenomena. It is inevitable that future generations will look back on films such as *The Matrix* (1999), with the same sense of cultural superiority (and perhaps visual boredom) that one might look back on John Travolta's disco clothes and jewelry in *Saturday Night Fever* (1977)—fashion statements that never evolved from fad to icon. Regardless, the fascinating question is what cultural epistemes create such profoundly powerful, historical subjectivities? How does the hip of today become the camp of tomorrow? In light of such questions, this collection explores the "deep structures" that lie beneath the phenomena of the cutting edge film. Although some of the films discussed may not be fashionable now or even twenty years from now, the underlying historical patterns that drive such changes will continue to be pertinent to future film scholars and applicable to all future waves of cutting edge films that Hollywood will create.

CHAPTER ONE

THE WILD ONE, BLACK LEATHER, AND WHITE FANTASY: OR, THE SEMIOTICS OF RACIAL DANGER IN 1950S AMERICA

LISA K. NELSON

Within the space of just a couple of years after the end of World *War* II, the image of the black leather jacket and motorcycle boots would be irrevocably associated with mayhem and violence, and the image of the black jacketed and dungareed thug would be established as a primary stereotype in the mid-twentieth century's collective consciousness. (Farren 38-9)

From *The Wild One,"* a movie few people saw based on a riot that never happened," an icon was born (Reynolds 72). The biker outlaw figure of Marlon Brando as "Johnny" dressed in black leather jacket, cap, and boots astride his motorcycle from the 1953 film is both the paradigmatic example of the visual representation of U.S. juvenile delinquency (always white, working-class, and male) from the early 1950s and a still-current icon of rebellion (figure 1).

This article offers an examination of the adaptation of black leather dress as a conflation of leather and race, a conflation that coincided with the rise of the civil rights movement, the battle over segregation, and was enabled by a silencing of that very conflation. It is the goal of this article to speak that silence and to examine the outlaw biker as an iconic embodiment within the specific historical and ideological contexts of post WWII United States and desegregation; the events and even the bikers themselves were probably less of an impetus for the birth of this figure than was the historical moment that called him into being. Second, by reinstating the figure in context, a focus on the semiotic significance of his donning of black leather becomes possible. And, finally, this project will examine how these semiotic valences of black leather wear continue in more recent U.S. cultural forms.

Figure 1.1 *The Wild One* film still

Historical Contexts

I am tempted to read our monsters allegorically, as the materialization of new anxieties.
—David Savran, "Haunted Stage" 2.

During these years of the "Red Scare," when the Soviets gained atomic technology and European colonies in Africa and Asia gained their independence as nations, global powers shifted and U.S. policy-makers configured these changes as conflict between the "free world" and communism. Especially at issue in this binaristic view of the world was taking sides: to which side does a nation show allegiance? This same configuration was used to structure the home front: Alger Hiss was tried for perjury and convicted; the Rosenbergs were arrested, tried, convicted, and executed for conspiracy to commit treason; and Hollywood's texts and its mythmakers were put on trial, having been subpoenaed by The House un-American Activities Committee [HUAC] on charges that they were communists or communist sympathizers. The United States was a culture terrified of its own potential for subversion, imagining it everywhere, and reacting with a tyrannical self-policing.

Fermenting in these years of imagined subversion, however, was also actual dissent, particularly racial unrest. It was the beginning of the civil rights movement and desegregation: unlike during WWI, U.S. blacks had refused to table race issues until after WWII. As a result, a new militancy had grown from within black communities (Sitkoff). The National Association for the Advancement of Colored People's [NAACP] membership increased tenfold during the war and publicized the systematic racism of the armed services. The war brought southern whites north and northern blacks south, both refusing conduct of the others' racial etiquette.[1] The result was an intensification of racial tensions throughout the war which "exploded in an epidemic of interracial violence" in 1943, resulting in race riots in Detroit (34 killed), Harlem, and various other cities (Sitkoff 671). In 1945, when WWII ended, 1,154,720 black U.S. servicemen and women returned home. In 1946, the Supreme Court banned segregation in interstate bus travel. In 1947, The Congress for Racial Equality [CORE] sent 23 black and white Freedom Riders through the south to test compliance with court orders. The year was also marked by widespread violence against blacks; particularly returning servicemen, for this black activism drew a vehement racist backlash. Although white students protested against integration at various city schools, segregationists recalled and played on the racist fantasy of the black rapist (an antebellum construct) to point out the ultimate peril of desegregation—miscegenation. In 1948, under pressure from the NAACP, Truman proposed anti-lynching legislation, but Congress refused to act on it. Truman also issued an Executive Order barring discrimination in the armed forces. The nation was a battleground, and race was the subject of battle. In 1954, racial tensions exploded with the Supreme Court's decision in Brown versus the Board of Education, which ended legal segregation.

Arising from this simmering contemporary stew was a culture of fear and violence. "In this era, a specter was haunting America [which] ... had traced ... fault lines of politics [that] seemed to be cracking open the American Landscape" (Whitfield 1-2). It was along these fault lines that the specter of the motorcycle outlaw rode into the U.S. imaginary because it is haunted by desegregation's imaginary monstrosity, the black rapist. The outlaw biker provided a nation's nightmares with a human form.

From Motorcyclist to Monster

Clearly, motorcycles and motorcyclists existed before the film, *The Wild One*. The motorcycle was invented at the turn of the century but was used primarily as a specialty sporting vehicle because its cost and bulk were prohibitive, manufacture was limited, and parts were generally tooled on an as-needed basis. Despite this, a small but avid culture of sport motorcyclists developed, mostly the rich and adventurous. All of this changed with the end of WWII. Technical advances improved reliability of motorcycles, lessened bulk, and substantially decreased the cost of ownership. These improvements, combined with an increased familiarity with motorcycles in the service, made them both a possibility and a choice for many young U.S. men after the war. Not only did the motorcycle offer a relatively inexpensive mode of transportation, but it provided mobility to a group of young men who, only a few years before, would have been confined to their city, if not their neighborhood.

Although sport organizations had been a part of motorcycling and racing culture since the 1920s, these organizations ballooned in the post-war climate. As membership grew, the median age and income level of the members dropped, and the function of the organizations changed. Although original sport organizations merely brought riders together at sporting events, these new organizations were more literally motorcycle clubs, social venues consisting of groups of young men who rode together, raced together, and socialized together both on and off their bikes.[2] These fraternities first formed in the mid-forties, primarily in coastal California industrial areas, its members mainly working-class white men in their twenties and early thirties, mostly returning veterans. The clubs were all chartered through The American Motorcycle Association [AMA], adopted bylaws espousing motorcycling as a family activity, and donned team uniforms of matching sweaters or jackets—attired like high-school lettermen. For the most part, the motorcyclist of the day, although thought to be a bit uncouth, was far from the folk villain he was soon to become.

The primary social activities of the clubs were rallies, races, and "runs," group road-trips into the countryside, and the favored day, the Fourth of July. It is from this date in 1947 that the story portrayed by the film *The Wild One* is derived—the infamous Hollister Riot. Since WWI the AMA had hosted Gypsy Tours, long rides to rally destinations. These tours had been suspended during WWII, but in 1947, as part of its yearly Fourth of July celebration, Hollister California was scheduled to host a tour and to stage races. Hollister was already a bike town by 1947, sporting 27 bars and 21 gas stations, although this fact is usually erased from narratives of the events.[3] The 1947 events brought roughly 4000 bikers to Hollister, among them several hundred "outlaws," the term used to designate bikers who belonged to clubs unaffiliated with the AMA.[4] Although the races at the track went according to schedule, and the track was filled to capacity, there was also a fair amount of action in town, from impromptu racing, to drinking and fighting. Some histories state that at Hollister only the outlaw bikers drank, raced on the town's main street, drove into bars, looted and brawled—though (or because) they were excluded from the formal racing events. However, other histories are less eager to attribute the behavior to contingents of good or bad bikers.[5] In any event, on Sunday, the third day, overwhelmed by the crowds, noise, and general nuisances, Hollister's six-man police force had had enough and called in reinforcements. The jail was full of drunken bikers sleeping it off, and the hospital was full of injured bikers—a normal occurrence at AMA events because the sport was dangerous. The California Highway Patrol arrived Sunday evening, herded the bikers together and, then, not knowing what else to do with them, set up an outdoor dance to keep them busy. Although the authorities had teargas, hoses, and guns at hand—race riot ready—the bikers simply danced as ordered and the night went forward without incident.

In the morning, the bikers dispersed. The weekend resulted in only 50 arrests, no serious crimes, and no fatalities.[6] However, the incident sparked media attention, was dubbed "The Hollister Riot," and was picked up by major news publications. That the Hollister incident should be represented as a "riot" is ridiculous because as Tom Reynolds comments, the number of violent race uprisings and labor strikes of the 1940s "made Hollister look like a prom dance" (54).

The most widely read account was in *Life* magazine, which carried a posed image and the following title and caption:

CYCLIST'S HOLIDAY: He and friends terrorize a town

On the Fourth of July weekend 4,000 members of a motorcycle club roared into Hollister, Calif. for a three-day convention. [....] Police arrested many for drunkenness and indecent exposure but could not restore order. Finally, after two days, the cyclists left with a brazen explanation. "We like to show off. It's just a lot of fun." But Hollister's police chief took a different view. Wailed he, "It's just one hell of a mess."

Ignoring the long tradition of motorcycle sport, or Hollister's position and economic boon as a motorcycle destination, the media instead represented the town as 'invaded' by an army of violent thugs who overwhelmed its six-man police force and destroyed order, property, and propriety. Not buying the post-war U.S. dream, these bad-mannered, roughcast veterans had formed their own societies that noisily ventured into small towns, disrupting any semblance of continuity and the domestic tranquility that the war was supposed to ensure. Although the media reports contained ridiculously exaggerated numbers in terms of damage, injuries, and arrests, their hyperbole worked well to codify the image, and to justify the terror the clubs were imagined to pose for 'decent' Americans. And, as a result, a new, uniquely U.S. monster was born – the outlaw biker.

From Monstrosity to Icon

A short story based loosely on the Hollister event caught the attention of young maverick producer, Stanley Kramer and lead to his version of the Hollister event, as represented in *The Wild One*.[7] Although few have seen the film and even many who have do not recall the narrative, *The Wild One* achieved not only a stable place within U.S. imaginary, not for the story it depicted, but for the image it spawned, a primary cutting edge icon of Americana, the black-leather jacket clad "Johnny" astride his Triumph Matchless, an icon of rebellion.

From the opening shot down the highway, bikers on both sides of the dividing lines, with engines roaring, the filmic trope of territories transgressed is mobilized.

Figure 1.2 *The Wild One* film still

The rebel's world is both errant and single-sex. Further, this invasionary force, Johnny and his Black Rebels also mobilize racial anxieties through multiple references to blackness that raise the specter of a racialized threat. The film's opening shot also foregrounds this resonance. Juxtaposed with the bucolic view of the countryside, the rumble of engines is heard from the distance. Slowly, the bikers become visible, emerging from the horizon. From the outset, the bikers are marked as excessive, dangerous, and transgressive, ignoring the highway's dividing line and, in a military-like formation, occupying both sides of the road. Although there is some variation in the bikers' dress, they all wear dark jeans and some kind of hat, and, without exception, they don identical black leather jackets, a uniform that both enforces the military association and marks the rebels through their non-normative group allegiance.

The key distinction of *The Wild One's* bikers is their dress—they all don black leather jackets as their uniform. Although the history of leather biker-wear is anything but straightforward, this costuming was a filmic invention. Original bike wear consisted of long oilcloth coats like the Australian cattleman's. After the war, as the bike became more sport oriented, these coats were replaced by boiled-wool and leather jackets like high-school letterman jackets for the AMA sanctioned clubs. Many bikers, however, both outlaw and AMA, had military surplus brown leather bomber-type jackets, and they began to wear these. Several men began designing jackets specifically for bikers, among them Ross Langlitz, who designed the jacket worn (and made famous) by Brando's Johnny. Although the general reasoning that leather offers a protective "second skin" dominates popular contemporary biker literature, this reasoning does not account for either the coloring of that leather or its inherent drawbacks. Ultimately, it is precisely the color of this uniform that constitutes the bikers as a decidedly dark invading force, and one that evokes the specter of the returning black servicemen and the anxiety they raised in white United States. So ubiquitous was black leather to the film's representation of the biker, one critic was lead to comment that the film "starred a 650cc Triumph, a black-leather jacket, and Marlon Brando in that order" (Sanger 1).[8]

Of course, leather wear had significance prior to *The Wild One* because wearing of black leather supported fascist and Nazi associations, associating the bikers with an abhorrent militarism.[9] This reading of the wearing of black leather is the standard one, linking it to foreign evils abhorrent to U.S. practices and values. All of the discussions of black leather that I found, including Hebdige's *Subculture: the Meaning of Style*, Theweli's *Male Fantasies*, and Farren's *History of the Black Leather Jacket* evoke the German military as the source of U.S. leather wear. Even Farren's history, which begins with film stills from *The Wild One* under the designation of "legendary leather," historicizes the garment as German in origination.

The garment, however, has uniquely U.S. semiotic valences as well. Historically, the early frontier man and the trapper dressed in leathers, and it has been tradition to take this dress as the mark of a more primitive nature. As early as 1782, in his *Letters from an American Farmer*, St. Jean de Crevecoeur explained this relationship between leather and primitivism as an effect of moral degeneration resulting from life in proximity to the woods which "produce[s] a strange sort of lawless profligacy...a mongrel breed; half civilized, half savage...degenerate...new made Indians...a set of lawless people" (617-619). This tradition has continued in both literature and popular culture with the use of leather in Cowboy and American Indian representation. From James Fenimore Cooper's *Leatherstockings* to the Western, the film *genre* so popular in the

1950s, the cowboy wore the hide of the cow as vest, chaps, and hat just as the Indian wore the loincloth of leather and fur. In these traditions, leather was linked to its source as animal skin—"hides"—and rendered animality to the wearer. Thus, these leathers of U.S. tradition were "skins" in two senses: they came from an animal as its skin; and they provided for the wearer a second "skin." Although this tradition of skins was more often than not softer suede-like than the highly polished leathers of the black rebels' machine-tooled jackets, this distinction itself can further strengthen the linking of leather to black skin. Whereas animal skins of the frontier ilk bore a softness and "fuzzy" quality that reminded one of the fur-covered animals that they came from, machined black leather was smooth and hairless, more sleek than soft. In this way, it more closely resembled human skin than animal hide.

Read within this U.S. context, the donning of leather is functionally the assumption of another's skin, and the donning of black leather is functionally the assumption of a black skin. As Dick Hebdige argues (about British Rasta style), through the donning of a garment—in this case a black leather jacket—"blackness is recuperated and made symbolically available ... [as] a sign of otherness" (42). And, in 1950s America, a culture fixated on mythologies of race at a moment of intense conflict over precisely those mythologies, the fact that the leather garment is black renders it overdetermined with racial signification. Thus, the motorcyclists, in cloaking themselves in black leather, enact a "semiotic guerilla warfare," one in which they appropriate an imagined blackness (Hebdige 105). This link between leather and race is further emphasized in *The Wild One* by the bike club's name, the Black Rebels Motorcycle Club. A purely fictional construction, Kramer's Black Rebel rebellion was at least in part marked as a racial one, for the logic of *The Wild One relies* heavily on racial imagery and mythology, a reliance through which black leather stands in as a proxy for black skin. Using this proxy (which Randall Kennedy defines in *Race, Crime, and the Law* as "a trait ... which is (or is believed to be) correlated with some other trait" [137]), the logic of the film and the cultural fictions of the day use black leather as a semiotic referent to blackness. As Kennedy argues, blackness itself is a proxy for criminality and danger, particularly a sexualized danger of violence in this rendering.

Put another way, in *The Wild One* the bikers' uniform of black leather functions as a kind of black-face or group minstrelsy, lending to these white men the semiotic valences of black masculinity. Minstrelsy is not simply about dressing up like the other, but performing imagined otherness itself. As Eric Lott argues in "White like Me: Racial Cross-Dressing and the Construction of American Whiteness," "to put on the cultural forms of 'blackness' was to engage in a complex affair of manly mimicry" (479). This racial "mimicry" structures the film's representation of the bikers. For instance, the bar scenes in which the bikers repeatedly use a language imagined to be "black." In Johnny's first conversation with Kathie, for example, when she asks whether the bikers are going to a picnic, Johnny replies: "A picnic, man! You're too square. You just go...the idea is to have a ball. Now, if you stay cool, you gotta wail."[11]

With the constant evocations of "jive" and "daddy-o," the loud music, rowdy drinking and smoke-filled bar, it is clear that the language of the bikers is meant to reference the languages of jazz and bebop. Here the Black Rebels' performance is meant to demonstrate that they have, as Lott says of minstrelsy, "become black, inherit[ed] the cool, virility, humility, and abandon that made up white ideologies of black manhood" (479). Exaggerated in the bar scenes is both the outsider status of the bikers and their urban origin: they are clearly meant to come from the city at a time when racial unrest in U.S. cities was bursting into riots and when U.S. suburbs were being constituted as white middle-class havens. These "blacks" have ignored segregation's logic and are roaming the placid countryside of the United States.

Most indicative of segregation's anxiety and logic, however, is the film's reliance on the myth of the black rapist and the specter of lynching to represent the outlaws' blackness. For ultimately, it is the bodies of white women who, even more than town boundaries, the rebels threaten to violate. The lynching script typically follows a set narrative structure: a black man is accused of raping a white woman and is arrested, but the horrific nature of the crime has so scandalized the community that its good citizens cannot contain themselves. Chaos erupts as they, now a wild mob, seize the rapist from proper authorities and mete out their own justice, beating, mutilating, and ultimately killing the "villain."

In *The Wild One,* the action is carried out precisely along these lines in adherence to the mythology of the black male rapist. Near the end of the rising action, trouble arises when a conflict between the bikers and a group of vigilante citizens escalates. A fight breaks out; and the biker is arrested; however, the citizens are not held accountable. As dark falls in Carbondale—a carbon copy of white America?—tensions mount and the bikers carouse on the streets.   In the meantime, Kathie—the town sweetheart, sheriff's daughter, and respectably dressed middle-class good girl—is sent off to find her father. On the way she is spotted and pursued by the rebels.   Although the threat of rape by these "black rebels" is depicted in the grainy, dark sequence where the rebels chase Kathie into a dead-end alley and circle her ever more tightly, the sequence is also heavily indebted to the filmic *genre* of the Western so popular in the 1950s with its depiction of the Indian savage on horseback, circling and capturing the white woman away from her protectors.

Figure 1.3 *The Wild One* film still

In *The Wild One,* this sequence comes complete with the Western's evocative "whooping" soundtrack.

Shot in the shadows, this scene shows black figures pursuing, circling, and closing in on Kathie.   The threat to her is obvious, if unstated. Although Johnny rides up and "saves" Kathie from his pals, the specter of his own potential for sexual danger looms.[12] But ultimately it is he who rejects Kathie's advances, causing her to flee from embarrassment. Kathie's flight from Johnny is seen by one of the town men and is interpreted as her escape *after* some kind of sexual assault. It is here that the lynching script is put into full effect. A mob nabs Johnny and beats him for his supposed sexual offense against Kathie. Johnny breaks loose and is pursued by a mob growing with frightening speed. He makes it back to his motorcycle and tries to leave town, but the mob pursue him, knock him from his bike, and are about to exact their own justice when the 'militia' arrives and pulls him from the crowd's grip. Thus, Johnny barely avoids being "lynched" for the assumed rape of Kathie, and, as in lynchings historically, the supposed sexual assault was nothing more than an excuse to do violence to the one accused.

Sexual violence was very much at issue in the film's reception. Banned in Britain for nearly 20 years, the film received much criticism at home for its perceived violent content. But, as Farren argues, "what seems most likely to have disturbed critics was that the violence went hand in hand with the *threatening sexuality* of the badass, leatherclad bikers" (italics mine, 39). Although Farren never suggests the source of this threat, the film itself, as I have been arguing, creates this threat by representing the bikers, through a racist mythology wherein blackness signals sexual danger, and this blackness is semiotically embedded in the black leather jacket, which had become "the symbol of the hood, the greaser, slightly mad, smirking one who destroyed and raped like a wheeled Atilla the Hun (Sangier 4).

Iconic Mimicry

This figure of the white man cloaked in black leather mobilized cultural anxieties, but he also drew adoration, becoming at once an object of desire as well as emulation. Herein lies the problem: the figure spawned mimicry, and the act of copying the rebel became a vehicle for the dissemination of this racist minstrel imagery at the same time that his carbon-copy mimicry served to detach the performance from its own social and historical contexts. As Patricia Bosworth so aptly puts it, "the film's ultimate impact" was the sale of "thousands of T-shirts, black leather jackets, and blue jeans," the new "outfit" that had become "symbols of rebellion" (100).[13]

Although this rebellion was imagined to be at once violent, sexual, animalistic, and militaristic, it was not bestowed with any actual content. Thus, although a rebel had been born, his rebellion was less of a program for change than it was a resistance to the status quo. Best articulated by

Robert Lindner in *Prescription for Rebellion*, this was "a rebel without a cause," who eschews the imperative to "adjust" leveled at him by every turn and through every social and familial institution, choosing instead "rebellion, as a pattern and way of life" (25). In Johnny, *The Wild One* offered the epitome of this type of rebel, immortalized in the famous exchange:

> *Girl in bar:*   "Whatcha rebellin' against Johnny?"
> *Johnny:*   "Whatcha got?"

In point of fact, the film had originally contained language that attributed the Black Rebels' rebellion to class discontent. The censors, however, determined that this violated censorship laws and required that all references to class be removed from the film. All that's left is Johnny's vague line that "it just builds up all week, then on the weekend you gotta wail." Thus, much like the highjacked trophy so contentiously prized in the film, the rebel himself appears as "beautiful object signifying absolutely nothing," rendered mute rather than choosing stoicism.

Although the rebellion offered no program, or maybe precisely because it offered no program, the stance of the rebel was immediately adopted by young men coast to coast, and the leather jacket provided the fledgling juvenile delinquent with a uniform. There's "no need to actually be rebellious," as Suzanne McDonald-Walker points out, because the leather jacket is "sufficient for the appearance of rebellion" (24). In the cultural imagination, the garment itself was bestowed with a transformative power: carrying "unacceptably strong overtones of violence, criminality and, in some quarters, even homosexuality" (Farren 10). The donning of the black leather jacket transferred these overtones to the wearer. Writing about the purchase of his first black leather jacket, Mick Farren remembers that donning the jacket "was something of a ceremony" of transformation:

> I immediately felt different. The reflection that glanced back at me from the shop windows and the occasional mirror showed a whole new shape. Boy, at least in his own imagination, had been turned into Man. The whole top half of my body was heavier and more capable while my legs were free, in their tight jeans, to play any games that they could think up. I swaggered, I scowled. The jacket molded to my moves. The highlights in its finish seemed to accentuate those moves and I fondly believed that I was bad, maybe even menacing. (Farren 10)

The jacket alone was enough to make people nervous, a power attributed to the man who wore it.

Although Farren's history of the black leather jacket is in many ways outstanding, he makes two startling omissions: he never explores any precedents in frontier, cowboy, or Indian wear, and he never makes a connection between leather and race, even though he discusses black leather explicitly as "a second skin" (66).[15] Admitting that "it isn't just the visual on its own that gives black leather its impact," Farren dehistoricizes the leather jacket's power, likening it to an "active talisman" or a "totem" of "modern magic" which bestows on its wearer those very significations it is believed to carry (66, 18).[16] Thus, Farren's argument is indicative of the more general cultural trend that uses black leather without consciousness of the racial resonances it carries.

What does it mean that white masculinity, simply by cloaking itself in black leather, accrues the cultural capital of the rebel without any of the costs of rebellion?[17] If the icon of white masculine rebellion and delinquency (and the fetishized image of homoeroticism) is actually a figure of racial cross-dressing, then (while the rebellion might not have a content and the rebel might not have a cause) the fear this rebel inspires and the danger he signifies do not arise from the costume of his rebellion but in the anxieties that his costuming provokes. It is because of the ability of the figure to draw on his culture's racist imaginary, to mobilize its racist mythologies, to draw on familiar tropes of black masculinity, and to embody those dangerous tropes, that he gained both his ultimate desirability and his fantastic danger.

Ultimately, the white man in black leather, as he arose in the U.S. 1950s, was a figure whose "threat" traded on white anxieties about the general danger of race mixing in the context of desegregation (the specific danger of an imagined black male sexuality); the icon of the white man in black leather arose as a semiotic progeny of the era's imaginary. Thus, once we examine the semiotics of this icon, we need to concede the U.S.'s racial history, or the history of U.S. racism in the making of our beloved icon and our romance with black leather.

Today's Johnnies

Black leather wear continues to rely on a racialized semiotic, and furthermore, those semiotics remain unspoken and unexamined. One context in which the black leather clad white man has been consistently imagined, from the 1950s to today, is gay representation, particularly as the outlaw biker. I choose this context, not because gay use of the figure is more problematic than in other contexts, but because there has been much self-examination of sexuality within this sub-culture and because of the centrality of these images within the subculture itself.[18] In this subcultural space he has been appropriated, evoked, imagined, and desired since his original appearance on the cultural horizon. From Tom of Finland's illustrations of biker boys, to the formation of the Satyrs—the first gay motorcycle club in Los Angeles in 1954, to Kenneth Anger's fetishistic rendering of biker masculinity in *Scorpio Rising* (1963), to today's gay pride celebrations, the figure of the leather clad biker has been a staple icon in gay culture.[19] In large part, the biker's place in gay iconography was due to the work of artist Tom of Finland, who simultaneously represented the biker's coveted status in the burgeoning gay lexicon and helped to reify that status, the growth in the popularity of Finland's work paralleling the growth of the gay sub-culture. The biker was a staple in an iconography of hypermasculine homoerotics.[20] Finland's images provided an inversion of the stereotype of gay effeminacy, producing what Micha Ramakers called "a (pretty butch), fairy-tale gay universe in which masculinity was held up as the highest idea," and that ideal was gay (xi). Bikers were among Finland's earliest works from 1947 (figure 4), then a solid feature of his work by 1954 (figures 5 and 6), (and a continued favorite until his death in 1991).

Figure 4, dating from the Hollister incident, reflects the pre-*Wild One* biker, a militaristic biker somewhat evocative of a state trooper. The later biker drawings (figures 5 and 6) date from the months after the release of *The Wild One,* and the biker "style" now clearly reflects a Brandoesque aesthetic with tight T-shirts, cuffed jeans, and black motorcycle boots.

Whereas the earlier image paired the macho biker figure with the more stereotypically effeminate gay men, the later images have recast the appeal of bikers in a strictly butch/butch erotic, thus affirming both the virility of gay men and the desirability of that virility.[21]

Tom of Finland was not alone in his choice of the biker as subject matter for gay imagery. The biker was a coveted character in the work of other artists and photographers in the growing gay press. According to F. Valentine Hooven's history of U.S. Muscle Magazines, *Beefcake,* "[e]asily the most popular role with both the photographers and the models was that of the leather-clad and booted biker and the favorite prop was the motorcycle, which has been called 'the ultimate piece of masculine jewelry'" (141). Images of bikers were standard fare in these proto-gay-porn publications.

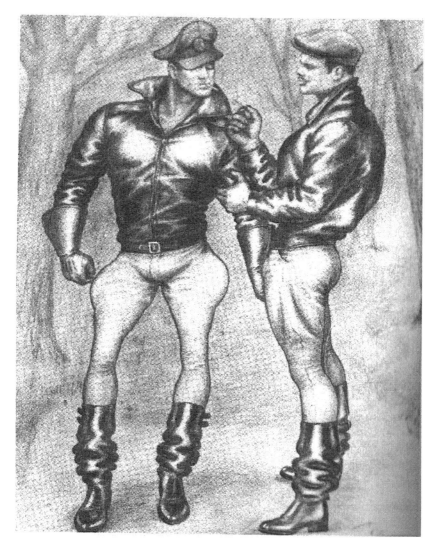

Figure 1.4 Tom of Finland, untitled, 1954

Thus the biker was a central figure in Finland's work and in gay cultural erotics as well. Ramakers attributes the biker's popularity in gay culture with his ability (when rendered gay through an image like Finland's) to couple gayness with this ur-symbol of "potency and masculinity" (134). Describing the biker "[d]ecked out in black leather and jeans, a tight white T-shirt covering his curvaceous chest, adorned with metal studs and insignia, heavy boots on his feet, he roams the wide landscape, free, unattached, not hindered by social regulations," Ramakers participates in the romance rather than critiquing it (134). The allure of the biker is taken to arise simply from his hyper-masculinity without any exploration into how that masculinity comes about.

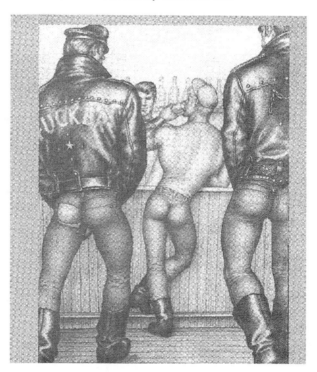

Figure 1.5 Tom of Finland, untitled, 1965

Diverging little from the bikers of *The Wild One,* Tom of Finland's fantastic men are encoded through a dual semiotic of black leather and homosexual desire. Yet discussions of Finland's drawings fail to locate them in either the historical frame of "actual" bikers or in any discussion of the racial valences of black leather wear.[22] When Ramakers does focus on the issue of race in Finland's work, his topic is more specifically Finland's use of black models.[23] Crediting Isaac Julian with the only other discussion of race in Finland's work, Ramakers follows Julian's lead, locating a racial dimension to Finland's work only with the introduction of black figures (1989). Seeing Finland's use of black men as participating in "a tradition of images that reduces black men to their sexuality," a tradition that "strongly emphasizes the size of black men's genitals and a connected 'insatiable, bestial sexuality,'" Ramakers concludes that "Tom's choice, conscious or unconscious, may then point toward a motivation in which precisely black men were chosen because the stereotypical associations that equate black men as a *pars pro toto* with a phallic and animal 'black sexuality' are so self-evident" (91-92). Thus, locating the erotic value of blackness only in the use of black models, Ramakers line of reasoning erases the dominant mode through which blackness participates in Finland's work—the donning of black leather. In fact, it is not simply the biker who wears black leather in this *genre*, but the leather boy and the leather man (a dominant/submissive or top/bottom pairing); moreover, this leather man is ascribed the mythical sexual prowess generally attributed the black man in U.S. popular culture—"a leather-clad [sexual] Superman" (Figure 7) (Ramakers 143).

That the sexual transgressivness of this figure is marked by his wearing of black leather does not register as a racial issue even when U.S. mythologies of race are seen to underwrite representations of blackness. Tellingly, the artist himself articulates some of the unstated link. According to Ramakers, "Tom absolutely loved (black) leather and spoke of it in strongly sensational terms: 'There's something alive in leather. It's the skin of an animal, and there's a sense in the touch, the feel, the smell that is the opposite of plastics and rubber, which are too mechanistic.[24] Black *is the color of masculinity,* of strength, and of sin. That's something we learned from the past; we didn't start it'" (Italics mine 139). Clearly, for Finland the value of leather lies in its blackness, and that is indistinguishable from its sensual and visual effects. The values that Finland ascribes to black leather—"animality and masculinity"—are the identical values ascribed to black men and attributed to the problematic inclusion of black models in his *oeuvre* (Ramakers 140). But because

Figure 1.6 Tom of Finland, untitled, 1982

critics get sidetracked focusing their discussion of race only in relation to black bodies, they fail to acknowledge how the use of black leather performs a racialized erotics by proxy. Through the wearing of black leather, the cultural values of animality and masculinity are appropriated by the gay man for his own subjectivity in a mode of self-fashioning that at once draws on all the semiotic resonances of black masculinity and makes them the property of white gay masculinity. And in a culture arguably as homophobic as it is racist, black leather provided a gay armor, a shield that both protected him and frightened those who would harass him.

The donning of black leather, straight and gay, in the 50s and today demand an interrogation, or at least a consciousness of the citational chain from which black leather wear emerged and an acknowledgement of how the eroticization of black leather participates in an eroticization of race.[25] This acknowledgement is ever more imperative in this day of commodity identity, the mass marketing of black leather wear to the SM, Goth, Punk, Rock, and Metal communities, the cookie-cutter Harley riding new biker (executive by day), to every imaginable demographic, even leather jacket baby wear. In all these forms, black leather's semiotic valences linger, still evoking racial anxieties 50 years after Brown versus The Board of Education, 50 years after Brando, donning his now-emblematic black leather jacket, rode into the U.S. consciousness. These resonances are dangerous particularly because of the silencing of their sources, a silencing that leads to such outrages as the group of Merrill Lynch executives who bike together—and have officially named themselves the "Lynch Mob"— then ride about the country in their black leather; the violence they suggest is particularly racist. For too long black leather has provided racist fantasy with both a costume and a cloak of invisibility.

Works Cited

Anger, Kenneth, dir. *Scorpio Rising.* Puck Productions, 1963.
Benedek, Laslo, dir. *The Wild One (1953).* Columbia Pictures, 1953.
Boaworth, Patricia. *Marlon Brando.* New York: Vintage, 2001.
Farren Mick, The *Black Leather Jacket.* New York: Abbeville, 1985.
Fubglsang, Fuglsang. *Motorcycle Menace: Media Genres and the Construction of a Deviant Culture* (1997 Dissertation) 2004. 26 Sept. 2001. <http://webs.morningside.edu/masscomm/DrRoss/ Research.html>.
Gossvogal, David I, Vishnu in Hollywood: The Changing Image of the American Male. Lanham: Scarecrow, 2000.

Gutkind, Lee. *Bike Fever*. Chicago: Follet, 1973.

Harris, Maz. *Bikers: Birth of a Modern-Day Outlaw*. Boston: Faber, 1985.

Hebdige, Dick, *Subculture: The Meaning of Style*. New York: Routledge, 1979.

Hooven, III F. Valentine. *Beefcake: The Muscle Magazines of America, 1950-1970*. Cologne: Benedikt Taschen Verlag, 1995.

Kennedy, Randall. *Interracial Intimacies: Sex, Marriage, Identity, and Adoption*. New York: Pantheon, 2003.

Linger, Robert. P*rescription for Rebellion*. Westport: Greenwood: 1952.

Lott, Erict. "White Like Me: Racial Cross-Dressing and the Construction of American Whiteness." *Cultures of United States Imperialism*. Eds. Amy Kaplan and Donald E. Pease. Durham: Duke UP, 1993: 474-495.

McCann, Graham. *Rebel Males*. New Brunswick: Rutgers UP, 1993.

Macdonald-walker, Susan. *Bikers: Culture, Politics, and Power*. New York: NYU P, 2000.

Ramakers, Micha. *Dirty Pictures: Tom of Finland, Masculinity, and Homosexuality*. New York: St. Martins P, 2000.

Renyolds, Tom. W*ild Ride: How Outlaw Motorcycle Myth Conquered America*. New York: TV Books, 2000.

Ronny, Frank. "Cyclists' Raid." *Harpers,* July 21, 1947, 31.

Sabger, Thierry. *Bike! Motorcycles and the People Who Ride Them*. New York: Harper, 1974.

David, Savan. "The Haunted Stage," from *The Playwright's Voice*. Ed. David Savran. New York: Theatre Communications Group, 1999. xiii-1.

Sirkoff, Harvard "Racial Militancy and Interracial Violence in the Second World War." *The Journal of American History* 58.3 (December 1971), 661-681.

Thwwelileit. Klaus. Male Fantasies Volume 1: Women, Floods, Bodies, History. Minneapolis: Minnesota UP, 1987.

Thompson, Mark, ed. "Introduction." *Leatherfolk: Radical Sex, People, Politics, and Practice*. Boston: Alyson, 1991.

Whitfeld, Stephen J. *The Culture of the Cold War*. Baltimore: Johns Hopkins UP, 1991.

Notes

[1] Harvard Sitkoff's essay "Racial Militancy and Interracial Violence in the Second World War" offers a nuanced account of this trend with detailed attention to how the treatment of blacks in the military not only mirrored treatment of blacks in society at large but also gave rise to a new sense of black militancy, which was then directed against social treatment. Although Sitkoff's argument goes on to trace how this militancy ultimately sells out to a liberal politics of gradualism espoused by inter-racialism, of interest here is the currency with which the figure of the black soldier would have evoked anxieties expressed through racial aggression.

[2] The history presented here is a standard one, culled from a variety of sources, many of which are more mythological glorifications of outlaw origin narratives. I found the most straightforward accounts in Ross Fuglsang, Tom Reynolds, Maz Harris, Lee Gutkind, and Thierry Sanger.

[3] Reynold's history is particularly nuanced in accounting for Hollister's complicity in the "riot."

[4] Because of the AMA's goal of representing motorcycling as a family venue, granting of affiliation was a means of controlling member behavior. A group's name and members had to be approved and the group had to have been granted a charter in order to participate in sponsored activities. Groups such as the Boozefighters and the Pissed off Bastards of Berdo (POBOB) were denied a charter, yet many of their members also belonged to affiliated clubs in order to participate in AMA events. Reynolds' history speaks to this point.

[5] Unsurprisingly, the AMA maintains that it was an instance of "a few bad apples." See Reynolds.

[6] Of all the arrests, the most serious charge – and the only one to result in jail-time beyond the weekend itself – was indecent exposure, a charge leveled for public urination and carrying jail time of 90 days. See Reynolds and Fuglsang.

[7] This story Kramer read was called "Cyclists' Raid," written by Frank Rooney, and published in the July 21st 1947 edition of Harper's.

[8] The Beetles who are the other motorcycle club in the film, unlike the Black Rebels, were dressed in an assortment of costumes without any particular commonality. Interestingly, the Beetles' dress was actually much more representative of motorcycle culture of the day and would be the style emulated by the "real" outlaws.

[9] Ironically supporting this claim, the only other representation of a motorcycle in the July 21, 1947 issue of Life discussed earlier is part of a photo from "Eva Braun's Album," a story of her girlhood and romance with Hitler. The photo shows Eva and two friends astride a motorcycle while the caption describes "her gay life with top Nazis" (53).

[10] One critic (Grossvogel) claims that BRMC stands for "Blind Rebels Motorcycle Club," a misreading emblematic of the systematic erasure of blackness in readings of the text.

[11] Although Bosworth emphasizes Brando's improvisation in the film, drawn on his conversations with "real bikers" in Hollister before filming, she also correctly

attributes this speak to a lingo of uptown Harlem chic familiar to Brando. Less enamored of Brando than Bosworth, Reynolds defines Brando's ad-libbing in the bar scenes as "white bohemian quasi jazz-speak" of the ilk only found in movies (69-70).

[12] Beyond the film itself, Johnny as potential rapist is supported within the viewer's mind by his stand-out performance in Elia Kazan's 1951 film of Tennessee Williams' *A Streetcar Named Desire* (1951), a role in which he portrays both a racially marked character and a rapist. Further, as McGee and Robertson point out, ads for *The Wild One* drew on the connections between the films, claiming "That 'Streetcar' man has a New Desire" (27).

[13] Ironically, this was not the first time Brando's character caused a fashion revolution, for as Stanley Kowalski in *A Streetcar Named Desire* Brando had made "the torn t-shirt a symbol of virility" (Cohan 244). Bosworth goes into wonderful detail here, discussing Brando's personal style, how the tight-fitting jeans were tailored, and arguing how Stanley's ripped t-shirt and jeans "became a part of Brando iconography, the new symbol of American maleness, and the decade's biggest fashion symbol" (49).

[14] McCann offers an interesting discussion of this censorship in relation to the film.

[15] Farren reads leather as a dead skin whose wearing provides "a form of protection [through which] ... living, vulnerable flesh is covered by an invulnerable dead hide" (66).

[16] This is much the same type of talisman that Norman Mailer became infamous for valuing, that he fetishized in his essay, "The White Negro: Superficial Reflections on the Hipster" and in his novel, *An American Dream,* and that he has consistently been taken to task for over the years.

[17] It would not be until this figure was appropriated by such groups as the Black Panthers or Dykes on Bikes that an expressly political rebellion was its goal.

[18] I want to stress that I focus on this gay imagery, not to single out gay usage of black leather, but because of my engagement with this imagery and this subculture. They are not "worse" than other appropriations; they are, in fact, aesthetically (and I could imagine an argument for ethically) superior.

[19] See Mark Thompson for a discussion of the Satyrs (xv).

[20] The iconography first developed in the bodybuilding magazines that rose to popularity in the '50s and eventually gave way to the gay pornography industry. See Hooven.

[21] According to Ramakers, this rebuttal to the correlation between homosexuality and femininity was Finland's aim: "he wanted to demonstrate that, first of all, gay men were men, virile men. His entire body of work was intended as a militant affirmation of gay men's masculinity and virility" (81).

[22] Those who discuss "actual" bikers are invested in maintaining their heterosexuality to the extent that they ignore these biker representations arising from gay contexts. And those who see these images as "gay" (like Hooven or Ramakes) happily elide the source of the figure through a (hopefully) unproblematic situating of the figure as "fantasy" rather than "real".

[23] Ramakers takes on the role of apologist, repeating Finland's claim that he was precluded from drawing black men until after 1986 because "they didn't sell." (84-85).

[24] As Finland claims, it may be an Animal's skin, literally a cow, but its erotic investment is not an effect of its bovine origin, but its reference to human skin, smooth, hairless, and black.

[25] My current project is just this, an examination into straight or mainstream appropriation of leather wear.

CHAPTER TWO

WALDEN IN THE SUBURBS: THOREAU, ROCK HUDSON, AND NATURAL STYLE IN DOUGLAS SIRK'S *ALL THAT HEAVEN ALLOWS*

DONNA CAMPBELL

In *The Bell Jar,* Sylvia Plath's autobiographical novel of the 1950s, her heroine Esther Greenwood announces at one point "I hate Technicolor" (43) because of its "lurid costumes" and the way in which characters tend "to stand around like a clotheshorse with a lot of very green trees or very yellow wheat or very blue ocean rolling away for miles and miles in every direction" (43). Esther's comment is important because it signals her understanding of the essential disconnection between Hollywood's images of a placid, prosperous 1950s and the reality of suicidal despair that she and others with artistic temperaments confronted in a culture determined to deny such feelings. In the hands of a great director like Douglas Sirk (1900-1987), however, the seeming tension between a glossy Technicolor surface and the despair-laden depths beneath become in themselves the subject of the film, an instance of meaning conveyed through the seeming disjuncture of film style and substance. In none of Sirk's films is this method of expression more evident than in a group of domestic dramas he made at Universal Studios in the 1950s: *Magnificent Obsession* (1954), *All That Heaven Allows* (1955), *Written on the Wind* (1956), and *Imitation of Life* (1959). In their solemn blend of extravagant, near-kitsch style with the themes of classic drama and melodrama, each offers a window into Sirk's at once admiring and ironic take on U. S. culture. Of this group, *All That Heaven Allows* stands alone as the most celebratory, and the most critical, of Sirk's visions of the United States, because it echoes the work of Thoreau in its characters, themes, settings, and visual style. In choosing Thoreau's philosophy as his model, and in casting a Thoreau figure as his hero, Sirk posits a redemptive, if flawed, prescription for rescuing one woman in the suburbs, and by extension others in a similar situation, from the arid artificiality of 1950's culture.

All That Heaven Allows is the story of Cary Scott (Jane Wyman), a well-to-do fortyish widow who is not yet ready to retreat to the somnolent comfort of the television set, despite the insistence of her friends that it is the best refuge for lonely women. As the film opens, Cary's best friend, Sara (Agnes Moorehead), stops by her white Colonial-style house to return Cary's dishes and say that she cannot stay for lunch. As Rainer Werner Fassbinder describes the scene in his influential "Six Films by Douglas Sirk", there is "A traveling shot past the two of them, and in the background stands Rock Hudson, as an extra would stand there in a Hollywood film. And because the friend can't stay for a cup of coffee with Jane, Jane has coffee with the extra" (Fassbinder 97). Rock Hudson, "the extra," plays Ron Kirby, the nurseryman who cares for Cary's trees. Unlike Cary, who is at a loss for occupation because her children are grown and she is "not a clubwoman" like Sara, he is passionate about his calling. When she asks about the trees at her house, he tells Cary that she has a rare *Koelreuteria* or Goldenrain tree, which according to legend only thrives in a house where there is love. He clips off a branch and gives it to her, the first of a series of natural, meaningful gifts that contrast with the sterile friendship, as signified by the empty dishes, that others offer her. The film develops through a series of such contrasts: in the very next scene, Cary looks at the golden branch, glowing with Technicolor radiance on her dressing table, before turning into the darkness to greet her grown children Ned (William Reynolds) and Kay (Gloria Talbot). Both seem quite happy to see Cary remaining in this darkness, entombed in her role as widow and mother. Kay tells her that according to Freud "sex after a certain age becomes incongruous."[1] Following his sister's lead, Ned voices his approval that his mother's date for a cocktail party at the country club is the ancient and sexless Harvey, who tells Cary that at her age, "companionship" is more important than romance.

The antinomies continue as Cary is pulled between the vitality, sexuality, and genuine feeling that Ron represents and the artificial, death-in-life atmosphere of the upper middle-class represented by Harvey. Sirk renders these interior conflicts visually through repeated scenes of Cary driving between the symbolic settings that represent the different worlds. At the Stoningham Country Club, Cary confronts the vicious world of catty gossips like Mona Plash (Jacqueline De Wit), who insults Cary for wearing a red dress, and predatory married men like Howard Hoffer (Donald Curtis), who sexually assaults and propositions her. By contrast, visits to Ron's world show Cary the vibrant life that she has been missing. As she travels to the old mill and tree nursery where Ron lives and to the tree farm of his friends Mick and Alida Anderson, who dwell in unpretentious simplicity, Cary falls in love with Ron's way of life as she falls in love with him. During a visit to the Andersons' home, Cary finds a book that Alida tells her is the key to happiness and to understanding Ron's inner peace: Henry David Thoreau's *Walden*. The scene is a turning point in the film, for Cary only then awakens to the possibilities of a new way of life, one not bounded by the country club and its rigid protocols of behavior. Strengthened by her love for Ron and his Thoreauvian ways, Cary bravely defies the gossip of the country club set and agrees to marry him. She shrugs off Sara's arguments about Ron's lower social class, his lack of wealth, and the age difference between them, but she cannot easily shrug off the objections of her monstrously selfish children. As Jon Halliday notes, in Sirk's films children "are to be seen not as the *new* generation, but as the imitators of the old, the perpetuators of tradition and repression" ("All That Heaven Allows" 61). Sacrificing her own happiness for their demands, she breaks off her engagement to Ron only to see them leave home and ignore her, leaving her with nothing but a television set for company.

In giving up Ron and seeming to settle for the television set, Cary has been defeated by her children, because they have consigned her to a simulacrum of life rather than the real life she could have led with Ron. But if her mind has acceded to their demands, her heart and body have not: repressing her feelings has given Cary migraine headaches. Consulting her friend and doctor, Dan Hennessy (Hayden Rourke), Cary learns that she is punishing herself for her pointless self-sacrifice and lack of love. As Fassbinder puts it more bluntly, "Jane goes back to Rock because she has headaches, which is what happens to us all if we don't fuck once in a while" (97). A chance meeting with Alida convinces Cary that Ron is still free and waiting for her, and she happily drives out to the mill once more. Because this is a melodrama, however, more suffering and expiation must ensue before the lovers can be reunited. In a series of coincidences that echo and reverse Cary's previous trips to the mill, this time Ron is out hunting instead of waiting to welcome her. Having second thoughts, she turns her car around and drives away, unaware that Ron, in hailing her from the snowy top of a cliff, has fallen into a snow bank and sustained a concussion. Informed of his accident by Alida, Cary travels to the mill for the last time, this time to watch over him as he recovers and to reassure him that she has "come home" at last. The surface level of the ending suggests that the two lovers leave behind the artificial and lifeless world of the suburban town, aptly named Stoningham, for the forces of life that Ron represents, yet as Fassbinder remarks, Cary may "miss the style of life she is used to and which has become her own. That's why the happy ending is not one" (97).

As even this brief summary of the plot suggests, *All That Heaven Allows* operates on multiple levels, complying with yet undercutting the principles of melodrama as it both delivers and withholds the expected happy ending. Stylistically and visually, it demonstrates Sirk's mastery of the idiom of melodrama and his use of the melodramatic "woman's weepie" formula for complex purposes. As he discussed in *Sirk on Sirk*, a series of interviews with Jon Halliday, Sirk believed that melodrama had lost the "melos in it, the music" (93) and that many classic plays were fundamentally melodramas. Thus Sirk's conception of his 1950's films was that they could be greater than what he frequently derided as "confused" or "nothing" stories would indicate: the *Alchestis* of Euripides, for example, provided the metaphysical basis for the movie that he made from the "confused novel" *Magnificent Obsession (Sirk on Sirk* 95), just as *Written on the Wind's* "Euripidean manner" reveals the end of the film at the beginning and forces the audience to attend to "structure instead of plot, to variations of a theme, to deviations from it, instead of the theme itself" (*Sirk on Sirk* 119). As Laura Mulvey contends in one of the many critical treatments of Sirk and melodrama, Sirk understood that 1950s melodrama acts "as a safety valve for ideological contradictions centred on sex and the family" (Mulvey 75) but that its *mise en scène* provides "a transcendent, wordless commentary, giving abstract emotion spectacular form" (77).[2]

It is this interplay between over-the-top emotion and multiple distancing techniques, between conventional stories and multiple points of view signaled by features as subtle as lighting and color that led critics such as Paul Willemen to describe Sirk's technique as "distanciation." This "secondary reality" in Sirk's films "alter[s] the rhetoric of the bourgeois melodrama, through stylization and parody" and causes them to distance themselves from "bourgeois ideology" (Willeman 29). Because of his innovative use of the form, Sirk has become a touchstone for work on melodrama, the basis for work such as Jackie Byars's *All that Hollywood Allows: Re-Reading Gender in 1950s Melodrama*, and, more recently, critical perspectives on Todd Haynes's 2002 *Far from Heaven,* an acknowledged homage to Sirk's *All That Heaven Allows.*[3] As Barbara Klinger shows in her reception study of Sirk's work, *Melodrama and Meaning: History, Culture, and the Films of Douglas Sirk,* the meanings of Sirk's films have changed with the ideological positions of critics in each decade: they have been "historically characterized as subversive, adult, trash, classic, camp, and vehicles of gender definition" (xv). Despite their disagreements about the films' meanings, critics have consistently identified certain elements as classically Sirkian in style, including "pessimistic themes, artificial *mise-en-scène,* distance, self-reflexivity, and false happy ends" (Klinger 12).

Thoreau in the Suburbs

Despite the critical debates flourishing over Sirk and melodrama, few have considered at length the role of Thoreau as image and idea in the films. Jon Halliday notes that Cary Scott's New England, "the home of Thoreau and Emerson," is also "the starting point of white, WASP America," with Ron Kirby and "his trees" as "both America's past and America's ideals" ("All That Heaven Allows" 60-61). Focusing directly on Thoreau, David Justin Hodge presents a more complete interpretation in "A Desperate Education: Reading Walden in *All That Heaven Allows.*" He reads the film through Thoreau's and Ralph Waldo Emerson's philosophy and sees it as a *bildungsroman,* the story of Cary's education away from conformity and toward the "re-education in independence" (Hodge 11) that Thoreau proposes as necessary for Americans. Hodge links this to Sirk's technique of distanciation as a means of conveying Thoreau's purpose of "waking up" Americans "asleep" to the real possibilities of life. But Sirk looked to *Walden* for more than philosophy. As he explained to Halliday:

> The picture is about the antithesis of Thoreau's qualified Rousseauism and established American society. . . . You know, when I first read *Walden* it was like a sun going up over my youth: this strangely *clean* language. And then in the wake of Thoreau I read Emerson, a bit later. . . . This kind of philosophy dwells in my mind and had to find an outlet eventually. (*Sirk on Sirk: Interviews* 99-100)

Sirk's emphasis on "*clean* language" and the contrast between "qualified Rousseauism" and conventionality suggest his interest in Thoreau as style and theme as well as philosophy. Originally conceived to capitalize on the phenomenal success of the Jane Wyman-Rock Hudson pairing in *Magnificent Obsession, All That Heaven Allows* lacked what Sirk called the metaphysical overtones of the earlier film, yet, as he explained in an interview with the BBC, "I got interested in the film in spite of the poor story." Later, he explained why:

> I put . . . a lot of my own—I would like to call it—handwriting into that film, you know. I put, for the first time, my mirrors, my symbols, my statues, my literary knowledge about Thoreau and so forth. I was trying to give that cheap stuff a meaning. And, in a way, strangely enough, it came off, I believe. (Sirk)

Sirk's sense of visual style, his interest in objects—his mirrors, symbols, and statues—are, like the literature, both method and subject in the film. Much like the motifs of illness and blindness for which he is noted, they help to render such Sirkian themes as self-recognition and the distancing of self from desire.

Such themes, like the "clean language" of Thoreau's style, suggest the value of a closer reading of the film's style and themes as they are grounded in the text of *Walden,* a key text in the movement known as American Transcendentalism (1830-1855). American Transcendentalism was a literary and social movement that, like Romanticism, promoted a belief in the innate goodness of human beings and the idea of the "god within." Transcendentalists such as Ralph Waldo Emerson, in *Nature* (1836), and Thoreau, in *Walden* (1854), claimed that transcendence or communion with the divine could be achieved by the individual directly rather than through the intercession of churches and preachers. Instead of relying on Enlightenment values like reason and logic, individuals should trust intuition and feelings as a guide to right living; as Emerson writes in "Self-Reliance," "Trust thyself: every heart vibrates to that iron string" (94). Transcendentalists believed that nature was the best teacher and that present experience, rather than the rules of the past entombed in books, should dictate behavior. As a result, they prized individualism and nonconformity, for, according to Emerson, "Whoso would be a man, must be a nonconformist . . . No law can be sacred to me but that of my nature" ("Self-Reliance" 96). In *All That Heaven Allows,* Sirk employs the ideas of a classic American philosophical movement, Transcendentalism, and the themes and symbols of its most iconic text, *Walden,* to foment a quiet revolution against conformity, thus using the culture's own tools to dismantle its repressive and damaging social structures.

Although the crucial *Walden*-reading scene does not occur until halfway through the picture, from the beginning Ron is established as a Thoreau figure. As Fassbinder suggests, he initially occupies the position and the clothing of an extra, moving from background to foreground only as Cary is left behind by her friend Sara. Sirk's shots in this sequence play a trick on the audience, focusing not on Ron but on Cary and Sara, notably on whether Sara will invite Cary to be the date for an eligible bachelor her husband is bringing home. "Oh, now, look, he's 40, which means that he'll consider any female over 18 too old; we may as well face it," Sara says. She is trying to smooth over not asking Cary to be the man's date but succeeds primarily in reinforcing the social rule that, at 40, single men are eligible and that at 40, single women are outcasts. That Stoningham society considers a 20-year difference in age between men and women to be just right is emphasized when Sara invites the elderly Harvey to be Cary's date for the country club dance. But when Ron emerges from the leafy background and offers to carry a box of dishes for Cary, the rules are broken. From the beginning his position is fluid: no longer a gardener yet not an avid capitalist, Ron announces his intention to grow trees, owning a business that makes him neither a master of men nor a wage slave. Cary, too, breaks the rules: she asks him to lunch, thus putting him on a social standing equal to that of Sara and herself. He accepts a roll and coffee, neither entirely accepting nor entirely rejecting her offer.

The Thoreauvian overtones are subtle: as Cary tries to make conversation, Ron, like Thoreau a guardian of trees, answers brusquely, almost rudely, until she shows a genuine interest in nature. What may seem a conventional strategy to reinscribe class into the relationship—the brusque manner being the workingman's way of showing independence in typical films—becomes in Sirk's hands another reference to Thoreau, who, like Ron, is a "speaker and actor of the truth" (Emerson, "Thoreau" 322), as his friend and mentor Ralph Waldo Emerson described him. Like Thoreau, Ron chooses as his favorite dish "the nearest" (Emerson, "Thoreau" 321) and refuses to waste time in idle conversation and to say the expected thing. When Cary, as a conversational gambit, asks Ron whether she should take up gardening, he replies, "Only if you think you'd like it," thus refusing the conventional response of waxing eloquent about gardens in favor of simple truth. Like a true Transcendentalist, he believes that individual desires, not social norms, should rule one's actions and that time spent in social niceties is time wasted. Only when Cary ventures a genuine question, asking whether she has any of the trees he has described, does he respond with conversation and a gift, the golden raintree branch she places in a vase on her dressing table. Ron is different from the other men she knows, for unlike them, he does not divorce sex from companionship as do both Harvey and Howard. They are two sides of the same pernicious ideology, for each wants one thing from her—for Howard, sex, and for Harvey, companionship—without taking Cary as an individual into account at all. By contrast, Ron treats Cary as a person throughout their relationship, encouraging her to make up her own mind and refusing to force her to act against her will. His Transcendentalist form of respect is more valuable than the superficial courtesy of the country club set.

"It May be the House that has Got Him"

As the film progresses, Sirk chronicles the stripping away of Cary's old way of life in a manner that recalls the opening chapter of *Walden,* "Economy." Thoreau's method in this chapter is rhetorical, a process analysis that guides the reader through the stages of shedding what is not essential. Shortly after diagnosing the problem, which is famously that "the mass of men lead lives of quiet desperation" (5), Thoreau begins identifying causes of and solutions to this dilemma. Repeatedly he uses the image of possessions weighing down or burdening the owner: "We do not ride on the railroad; it rides upon us," he writes, after commenting that "men are not so much the keepers of herds as herds are the keepers of men" (62, 38). Ownership, for Thoreau, is a trap, much as it seems to be for Sirk's characters. Thoreau "owns" farms in his imagination but purchases none, because "when the farmer has got his house, he may not be the richer but the poorer for it, and it may be the house that has got him" (22). Sirk, too, depicts the trap of ownership in his films. As he explained to Michael Stern:

> I considered that the homes that people live in exactly describe their lives. They are always behind those window crossings, behind bars or staircases. Their homes are their prisons. They are imprisoned even by the tastes of the society in which they live. In *All That Heaven Allows,* this woman is imprisoned by her home, her family, her society. They are imprisoned in two ways—by their personal habits, and by the class to which they belong, which is slightly above the middle-class. ("Sirk Speaks")

To help his readers avoid this trap of imprisonment by objects, Thoreau addresses each of the elements required for life—housing, warmth, clothing, and food—and in each case demonstrates that too much is as bad as too little. Taking his readers through stages from surfeit to sufficiency, he strips them of their psychological armor, preparing them for the message of simplicity that they might at first resist, much as Sirk draws his reader into Ron Kirby's world by degrees.

Houses and interior spaces, and the objects that clutter them, are always significant in a Sirk film, and nowhere is this more true than in *All That Heaven Allows,* where the theme of transformation applies to houses as well as to people. Sirk explains his care in choosing décor to Michael Stern:

> That living room in *All That Heaven Allows* has a certain elegance. I worked for UFA as a set designer, you know. I believe my pictures reflect this, even in a sort of continuity. In *Written on the Wind* the mirrors that run throughout are marbleized. They are not clear mirrors any more. Even the reflections have become clouded. ("Sirk Speaks")

What Sirk does not mention is that those same marbleized mirrors, and symbolically clouded reflections, surround the fireplace in the Scott family home, a colonial-style house painted in neutral white-on-white tones. The gold-flecked marbleized mirrors that surround the fireplace, traditionally the heart of a home, rarely reflect the flames of a fire, because fires are rarely made in this house of little cheer and less warmth. What these mirrors do reflect is the massive silver loving cup, well polished and emblazoned with "Talcott Smith," the name of Cary's deceased husband, placed prominently on the mantelpiece. The trophy, which as Stern observes looks like an urn for cremated ashes (*Douglas Sirk* 116), figures prominently in the scenes with the film's two tradition-loving men, Cary's elderly suitor Harvey and her son, Ned. Caressing the cup after taking it from the mantelpiece, Harvey recalls drinking champagne from the cup after winning a race, a memory that suggests continuity with the past and, in this context, with the dead. When Cary carries the loving cup into the cellar after she becomes engaged to Ron, symbolically burying the dead past beneath the earth in preparation for rejoining the world of the living, she follows Thoreau's injunction to "simplify, simplify." "I had three pieces of limestone on my desk," Thoreau writes, "but I was terrified to find that they required to be dusted daily, when the furniture of my mind was all undusted still, and I threw them out of the window in disgust. . . . Before we can adorn our houses with beautiful objects the walls must be stripped, and our lives must be stripped" (26). But Ned, the antithesis of Thoreau with his worship of tradition and the dead past, misses the loving cup immediately and, in an outburst little short of a tantrum, explodes: "Mother, what happened to Dad's trophy? Is the trophy part of the *clutter* you were putting away?" Although Kay has assured her mother that she doesn't approve of the "old Egyptian custom" of burying widows alive with their dead husbands (though her actions belie her words), Ned has no such qualms. "Haven't you any sense of obligation to father's memory?" he rages. Trying to free herself of the trophy, and by extension, the house and the past, Cary finds herself fettered by both. Like Thoreau's farm that owns the farmer, Cary is owned by her dead husband's house and the power of tradition. Sirk comments:

> In *All That Heaven Allows* the town is shown as being arranged around the church steeple. You don't see them going to church, because that would be too much on the nose. People ask me why there are so many flowers in my films. Because these homes are tombs, mausoleums filled with the corpses of plants. The flowers have been sheared and are dead, and they fill the homes with a funeral air. ("Sirk Speaks")

In leaving her house, Cary chooses to go from dead flowers to living trees, from the tomb that enshrines her dead husband's memory to the life-giving woods that Ron represents. "[A] taste for the beautiful is most cultivated out of doors, where there is no house and no housekeeper," writes Thoreau. In moving out of doors, away from her mausoleum of a house, Cary also moves toward a taste for the beautiful and the Transcendentalist ideal of knowing one's true self.

The old mill that Ron transforms into a home also reflects the influence of Thoreau. First, it is situated beside a pond, evoking Thoreau's home at Walden Pond. Like Thoreau's house, it is built from the remains of an older building, the flour mill that had belonged to Ron's grandfather. Although as Hodge points out, Cary is often the one who is instructed rather than the instructor, here it is her quick eye for the value of the past that sees potential in the fireplace, loft, and broad-beamed floors. Like the brusque, nearly rude speech that Ron uses early in their relationship, his initial reaction to the mill brands him as someone who, by living in the present (rather than in the past and the future, as Cary does), fails to see value in the past. In a dismissive response that recalls Thoreau's similar disdain for the fetters of the past, Ron explains that he plans to tear the mill down and plant some trees on the acreage. Aware that the past can have value, however, Cary conceives of turning the mill into a place to live. Authentic rather than artificial tradition is the key to its charm for her: the beams are oak, Ron tells Cary, and will "last another hundred years." Moreover, its materials, native to the land, are exposed: beams, stone floor and walls, and wide sawn planks are all evident beneath the dust of disuse. During this first visit, however, Cary can appreciate the past but is still frightened by nature: as she climbs the stairs to the loft, a pigeon startles her, catapulting her into Ron's arms. "Did the bird frighten you, Mrs. Scott?" Ron asks with a smile, to which she retorts, "It would have startled anyone!" The theme of Cary's fear, so constant in Ron and Cary's later conversations about their marriage, is thus introduced, as is its eventual cure: the refuge she finds in Ron's arms and Ron's ideas.

As Cary observes during her second and subsequent visits, Ron gradually transforms the space of the dead past into a living home. He restores the hand-hewn beams, makes a welcoming fire in the fireplace, and adds classic, natural, wood-and-leather furniture in tones of red and gold to complement the mill's gleaming oak floors, a reversal of the lifeless whiteness of Cary's already-perfected house. "There is some of the same fitness in a man's building his own house that there is in a bird's building its own nest" (31), Thoreau observes, and one of the principal, if largely unseen, actions of the movie is Ron's reconstruction of the old mill to reflect his rather than the world's idea of beauty and utility. As at Cary's house, a single object comes to represent both the past and a relationship: a Wedgwood teapot that Cary finds in the dust of the old mill during her first visit. Cary confesses that if she found the other pieces, she would steal it: "I love Wedgwood." Reluctant at this early stage of their relationship to admit the value in anything past or perhaps anything domestic, Ron says, somewhat sternly, "It was probably thrown there because the pieces were missing. Better leave it." Later, however, he finds the pieces and mends the teapot, giving it to Cary during her second visit, during which he proposes to her. The action demonstrates that Ron listens to Cary and remembers what she likes and values, something that no one else, incuding her children, has done in a long time. When she declares that marriage is impossible, however, she inadvertently brushes the teapot off a table and smashes it to bits. "The hours and hours you spent on it," Cary mourns, to which Ron replies, "It doesn't matter," one of many times when he and those in his circle reassure her with their Thoreauvian "the past is past" philosophy. Cary, like the audience, may assume that the teapot represents their relationship, once perfect but now symbolically broken by her initial rejection of his proposal. But only after this elegant symbol of tradition is smashed does Cary turn to Ron and blurt out, "Oh, Ron, I love you so very much," after which they consummate their relationship, an act signaled discreetly by cutting away to the exterior of the mill where Ron's tame deer is standing and then back to the interior, where Cary relaxes in Ron's arms. Unlike the indestructible silver trophy, the teapot assumes its proper place as an object that, like all mere things, is

decidedly secondary in value to human relationships, however multivalent
its symbolism and precious its link to the past.

"Beware of all Enterprises that Require New Clothes"

Clothing is also among the elements that Thoreau addresses, and here,
too, *All That Heaven Allows* follows the themes of "Economy." Although
Ron wears a woodsman's flannel shirts and work pants for much of the
film, Cary dresses in ways that reflect her inner state of being. Clad for
much of the film in a series of gray suits and black cocktail dresses, she
deviates from this pattern only twice, wearing a provocative red dress to
the cocktail party at the club and a brown knit dress with orange accents
during her second trip to the mill. A departure from her usual wardrobe
that recalls Thoreau's injunction to "beware of all enterprises that require
new clothes" (15), the red dress makes her visually and conversationally
the center of attention before and during the party, and all read it as a sign
of sexual availability. Ned comments that it is "cut kind of low"; Mona,
the town gossip, insults her; and the boorish Howard kisses her roughly
before propositioning her, saying "I'm not sorry for desiring you."[4] They
undress her, metaphorically speaking, whereas Ron and his circle, as if
equating clothing with protection, nurture her. Both Ron and Alida
remind her to put on a coat at different points in the movie, and Ron
tenderly puts on and takes off her snow boots. Chastened, perhaps, by the
others' reaction to the dress at the cocktail party, Cary henceforth wears
color, typically reds and pinks, only in the privacy of her own home. The
sole exception is the brown dress, which signals a break in Cary's usual
gray suit of ladylike armor when she wears it on the afternoon that she and
Ron become lovers. Notable for its natural color amid the Technicolor
gaudiness that characterizes the others' clothing, the brown dress blends in
with the equally natural browns and reds of Ron's restored mill, visually
linking Cary not only with the place in nature but with the animal that
signifies it, Ron's tame deer.

The brown dress is notable for another reason, too: it marks the only
occasion on which Cary does not wear any jewelry. Thoreau had called
the wealthy the "most terribly impoverished class of all, who have
accumulated dross, but know not how to use it, or get rid of it, and thus
have forged their own golden or silver fetters" (10). Tellingly, Cary
consistently wears a symbolic fetter in the form of a string of pearls ringed
tightly around her neck. On social occasions such as Sara's party and the
country club cocktail party, she wears three tight strands of pearls, an

action that on the literal level denotes her sense of fashion but on a symbolic level suggests the intensification of social pressures, the "golden or silver fetters," that imprison her. Such fetters are also echoed in the film's darkest moment, when Cary, having broken her engagement to Ron, greets her children at Christmas only to learn that Kay is engaged and that Ned will be moving to Paris and then Dubai. With no regrets or sense of contradiction, both plan to abandon the house/mausoleum that they had insisted that their mother inhabit. "Don't you see, Kay? It's all been so *pointless,*" Cary says, holding her temples as though another migraine has struck her. Her black dress in this scene, appropriate for a widow, contrasts with Kay's red dress, a signifier of the sexuality that Kay has resented in her mother and now has appropriated for herself. Cary's dress is decorated with tiny silver balls, as though she is merely an object, an extension of the Christmas tree that is the visible emblem of her children's infatuation with tradition.

A Perfect Forest Mirror

Sirk's interest in windows and mirrors, and by extension reflection and perception, also has echoes in *Walden.* "I perceive that we inhabitants of New England live this mean life that we do because our vision does not penetrate the surface of things," Thoreau admonishes his audience. "We think that that *is* which appears to *be*" (65). Throughout *Walden,* Thoreau casts the pond as both transparent glass and reflective mirror, a doubling of surface and depth that extends to his analogy between sky and earth's water. Walden is "a perfect forest mirror . . . Sky water" (127), yet so clear that waterlogged canoes and pine trees are visible on its bottom. Referring to another pond in the region, Thoreau declares that "White Pond and Walden are great crystals on the surface of the earth, Lakes of Light" (134) or mirrors and lenses for correcting the vision and seeing clearly. In Cary's house, marbleized mirrors, draped and covered windows, and shiny surfaces reflect and refract her facial expressions of unhappiness. In the sole scene in which she actually looks out a window, which like all the others in her house is swathed in net curtains, Cary watches caroling children riding in a sled as the snow falls softly, and a tear drifts down her cheek as her double isolation—behind curtains and glass, bereft of her children—registers in her mind. The most celebrated instance of Sirk's reflective surfaces in *All That Heaven Allows* occurs shortly thereafter, when Kay and Ned purchase a television set for her. As the camera zooms slowly in on the television screen, the salesman's voice intones, "Turn the dial and you'll have all the company you want. Drama, comedy—life's parade at your fingertips." Framed by and reflected in the television screen, Cary returns its blank technological gaze, the ribbons and trappings of Christmas ironically surrounding her image and mocking the sense of isolation and loss that she feels.

In contrast, Ron's house features true windows, not reflecting mirrors of misery. The principal change that he makes to the mill is the addition of a floor-to-ceiling window overlooking the woods and pond. This giant window, which never has its curtains drawn to obscure the view, exposes the outer natural world of snow-covered hills and pond. Because they can focus on the vision of nature outside the window, and in Transcendentalist terms, the truth within nature that they see, Cary and Ron speak honestly to one another when standing before this window. Although Ron proposes to Cary when the two stand by the fireplace, both move to the window to confess their fears or unpleasant truths to one another: Cary admits her fear of marriage, Ron admits that he fears Cary's world could change him because of his love for her, and Cary charges Ron with forcing her to choose between him and her children. Unlike the marbleized mirrors of Cary's house, which reflect only the lies and denial essential to social conventions, the window allows true insight into Cary's and Ron's struggles. In what it reveals of nature and of the inner lives of Ron and Cary, it is Thoreau's "perfect forest mirror" as both a reflective surface in which the truth is laid bare and a transparent surface through which the depths of their feelings can be glimpsed.

The window also provides a redemptive vision of another symbol of nature and their relationship, the deer that Ron has fed throughout the picture. When Cary goes to the mill after Ron's accident, Dan tells her that he has had a concussion and must not be moved because of his serious injuries. Yet when the nurse opens the shutters, the deer returns and looks in the window, just as Ron's eyes flutter open and he recognizes Cary. The overstated rather than understated quality of the action is, in a characteristically Sirkian way, both emphasized and undercut by the soaring music and by the obvious artificiality of the set behind the window. As Sirk told interviewer Michael Stern, however, such artificiality was intentional, as was his use of obvious back projection screens for certain shots:

> Throughout my pictures I employ a lighting which is not naturalistic. Often the window will be *here*, and the light from *there*. With color, too, I did this, to attain a lighting that is almost surrealistic. . . . As Brecht said, you must never forget that this is not reality. It is a tale that you are

telling. The distanciation must be there. It creates an unreal quality, a certain heightening. You can't just show it. You have to shoot it through with a dialectic. ("Sirk Speaks")

The seeking out of multiple perspectives, the deliberate distortion of perception to achieve a higher truth, the confronting of facts, however unpleasant they are, and the ultimate knowledge that such a truth must be discoverable by, and personal to, the individual who seeks it all resonate in *Walden*. In true Transcendental fashion, the intuitive path to knowledge through the human heart trumps the rational objections that Cary and Ron confront in coming to terms with, and ultimately rejecting, society's values.

"The Hospitality Was as Cold as the Ices"

The most overt instance of the film's use of *Walden* is the scene in which Cary picks up a copy of the book at the home of Ron's bohemian friends Mick and Alida Anderson. She has already been established as a reader of unconventional literature, when Kay picks up an unidentified novel in Cary's bedroom and says with some shock and dismay, "You're reading *this?*" Now, however, the source of her reading is made apparent visually as well as aurally, for the dust jacket clearly identifies it as *Walden and Other Writings* by Henry David Thoreau. "The mass of men lead lives of quiet desperation," Cary reads aloud. "Why should we be in such desperate haste to succeed? If a man does not keep place with his companions, perhaps it is because he hears a different drummer. Let him step to the music which he hears, however measured or far away" (5, 217). Although Cary never turns the page, the first sentence actually occurs in "Economy," the first chapter of *Walden,* and the next three in "Conclusion," the last chapter. The screenplay thus neatly telescopes both problem and solution into one compact bit of philosophy, just enough to set up the conversation she has with Alida. When Cary asks, "Alida, what did you mean when you said that Ron 'taught' Mick?" Alida reveals that she and Mick had been on the verge of separation during Mick's years as a Madison Avenue advertising executive. However, when he met Ron, who neither had nor needed the trappings of wealth, Mick gradually came to understand Ron's secret: "to thine own self be true," an echo of Emerson's "trust thyself." Ron has not read the book, she adds; instead, "he just lives it" as the natural heir to Thoreau and a guide to a better, more authentic, New England. Yet coming after so much sincerity and simplicity from *Walden,* Alida's use of a quotation from *Hamlet* seems a touch of Sirkian double meaning for those who recall the context: the phrase comes from

Polonius's speech to Laertes early in the play, a speech at best full of platitudes and at worst tinged with some cynical if not selfish advice.

The lobster dinner at Mick and Alida's that follows this explanation confirms the rightness of Cary's choice to fall in love with Ron and contrasts with the two parties with the country club set that occur before and after it. The first country club party, the one at which Cary wears her red dress, ends with her being attacked by Howard; the second, an engagement party that Sara gives for Tom Allenby (the bachelor of the opening sequence) and his fiancée, reprises the first with even more insults and attacks. After enduring smoothly veiled insults that hint that Ron is marrying Cary for her money, Cary greets the dependably nasty Mona Plash. "Why, Cary, he's *fascinating*," Mona coos. "And that tan! It must be from working out of doors. Of course, he's probably handy *indoors,* too." Howard again grabs Cary and tries to kiss her, this time intimating that she is sexually promiscuous ("Line forms to the right"). But Ron comes to the rescue, knocking Howard into a chair and taking Cary away from the sterile cruelty that passes for entertainment in her world. The country club—symbol of 1950s social aspirations, racial homogeneity, and supreme safety for the upper middle-classes—becomes in Sirk's film a site of violence and unpredictability. In that milieu, every social exchange begins with provocation and ends in psychological or physical violence. Cary's only defender within that society, Sara, does what she can verbally to stem the attacks. However, her rejoinders—"Now what is *that* supposed to mean?" and an indignant "Really!"—fail to slow, let alone stop, the vicious amusement that the others insist on carrying on, awakened out of their torpor by the prospect of this suburban blood sport. That Ron's physical attack on Howard is condemned ("Poor Howard might have been killed!" murmurs one partygoer) while Howard's attack on Cary is not only condoned but used to blame her for his behavior indicates the level of corruption and inverted values in 1950s upper-middle-class culture.

Unlike the parties with Cary's circle of friends, the dinner at Mick and Alida's introduces Cary to a social gathering that is actually enjoyable. Notable for its heterogeneity rather than its class snobbery, the lobster dinner includes a Spanish fisherman with his wife and daughter, the head of the local Audubon society, and a beekeeper who is also an artist; all, like Ron, work at something tangibly related to nature. Significantly, it is one of the only scenes where food, and by extension spiritual comfort, is served in the film, and the food here is hearty, cornbread and lobsters, instead of the desiccated canapés that Cary serves when Ron meets her children. Drinking, too, is not the occasion for fetishism and ritual that it is in Cary's set. For example, Ned makes Talcottis for both Harvey and Ron when they come to take his mother out, but he turns this into a rite of class snobbery, commenting that his mother's brand of gin is "not as good as his usual brand" and ostentatiously noting that he adds "just two drops" of vermouth. When asked the recipe for his cocktails, Mick, by contrast, speaks in nonsense words, signifying that the company, not the content of the drinks, is what matters. Of course, quantity matters, too, since Mick and Ron bring up 16 bottles of Chianti for their guests. Dancing is not the staid foxtrot of Cary's set but a free-form, hilarious accompaniment to singing and to playing the piano and concertina. As Thoreau comments in the conclusion to *Walden,* "I sat at a table where were rich food and wine in abundance, and obsequious attendance, but sincerity and truth were not; and I went away hungry from the inhospitable board. The hospitality was as cold as the ices. I thought that there was no need of ice to freeze them" (221). *All That Heaven Allows* takes place throughout the fall and winter—signifying, of course, the autumn of Cary's life—but also extending symbolically to the freezing nature of the country club set, with its empty fireplaces and tastefully nondescript interiors. Their manner is indeed as "cold as the ices," a symbolic doubling of the cold without and within that makes the warmth of Ron's world all the more compelling.

Rock Hudson as a "Bachelor of Nature"

The figure of Rock Hudson starring as Ron Kirby further deepens and complicates the Thoreauvian themes in the film. Sirk's choice of Hudson is not accidental: he featured Hudson in at least ten of his films. As Sirk explains, Hudson was not yet a star when Jane Wyman proposed *Magnificent Obsession* as her next picture, but he saw in it a way to build Hudson's career as well as to create the kind of leading man needed for the complicated melodramas he wished to make:

> Rock Hudson was not an educated man, but that very beautiful body of his was putty in my hands. And there was a certain dialectic at work in his casting, especially after *Magnificent Obsession.* This film he did not understand at all. But after it, I used him as a straight, good-looking American guy. A little confused, but well-meaning. ("Sirk Speaks")

In an earlier interview, Sirk had expanded on his theory of the kind of character necessary for his melodramas and the ways in which Hudson fulfilled such a role:

[I]n melodrama it's of advantage to have one immovable character against
which you can put your more split ones. Because your audience needs—
or likes—to have a character in the movie they can identify themselves
with: naturally, the steadfast one, not to be moved. Now, this character
preferably ought to be the hero of the story—then it's Gary Cooper, John
Wayne, and so on. Or Rock Hudson . . . You couldn't make a split
character out of Wayne if you tried. I couldn't out of Rock Hudson. (*Sirk
on Sirk* 98)

Hudson's "immovable character" suggests Thoreau as Emerson
described him: fixed in his ideas, idealistic, humble and lacking in worldly
ambition, but more than a little self-righteous. Working with rather than
against Hudson's steadfast character and good looks thus allowed Sirk not
only to evoke Thoreau but also to present the split character of Cary in
more detail. As Fassbinder astutely remarks, "Women think in Sirk's
films" (97), and *All That Heaven Allows* is filled with shots of Cary
thinking as she subtly reacts to, works through, and responds to what she
hears, from the truths that Ron tells her to the attacks of her children.

Frequently remarked on throughout the film ("Look at that *man!*"
breathes one young socialite), Hudson's physical presence becomes a
point at issue in the film because of his youth and good looks, both of
which suggest to Cary's friends and family that her interest is purely
sexual. "I think all you see is just a good-looking set of muscles!" Ned
angrily hisses at her. "Ned, we mustn't let this come between us," Cary
pleads, but, like the decorative screen that separates the two visually, the
barrier of tradition is too great for Cary and Ned to see each other clearly.

In one of the movie's visual puns, Cary stops by the butcher shop after
she spends her first weekend with Ron. As Mona walks in the door, the
butcher is chiding Cary because she was not at home all weekend when his
delivery boy stopped by. "Where were you, dear?" Mona asks, to which
Cary replies "Upstate." To underscore the conversation, which reveals
that Cary and Ron are lovers, Cary has just picked up a huge package of
beefsteak, which she carries out to Ron's car. The visual analogy between
Cary's package and Ron, another hunk of beefsteak ("set of muscles!") in
the language of the day, is lost neither on the audience nor on Mona and
the butcher, who nod sagely to one another as Cary gets into Ron's car.
Revelations about Hudson's homosexuality have added an unintentional
layer of camp to some of the lines. For example, modern audiences
respond with laughter when Ron encourages Cary to be strong and she
replies, "And you want me to be a man?" As Barbara Klinger cautions,

however, camp sensibility in this context can create an awareness of the "constructedness of romance and gender roles" but may rest simply on "a sense of superiority to the past" without considering larger questions of ideology (156). More pertinent to the original context of the film is the 1950s publicity machine's packaging of Hudson as "the 'natural' man . . . living on top of a mountain in a redwood house . . . a quasi-Paul Bunyan figure who has maintained innate masculine characteristics unpolluted by fame or civilization" (104). Like Thoreau, who appears as the idealistic gardener David Sterling in Louisa May Alcott's novel *Work,* Hudson is presented as a "bachelor of nature," a figure innocently indifferent to women until the right one crosses his path.[5] Although contemporary audiences develop camp readings of the film from the extradiegetic elements surrounding Hudson's life and death, for 1950's audiences, who were largely unaware of Hudson's sexuality, the "bachelor of nature" idea was a satisfying explanation, even if it did have overtones of ambiguous sexuality. The same ambiguity surrounds the concept of the "bachelor of nature" as it appears in reminiscences by friends of Thoreau. For audiences of the 1950s as for those of the 1850s, the "bachelor of nature" concept permitted a vision of masculinity "unpolluted by fame or civilization" and, by extension, unpolluted by issues of sexuality, however unstable or ambiguous the identification of sexuality might otherwise be.

As one of Sirk's most celebrated melodramas, *All That Heaven Allows* draws deeply on Thoreau's *Walden* not only philosophically but stylistically and thematically. As Michael Stern suggests, the film is really "American folklore" because it is "told with the force of a moral argument" and features characters of a "mythic dimension" (Stern, *Douglas Sirk* 123). The crucial scene in which Cary reads the four sentences from Walden that comprise the film's core sensibility relies on Thoreau's prose much as a novel relies on the ekphrastic use of a work of art: as a touchstone for the rest of the work, a sign against which conflicts, judgments, and decisions can be tested. In its social critique of 1950's conformity, materialism, and spiritual malaise, *All That Heaven Allows* is not unique. Films such as *The Man in the Gray Flannel Suit* (1956) also chronicled despair and conflict from the perspective of the supposedly conformist lives of the middle-class. But *The Man in the Gray Flannel Suit* proposes to cure middle-class angst with a middle-class solution. Although the film argues for greater truth and understanding, as Tom Rath acknowledges the illegitimate child he fathered during the war, the Raths' solution to their problems is to pin their hopes on dividing the undeveloped land they have inherited into quarter-acre suburban housing plots. By contrast, *All That Heaven Allows* ranges beyond the boundaries of upper middle-class life to propose what Alida calls "stepping off the merry-go-round" altogether and living a life close to the land, nurturing rather than subdividing and exploiting it. *All that Heaven Allows* celebrates true, lifelong nonconformity rather than a momentary rebellion. Given the disjunctive nature of Sirk's conception of melodrama and the ironic perspective from which he creates its elements, the solution may not work, and the happy ending is consistently called into question by the artificiality with which Sirk undercuts standard features of melodrama. But *All That Heaven Allows* differs from the rest in its cutting edge approach: it provides not only an American problem, but an American solution, one rooted in the past but applicable to the issues of the 1950s. As Dan asks Cary when she visits him to find the cure for her headaches, "Do you expect me to give you a prescription to cure life?" *Walden* is that prescription to cure life, and *All That Heaven Allows* is Sirk's meditation on how that prescription might work for a 1950s culture that is ready to be healed.

Works Cited

Byars, Jackie. *All That Hollywood Allows: Re-Reading Gender in 1950s Melodrama*. Chapel Hill: University of North Carolina Press, 1991.

Emerson, Ralph Waldo. "Self-Reliance." *Ralph Waldo Emerson and Margaret Fuller: Selected Works*. Ed. John Carlos Rowe. Boston: Houghton Mifflin, 2003: 93-114.

—. "Thoreau." *Walden and Resistance to Civil Government*. Ed. John Rossi William, 2nd ed. Norton Critical Edition. New York: W. W. Norton, 1992.

Fassbinder, Rainer Werner. "Imitation of Life: Six Films by Douglas Sirk." Trans. Thomas Elsaesser. *Douglas Sirk*. Eds. Jon Halliday and Laura Mulvey. London: Edinburgh Film Festival, National Film Theatre, and John Player and Sons, 1972: 95-107.

Halliday, Jon. "All That Heaven Allows." *Douglas Sirk*. Eds. Jon Halliday and Laura Mulvey. Edinburgh: Edinburgh Film Festival '72 in association with The National Film Theatre and John Player and Sons, 1972: 59-66.

—. *Sirk on Sirk: Interviews*. London: Secker & Warburg in association with the British Film Institute, 1971.

Hodge, David Justin. "A Desperate Education: Reading Walden in All That Heaven Allows." *Film and Philosophy* 8 (2004): 1-16.

Klinger, Barbara. *Melodrama and Meaning: History, Culture, and the Films of Douglas Sirk.* Bloomington: Indiana University Press, 1994.

Mulvey, Laura. "Notes on Sirk and Melodrama." *Home Is Where the Heart Is: Studies in Melodrama and the Woman's Film.* Ed. Christine Gledhill. London: BFI Publishing, 1987: 75-79.

Plath, Sylvia. *The Bell Jar.* New York: Harper and Row, 1999.

Sirk, Douglas. "Behind the Mirror: A Profile of Douglas Sirk." Douglas Sirk Interview with Mark Shivas. Included on the DVD edition of *All That Heaven Allows*: BBC2, 1979. Ed. Mark Shivas, prod. and host.

Stern, Michael. *Douglas Sirk.* Boston: Twayne Publishers, 1979.

—. "Sirk Speaks." *Bright Lights Film Journal* 48 (2005): n.p. .

Thoreau, Henry David. *Walden and Resistance to Civil Government: Authoritative Texts, Thoreau's Journal, Reviews, and Essays in Criticism.* Ed. William John Rossi. 2nd ed. New York: W.W. Norton, 1992.

Willeman, Paul. "Distanciation and Douglas Sirk." *Douglas Sirk.* Eds. Jon Halliday and Laura Mulvey. Edinburgh: Edinburgh Film Festival '72 in association with the National Film Theatre and John Player and Sons, 1972: 23-29.

Notes

[1] Quotations from *All That Heaven Allows* are transcribed from the film. Fenwick, Peg, et al. *All That Heaven Allows.* videorecording. Criterion Collection, United States, 2005.

[2] Among the many treatments of Sirk and melodrama are several essays in Christine Gledhill's collection Home Is *Where the Heart Is: Studies in Melodrama and the Woman's Film* (London: BFI Pub., 1987).

[3] See, for example, the essays in James Morrison's *The Cinema of Todd Haynes: All That Heaven Allows* (London and New York: Wallflower, 2007) or Sharon Willis's "The Politics of Disappointment: Todd Haynes Rewrites Douglas Sirk." (*Camera Obscura: A Journal of Feminism, Culture, and Media Studies* 54 [2003]: 131-74)

[4] Mary Beth Haralovich discusses the use of color, especially in the characters' clothing, in "All That Heaven Allows: Color, Narrative Space, and Melodrama," pp. 57-72 in *Close Viewings: An Anthology of New Film Criticism*, ed. Peter Lehman. (Tallahassee: Florida State UP, 1990).

[5] For an examination of this concept, see Jane Goldstein's "A Daughter's Place: The Intertextuality of Gene Stratton- Porter's Laddie and Louisa May Alcott's *Little Women*." *Canadian Children's Literature/Littérature Canadienne pour la Jeunesse* 111-112 (2003): 50-59.

CHAPTER THREE

WHAT IS WOMAN?: TRANSSEXUAL LOVE IN *DIFFERENT FOR GIRLS*

BARBARA TILLEY

In the "Forward" to *Finding the Real Me: True Tales of Sex and Gender Diversity*, Stephen Whittle, a female to male transsexual, asks "How can a person born with a penis claim to be a woman, when to be a woman requires that you are not born with a penis?" (ix). For Whittle, gender identity does not mean simply being a biological boy or girl, but feeling and believing that one is not a girl even if one is born biologically a girl. Whittle writes that "[w]hen considering "sex" we group people according to whether someone has a vagina, breasts, ovaries, and so on, or a penis, testes, and so on" (x). However, sex and gender are two different binary categories. One is based on biology and the other, in our more modern perspective, is based on cultural and social definitions of what people believe to be their individual sexual identities. Most people cannot conceive of gender as being anything but boy/girl, male/female; there are two biological sex categories; therefore, there are only two gender categories. However, Whittle argues that "[t]rans [exual] people beg the whole question of human understanding at it currently is about gender and sex" (ix). The transsexual or transgendered person is someone who is seen by others as being one biological sex, but he/she *feels* to *be* something or someone else. As Carol Queen and Lawrence Schimel explain in *PomoSexuals: Challenging Assumptions about Gender and Identity,* "[p]ostmodern thought invites us to get used to the Zen notion of 'multiple subjectivities'—the idea that there is no solid, objective reality, that each of us experiences our [gender] reality subjectively, affected (or influenced) by our unique circumstances" (21). For many transsexuals, gender is a fluid state of existence; ultimately, gender encompasses more than biology, it is also sexuality and individual identity.

Film offers a provocative lens through which to examine new definitions of gender in late twentieth century culture. Like gender itself, film is an adaptive and malleable medium. As our understanding of gender subjectivity develops, it is possible to use film as a way to show gender in new and more complex lights. The image of the transsexual on the film screen becomes a lasting historical representation of the cultural moment. It does not matter whether the film is capturing fiction or documentary happenings; what matters is that the image is there to be seen. Films are a powerful and profoundly influential media source for social and cultural definitions of new genders. Although exploring sex and the body are not new to film, exploring the transsexual's body, his/her sexuality, and the complexities of the transsexual in love are newer to film plots and to film viewers. The 1996 British film *Different for Girls* explores the romantic relationship between Paul Prentice, a heterosexual male, and Kim Foyle, a male to female post-operative transsexual. In *Different for Girls*, the characters, their respective lives, and their individual experiences are portrayed as having a place in society. As viewers, we are never titillated by the knowledge of Karl's transformation to Kim, but are expected to understand and to accept this as one person's need to find her true gender identity. As one reviewer notes "*Different for Girls* is unique" because "[t]his is the first film in years about . . . transsexuals . . . in which the protagonist has absolutely nothing whatsoever to do with prostitution" (*Queer View* 1997). In other words, the transsexual is treated with respect and dignity in this film. Moreover, the director, Richard Spence, shows the evolution of emotional and physical discovery that occurs between two people who once shared a connection in their youth, and who rekindle this love in their adulthood.

The Evolution of the Transsexual Image in Film

Indeed, *Different for Girls* is a cutting edge film because it situates the transsexual experience of finding genuine love in a positive light within visual mainstream culture. Although it may seem contrary to call mainstream film cutting edge, in fact to recognize a transsexual as a positive figure in film *at all* is to change the way most films have portrayed the transsexual. Much of what is found in popular mainstream films prior to *Different for Girls*, in terms of transsexual characters, are actually women dressed as men or men dressed as women. An entire *genre* has been created in North American Hollywood cinema out of an interest by filmmakers to "fool" the audience by presenting a character as female when that character is definitely male, or vice versa. Most often these films are comedies and the "transition" from female to male or from male to female is assumed to be a temporary situation. In fact, this must be a temporary situation to make the character's actions of dressing and acting as another sex more palatable to the audience. In Vito Russo's book *The Celluloid Closet*, he states that "[m]en in silent comedies often took women's roles, but total character impersonation disappeared early. The use of female garb by male comics became just another device for a one-scene joke" (6). An early Katherine Hepburn film, *Sylvia Scarlett* (1936), presents Hepburn as a young male when, of course, the audience knows her to be female. Russo reads this film as suggestive of "homosexual activity," because Cary Grant's character is obviously interested in the young boy, Hepburn (14). Yet, it is also an early attempt at visual gender deception. Hepburn plays the young boy very well and the audience is asked to "believe" that Hepburn is indeed a young boy. The idea that Hepburn wants to be seen as male, (with all the distinguishing physical characteristics of a male person), however, does not mean that she is perceived as anything but a female trying to pass as male. Moreover, it is understood that for her to pass as male and for audience members to be receptive to this ruse, she must be heterosexual. As viewers, we know that Cary Grant is interested not in a young boy, but in Katherine Hepburn. Even in a mainstream Hollywood movie, the gender transition premise does not work unless the character is heterosexual. Interestingly, the transsexual in film is most often portrayed as heterosexual.[1]

Certain films—such as Billy Wilder's *Some Like It Hot* (1959), Sydney Pollack's *Tootsie* (1982), Blake Edward's *Victor/Victoria* (1982), and Chris Columbus's *Mrs. Doubtfire* (1993)—all use the premise of the "transition" from male to female or from female to male as a vehicle for comedy. As audience members we watch the transition occurring, (the change in clothes, hair, voice, mannerisms, and even body shape), to see if it is possible for these new men or new women to pass in the real world of set gender distinctions. We engage with the transitioning protagonist's plight, because there usually is one, for which they must disguise themselves as a man or as a woman to make a living, (*Tootsie* and *Victor/Victoria*), to see the children during a messy divorce (*Mrs. Doubtfire*), or even to hide after witnessing a crime (*Some Like It Hot*). We laugh at the trouble these characters go through to "be" a woman or to "be" a man, but we do not for one moment believe that they want to *remain* a woman or a man.

Similar to homosexual images in film, the transsexual image in film has often been punished, degraded, killed, driven insane, portrayed as a damaged human being, or been used as a figure to provide sophomoric humor about misunderstood sexual interests or even sexual desires. A film such as Jonathan Demme's *Silence of the Lambs* (1991) shows a classic image of the psychopathic transsexual. When Billy is turned down for sex reassignment surgery because of mental issues, he goes about hunting and trapping women to make a female body suit of sorts out of their skin. He wants to wear this suit so that he can live as a woman. More recent films showing true-life depictions of the transsexual experience are Kimberly Peirce's film *Boys Don't Cry* (1999) about Brandon Teena, a young woman who lived in Nebraska and dressed as a man; she was murdered after being discovered to be a woman. Also, there is Frank Pierson's, *Soldier's Girl* (2003), the story of a soldier who is beaten to death by his friends for dating and falling in love with a post-operative male to female transsexual named Calpernia Adams. Although these last two films came after *Different for Girls* and they are important in their representation of the experience of the transsexual, they still dwell on the negative aspects of gender transition. Therefore, it would seem that *Different for Girls* shows a unique and, certainly, cutting edge representation of the transsexual experience in film.

Authentic transsexual characters are extremely rare in films and even more rare are positive representations of transsexual characters. Two popular mainstream films that stand out as actually representing the possibility of more complex transsexual characters are Dil in *The Crying Game* (Neil Jordan 1992) and Orlando in *Orlando* (Sally Potter 1992). In Neil Jordan's film, Dil sees herself as a woman although she has not had a full sex change. Dil is always referred to as a woman and female pronouns are used to describe her. Fergus believes she is a woman, and the film plays to his belief up until their sex scene when Fergus realizes that Dil has a penis. Although this realization is marked with brutality and disgust on Fergus's part—he pushes Dil away roughly enough so that she hurts herself and then he begins to retch and vomit—Dil believed that Fergus knew about her penis and desired her anyway. The illusion of the transsexual is explored in *The Crying Game*, but in Sally Potter's *Orlando*, Orlando does actually change sexes. Yet, this sex change is marked with little fanfare. One night Orlando goes to bed as a man and the next morning she wakes up as a woman. This film, based on Virginia Woolf's 1928 novel of the same name, follows Woolf's plot fairly closely. The book reads almost like two novels, one from the perspective of a man and the other from the perspective of a woman. Sally Potter follows this format for her film. Although we never see the transition take place, the emphasis is on one person's perspective as both genders. As viewers, we know that Orlando understands what it feels like to be male and female. However, one film from the early 1990s portrays the transsexual in a more complex and positive light. This film is Stephan Elliot's *The Adventures of Priscilla, Queen of the Desert* (1994).

This film focuses on three Australian drag queens on their way to a drag show. The three buy a bus, christen it Priscilla, Queen of the Desert, and finally paint it lavender. In typical road trip fashion, they encounter many adventures along the way to the show, but they also develop important relationships with each other. The film plays up the camp of the drag queens and their act, but it also deals with some very serious issues that affect the three "girls". Although it is clear that two of the drag queens are men, the third "man" is obviously different. Stephen Elliot does not deal directly with the transsexual experience in the film, focusing much of the attention instead on Mitzi Del Bra/Anthony 'Tick" Belrose (played by Hugo Weaving), a man who got married and fathered a son, but who has never told anyone in the gay/drag queen community about his husband/fatherhood status. However, near the tail end of the movie, Elliot shifts gears and introduces more of Bernadette's character (played by Terence Stamp) and her interests in a straight man, Bob (played by Bill Hunter), whom the girls have taken on board to fix their bus. Throughout the film, Bernadette is referred to as a "tranny" or a "transsexual." She has breasts and is constantly taking female hormones to continue her transition from male to female. At one point we see her sitting with Mitzi with a bowl of pills in front of her, and as if we didn't already know that these pills are her female hormones, Mitzi tells her to "eat your hormones". In another scene when all the girls and Bob are cavorting in a lake, we see Bernadette's breasts through her white shirt. Although it is clear that there is a budding relationship between Bernadette and Bob, there is no overt discussion of this relationship. Bob begins to pay special attention to Bernadette; he brings her flowers, compliments her about her impersonation abilities, and singles her out to treat her more like a "lady". We are to understand from their behavior with each other that Bernadette is heterosexual and so is Bob. At the end of the movie, when the other characters leave to go back to Sydney with Mitzi's son in tow, Bernadette chooses to stay and "try it" with Bob. As viewers, we are left with a sense of hope that these two people will make it as a couple. However, that is as far as the film takes us into the transsexual journey. Perhaps these three films paved the way for Richard Spence's *Different for Girls* (1997); however, I would argue that it is really *Different for Girls* that has paved the way for many positive images of transsexuals in film.

The Transsexual in Transition

The subject of *Different for Girls* is love; in fact, in cinema *genres* this film is labeled a romantic comedy. However, this film is also a political story about definitions of gender and transsexual identity; *Different for Girls* is also a postmodern story of perspective and physical realities. The film questions perspective, both physical, lived perspective and the visual assumptions that create perspective. The perspective of others about gender, physical identity and sexual desire are explored in this unusually positive film about the transsexual experience. It is important to spend some time discussing the opening scene of the movie, which is presented even before we see the title of the film on screen. The "fluid subjectivity" of sexuality and gender identity is created in this very powerful opening scene of Kim in her former state as Karl. We are given a visual picture of the silent Karl; he utters no words, we only see his body, his experience, his alienation, and his pain. This opening scene is also one of only two violent moments in the film, and might be easily forgotten as the rest of the film unfolds. The very beginning of *Different for Girls* shows why this film is cutting edge in its examination of human sexuality and specifically in the transsexual experience.

The opening scene of *Different for Girls* shows a young, effeminate Karl Foyle showering in what looks to be an open, public shower. Obviously believing that he is alone, he stands under the shower with his legs crossed, hiding his penis and testicles between his legs. He caresses his own body, running his hands over his chest, along his legs, and then into his hair. In this position, it is hard to tell whether this person is a boy or a young girl. There are no breasts and the body is lithe and strong; this person could be either male or a prepubescent female. The moment is a striking one for viewers because there is an obvious tension in this opening scene; it is clear that the young person desires to be and to feel like someone or something else. Karl's reality is not his physical experience at that moment, but a desired experience that he creates for himself in the water of the shower. He is cleansing himself literally and figuratively; he seems to want to rid his body of that which has no place, the foreign male genitals. Yet, at the same time, he can only rid himself of the visual reality that he is a boy by hiding his genitals between his legs. This becomes very clear when he is caught by the other schoolboys, his peers, in the showers. This is one of two moments of clear violence in the film.

The clothed boys come from around the corner and sneak up on Karl quietly; the contrast between the clothed "normal" boy and unclothed "abnormal" boy is made quite clear at this moment in the film. One larger boy begins to hit Karl with a wet towel, taunting and shoving him at the same time. The camera moves in for a close-up as he shouts aggressively at Karl, "What are you doing pervert? Standing there like a eunuch. You want to play games in the showers, eh? Come on then!" Of course, the assumption here is that Karl's behavior is incredibly threatening to the other boys, but it is also confusing and outside their purview of physical and sexual knowledge. Karl's response is to say nothing; his silence makes the scene more uncomfortable and tense for everyone, including the film's viewers. In fact, throughout this scene Karl never says anything, except to cry out in pain when he is being hit with a towel, shoved by the other boys, and later in the scene, when one of the boys suddenly changes the hot water to extremely cold water. These visceral responses from Karl emphasize his physical vulnerability but also the sense of alienation he feels about his own body. What he does not want to see or feel, his testicles and penis, are the very part of his body that the other boys need to see in order to accept him as a male. When they come around the corner of the showers and he is obviously hiding his genitals between his legs, they are threatened by his rejection of his maleness. Karl's masculinity is in question; therefore, so is theirs by this rejection.

Suddenly around another corner comes a second group of boys, and at the head of the group is a strikingly good looking young student; he is bigger than the others and clearly more concerned about what is happening in the showers. This figure is the young Paul Prentice, and in more than a chivalrous gesture, he yells at the other boys to "leave [Karl] alone!" The immediate reaction of the boys to Prentice coming to Karl's rescue is to state, "Oh yeah, I forgot, you go out with him Prentice." At this stage of their relationship, there is no "going out," but Prentice is clearly concerned about Karl's welfare; at this moment in the film there is no sexual tension between Prentice and Karl.[2] When the boys continue to flout Prentice's presence and his command to leave Karl alone, he runs at the taunting group and fights them off of Karl. As Prentice places his school jacket around the naked and shivering Karl, one boy comes up to Prentice and says, "Oh, we're boyfriends now, are we Prentice?," obviously directing the comment towards his action of protecting Karl from the other boys.

As viewers we hear the word "queers" whispered in a dismissive, yet menacing tone around Prentice and Karl. However, Prentice and Karl are already shutting out the others' presence.

This is a serious moment as the two look at each other, one with sheer gratitude and the other with kind, smiling affection. Interestingly, Karl remains under the shower; he never moves as Prentice places the protective coat around him. He just stands and stares at Prentice as the water falls over his body, saturating the coat and himself. The water, which has acted as a sort of cleansing force at the beginning of this scene, emphasizing Karl's desire to reshape his body, now seems simply to be secondary to the momentous occasion of one boy saving another. This opening scene, although quite short, sets the stage for the intense emotional connection between these two people, which is rekindled when they meet as adults. However, by then Karl has become Kim Foyle.

Paul Prentice and Kim Foyle

After this very poignant scene in the shower, the viewer might be expecting the film to roll on in this manner, moving forward with the lives of the two boys and their relationship. However, as viewers we are suddenly jarred by a complete change of music and of scene. We see the title of the film on screen, hear for the first time rock music with a definitive beat and are confronted by the camera rising up over modern-day London city streets. Our first view of Kim, who was once Karl the boy in the shower, is in a taxi cab driven by an erratic and aggressive driver who keeps calling her "love." Kim, (played by Steven Mackintosh), is a thin, diminutive woman with sandy-blonde hair, wearing a plain, dark suit. Her body language is restrained, and it is clear that she is uncomfortable in the cab. As the cab driver swerves around the London roads, he hits a motorcyclist and the man goes over the cab's hood into the street. Thus ensues chaos and a rather funny exchange with the cab driver as he and the man, whom we later learn is Paul Prentice, (played by Rupert Graves), exchange words about who is at fault. When Prentice tries to get Kim involved in the discussion, she claims "it has nothing to do with me." Kim's immediate goal is simply to make sure that the motorcyclist is okay and to go on to her job as quickly as possible. Yet, in a moment of clarity she realizes that the man to whom she is speaking is the same person who saved her so many years ago from the vicious boys in the showers.

Prentice also senses something familiar about Kim but cannot place her. When he does come to the realization that Kim is Karl, he is hardly subtle about it; he calls out to "Karl!" on a public street while Kim walks past him. Over her shoulder, she declares emphatically, "not anymore!" as she walks away from Prentice before stopping to have a conversation. Kim is nonplussed at being "discovered;" however, when confronted with someone from her past she is obviously curious about him, now he is a grown man. Even during the first scenes between these two adults, director, Richard Spence focuses more on Prentice's struggle with Kim's new body than on Kim's idea of herself. Kim accepts herself and her identity, but she has not yet found a way to live a full and happy life. She is constantly worried about the world around her and the people whom she encounters. She seems to feel that the less she does to disturb the world, the easier it will be to live without being disturbed by others. But she has come to terms with her own identity; she is a woman; she feels and experiences her life from the perspective of a woman. On the other hand, it is Prentice who struggles with Kim's new body and identity. In trying to understand Kim's new self, Prentice is characterized as a rather insensitive clod; his first question to Kim is "Do you dress like this all the time?" Kim responds bluntly, "Well, I'm not a fucking drag queen!" Kim wants to be seen and treated like a "normal" woman, but Prentice first has to come to terms with her womanhood. When he is staring at her, she points this out to him, and when she says to him, "What do you think, Prentice?" he responds in a not too tactful way, "I suppose it's you, yeah." Prentice sees a woman's physical body, but he also sees his friend Karl. To say to Kim, "I suppose it's you, yeah," is to acknowledge not the woman Kim, but to suggest that Kim's "new" body is almost a sort of disguise over the once familiar male body. This first moment of "seeing" for Prentice mirrors the confusion between the categories of sex and gender. Prentice must merge his own understanding of his friend Karl with his new knowledge of Kim. This is one of the key themes that Richard Spence explores in this provocative movie.

Prentice's masculinity is portrayed almost as an extreme; he is a motorcycle courier so he is almost always dressed from head to toe in black and red leather. He is loud, and wears his emotions on his sleeve, constantly confronting those around him, most often other brutish males with whom he is happy to fight. Yet, he is clearly characterized as someone who takes notice of others, especially that someone with whom he was so close to in school. His reaction to Karl's transformation into Kim is one of confusion and even wonder. Their first "date" for drinks as adults shows Prentice and Kim's disparate personalities; Prentice is now a rather immature, emotionally volatile man who struggles to communicate easily with women, and Kim has become a self-protective, shy woman who wants to live her life without any public or private confrontations. During their "date" we discover a lot of information about their past relationship with each other. It has been sixteen or seventeen years since they have seen each other and in that time Kim has been to college. At one time, they both believed that Karl was gay; however, as Kim explains, she "got [that] wrong". Prentice is in a relationship with a woman at his workplace, Angela, and he has spent his time since their high school days moving from one job to the next without any real sense of permanency. The interesting irony is that Kim has "sort[ed] herself out" by transitioning from a man to a woman but that Prentice has never really succeeded in growing into a successful man. When they meet again, Kim has been living as a woman for "four years, three years pre-operative and one year post." Prentice's response to this revealing information is that Kim's decision was "pretty drastic", and he wonders why she couldn't have just lived as a "transvestite [and] pad [her] bra out at weekends." Kim's declaration that this was not possible and that she is "a woman and Karl was a girl" sends Prentice into an emotional tailspin. Confronted with a moment of confusion about Kim and her choices, and his clear interest in her physical changes he acts out aggressively in public and makes a scene in front of Kim. When Kim gets up to leave, Prentice runs after her shouting "Karl!" instead of Kim and tries to apologize for his behavior.

Outwardly and on a physical level, Kim's body is female, but Prentice must connect this very new knowledge with his own experiences of the male, Karl. Although this scene might appear trivial, compared to some of the other more provocative scenes that come later, it is actually pivotal in a larger discussion of gender and what it means to be male and/or female in society. In *Gender Politics: Citizenship, Activism, and Gender Diversity,* Surya Munro argues that "[d]iscrete forms of categorization form the basis for social identification" (3). Prentice sees a person who reminds him of Karl and because he has been in a relationship with this person, he names the obviously female person, Karl. Munro explains that "[a]lthough we tend to think that our bodies [and identities] are a 'given', actually our experience of them is formed by discourses" (29). Prentice's discourses are his own male experiences with women and his ideas about male and female bodies.

Understanding Gender and Sexuality, All Over Again

Although we never see Karl transform into Kim, the transformation is referred to constantly throughout the film, such as with an early exchange between Prentice and Angela. Prentice wants to understand Karl's decision to become Kim, as well as the desire he is beginning to feel for her and so asks himself what it means, genetically, to be a woman. In one scene, Prentice tries desperately to talk to Angela and work it out in his head. She embodies one of his "discourses" because he is having a relationship with her and, therefore, desires to engage with her and to get a woman's point of view. She barely pays any attention to what he is saying, brushing off the discussion because she is more interested in finding a particular green shirt to match his eyes. Prentice says to her:

> Did you know that we all begin life with identical genitals . . . it's like our sex chromosomes right, there is XX for [females] and XY for [males] . . . [and] apart from XX and XY, there is XXX and XXY, XXXY, X/XY, XY/XYYY, no wonder there's so much confusion . . . did you know that we're all basically female, men and women. Basically what makes maleness is just added on . . . so when it comes to who you're supposed to be, then *anything* could happen! (Prentice's emphasis).

Angela's sole reaction to Prentice's declaration of the male/female conundrum is to ask, "Who's confused? I sit down to pee, I know what I am." Angela's perspective about gender runs along the line of a very traditional heterosexual dynamic with Prentice. However, Angela is positioned outside of Prentice's newfound knowledge about gender identity; she can never hope to understand or to connect with what he is saying about sexuality. She knows who she is and defines herself through both a societal and heterosexual marker of womanhood; she sits to urinate. Prentice's attempt to have a "traditional" relationship with Angela is finally hindered by *her belief* that he cannot accept a more masculine role with her. When she questions him about the direction of their relationship, he responds that he doesn't "know what [he] wants." The implication here, by Prentice, is that he wants something other than a traditional, heterosexual relationship with Angela. Angela replies that "it's certainly not me, is it" whom he wants and Prentice grimaces with the knowledge that no, in fact, it is not Angela's body or femaleness that he desires. Spence suggests that Prentice and Angela's relationship ultimately is a failure. Interestingly, in this scene Spence also seems to suggest that the more substantive relationship is between Prentice and Kim. It is Kim whom Prentice is trying to understand, not Angela, and it is for Kim that Prentice shows an obvious attraction.

Prentice finds himself attracted to this new woman, Kim, in a way that he does not feel for Angela. However, in experiencing these new feelings, he begins to question his own sexuality. Throughout most of the film, Prentice tries to ignore his burgeoning sexual desire for a person whom he once knew as a boy. Prentice struggles with the knowledge that Kim was once Karl, and he emerges as a man with conflicting feelings for not only women but particularly for Kim. Prentice experiences what Queen and Schimel describe as "multiple subjectivities" in relation to his understanding of Kim's gender transformation. Queen and Schimel explain that:

> This mode of thought encourages overlapping and sometimes contradictory realities, a life of investigation and questioning as opposed to essentialism's quest for the One Truth, the innate quality, indubitable facts on a silver platter, the answer to everything. (21)

Kim's body does not represent "one truth," for Prentice, but many truths about herself and her gender identity. Kim sees herself as a woman because she has felt that way since she was very young. She sees her old self, her "man", self, and identifies it almost entirely with her penis. She states:

> I don't miss it. I never really wanted it. It was a growth coming out of me. You know the way you deal with growths, you get rid of them. It was ugly, it was all wrong. Everything felt wrong, it always had done.

Kim's gender identity has always been female; she was born male but feels and believes herself to be a woman. Yet, Prentice still has trouble reconciling his new physical and emotional feelings for Kim with his knowledge of their past as boyhood friends.

Understanding the Transsexual Body

At a pivotal point in the movie when they are having dinner together at Kim's apartment, Prentice asks Kim what parts of her body have changed since she began taking female hormones. He begins the conversation with Kim by stating, "This hormone business, it is quite interesting really. Apparently they gave doses of estrogen to male rats, and they started to build nests." He asks Kim "what has [estrogen] done for you?" Initially, Kim states that she's "a better driver now", but then she begins to catalogue her changes more seriously, describing in detail what happened to her physically:

Well, it changes your shape, obviously. You develop some things and lose others. It makes your skin softer. My breasts changed first and they've gotten even bigger in the last two years. My nipples are darker, the aureoles are larger. I've got hips now, my waist is slim, my belly's fuller. My buttocks are rounder, and my limbs feel lithe.

It is clear that as Kim describes how her body has changed, Prentice is visibly both uncomfortable with what she is saying, and he is sexually aroused by the details of change. Prentice ultimately becomes so sexually excited by what Kim is saying that he runs from the building declaring that he can't stay because she has given him a "hard-on". Kim's response is to say "it is not illegal" to experience sexual arousal, but Prentice will not stay to confront his new feelings for Kim. The sexual tension between Prentice and Kim at this moment is interrupted by Prentice's inability to rationalize his erect penis with the fact that Kim/Karl no longer has a penis as he once did and that Kim/Karl has sexually excited him. Outside of Kim's apartment, in the central courtyard of the surrounding buildings, Kim and Prentice yell at each other about what has just occurred between them:

Prentice: What was that? Your game of girl meets boy? . . . Karl's a woman after all? Shit! Didn't I notice, didn't you make me [notice]?
Kim: What? Scared your dick might end up in the wrong pigeonhole?
Prentice: If my girlfriend knew I was here!
Kim: Well, why doesn't she?—you keep pretty quiet about her. Now you know what it's like to be confused about your cock. Well, I got rid of my confusion, I had no choice. What are you going to do, get rid of me?
Prentice: Oh you think it is a big deal, do you? It's not, see?

At this point, Prentice unzips his pants to reveal his penis to Kim and the audience, and to declare that he doesn't "know what all the fuss is about . . . it just gets in the bloody way." This volatile scene between the two of them emphasizes the ambiguous nature of Prentice's feelings for Kim and his own confusion about his sexuality. Kim recognizes and confronts Prentice with his confusion by challenging him to accept her choice of a new body and changing genders. Prentice's overreaction to his "hard-on" is to pull out his penis in public, thereby presenting Kim with what she, herself, believed "was a growth coming out of [her]." He then begins to dance around the public courtyard screaming, enough so that soon there is a crowd of people staring at his penis. Confronted with the very appendage that Kim removed, Prentice asks her if she would like to go back into her apartment to "discuss [her] womanhood." Prentice's confusion, rage, and what seems to be almost embarrassment about his own sexual arousal culminates in his arrest for indecent exposure; he screams at the crowd and the police: "see the whole world is hung up on bloody genitals." Prentice's public outburst changes the tone of the film, which up until this point has been a developing love story. When Prentice and Kim are taken away in the police van, it is no longer possible to treat the film as a simple romantic comedy; now the film is about discrimination, the effects of police brutality, and the realities of gender difference.

James Berardinelli writes in a review of the film that "by becoming a woman, [Kim] has been forced to live with the stigma that society places upon those who change genders" (*Reel Views*, 1997). To emphasize this stigma, Spence uses violence to show viewers Kim's and, ultimately, Prentice's vulnerability at the hands of British police. After exposing his penis in public, Prentice is taken away by two police officers. Kim, too, is brought along, because she attempts to stop the police officers from apprehending Prentice. The tension among the four people in the van is palpable; Kim's body is stiff and pressed up against the police van wall because she has "never been in any trouble before". In the police van, one of the officers implies that Prentice and Kim are a gay couple and when asked what happened between them, Prentice replies "you got the wrong sexual orientation . . . she's straight and so am I." It is clear that one of the officers does not believe this when he declares, "oh yeah!" as if to say that he needs identifiable proof that Kim is a woman. The officer's comment, which is understood as antagonistic, culminates in him trying to feel under Kim's skirt in an attempt to discover "what's under here, then?" Evidently the officer believes that Kim is a transvestite. It is at this moment that Prentice steps in, as he once did in his youth, and protects Kim against abuse. In turn, the officer attacks Prentice and severely beats him, until another officer stops the situation from escalating even further. Spence films this scene so that only the close quarters of the inside of the police van are visible. Sound is amplified and the physical movements of everyone are exaggerated because of the space restrictions in the van. As viewers, we see pieces of bodies being thrown around because the scene is filmed so closely; we hear the anguished cries of Prentice as he is being attacked and Kim, as she desperately tries to get the officer to stop the violence. The dark colors in the van, (everyone is dressed in black and the back of the van is painted black), add to the cell-like atmosphere of the vehicle's space. The brutality of the beating is obviously connected to the officer's belief that Kim and Prentice are sexually involved. The officer reacts to them as if they are a threat not only to society but also to his masculinity and sexuality.

Subjective Perspectives

Perspective is, of course, subjective and during the scene in the van, Spence exaggerates the viewer's claustrophobic perspective by filming the scene very closely. Spence also plays on perspective through the eyes of the officers. In the van, the police officers do not see a woman; they see a man dressed in women's clothes; they assume Kim is homosexual and Prentice is his/her gay lover. Her outward appearance, then, is open to interpretation through the eyes of an authority group, the police. This new view of Kim changes the nature of her physical believability. In his review of the film, James Berardinelli points out that "Kim isn't a beautiful, petite woman, but someone whose features are still unmistakably masculine." However, by the time the viewer experiences the brutality of the van scene with Kim and Prentice, we believe in Kim's womanhood. She is no longer passing or pretending; we see her as a woman. But in the police van, we are confronted with a new visual perspective that Spence creates in the form of the police officers. This new perspective reveals the vulnerability and fear accompanying the subjective outward physical appearance of the transsexual. Throughout this scene between the officers and Kim and Prentice, Prentice refers to Kim as "she" and "her" with adamant conviction in a way that he has not done before. Prentice finally seems to recognize Kim's physical vulnerability because the officers insist on knowing absolutely whether Kim is a man or a woman. They want to see and feel, in a tangible way, Kim's penis, which they believe is under her dress. Perspective, in this scene, is not just about the visual, but it is about the tangible; what can be touched, must be real. This is the one scene in the film where there is a suggestion that Kim must be punished by society for her transition from male to female. Kim, herself, seems to believe that she will be punished for her new gender choice. When the officer tries to put his hand under her skirt, she actually does not push his hand away. Instead, she turns her head away in a passive gesture, waiting for the inevitable violation to occur. What happens, however, is that Prentice actively pushes the officer's hand away, yelling at him to "leave her alone!" This act leads to the brutality that defines this scene in the police van.

The violence that erupts around Kim and against Prentice changes their roles with each other. Prentice chooses to press charges against the police officer, and he asks Kim to help him. At first, she runs away to stay with her sister, fearing any involvement with Prentice and his volatile life. Her response to his repeated requests for help is to tell him that he brings "chaos, trouble, and fuss" into her life. She feels that in order to salvage her life and to keep her integrity as a woman, she "can't be involved [with him] anymore". This declaration to Prentice is Kim's way of withdrawing from the potential for more forays into the public eye. Kim feels exposed and vulnerable out in society; in the routine of life that she has come to know—going to work, coming home, visiting her sister—she feels safe and comfortable. Prentice invites change and Kim is frightened of any change that brings constant visibility. Kim defines herself as a woman, but she is very conscious of how others perceive her; she works in a large office in a very open space, yet she remains rather invisible to her co-workers. She chooses very plain, often beige, suits to wear to work. Her casual clothing is mostly in pastels and white. She wants to blend into the everyday world of male and female; she definitely does not want to call attention to herself and her body.[3] Although she fully accepts her body, she is keenly aware of what it means for others not to accept her body or her gender identity.

The tangible fear that Kim experiences in the police van and the police station force her into a position of almost supplication to the police. Judith Halberstam explains *In a Queer Time and Place* that "the *transsexual* body has been deliberately reorganized in order to invite certain gazes and shut down others" (97). When Kim is brought into the police station, it is clear that the male officers around her do not believe that she is a woman; she has no "proof of identity" as she tells them. The fact that she says her name is Kim and that she claims to be female, simply becomes a joke to the officers. They threaten to put her into a cell with "other people like [her] self," suggesting that she is an other, someone outside gender definition. The police officer's gaze is "shut down" by what he wants to see, not what is there to see in Kim's female body. Consequently, Kim simply wants to hide from their prying eyes and judgmental stares. They represent everything that she has been trying to avoid since boyhood when she was harassed in the showers for desiring to be different. When she is asked to side with the police against Prentice about the attack in the van, she does so simply to escape; as she says, she "avoids trouble" at all costs.

However, when Prentice reveals that he is going to leave the area after the court case, Kim changes her mind about escaping judgment and comes forward to testify against the police officer. It is Kim who comes to

Prentice's rescue, and who ultimately saves Prentice from a jail term for indecent exposure. This moment is a turning point for both Prentice and Kim, because it becomes clear that their love for each other traverses both society's prejudices against their relationship and Kim's change in gender identity. By uniting against the abusive police officer, Prentice and Kim are brought together on equal footing. The issue in their relationship is no longer about who does or does not have a penis, but about how much they mean to one another. During the courtroom scene, it becomes clear just how much Prentice and Kim believe in and rely on each other. When asked whether it was Prentice who "intervened to protect" Kim in the police van, Kim replies that yes it was "and not for the first time." This reply references the shower scene at the beginning of the movie and connects their boyhood experiences with their present experiences together as man and woman. Kim tries to define her relationship with Prentice and states, "well, you know what it's like when you lose a sock? The one that's left is odd. Well, Prentice is like the other sock turning up again . . . our relationship doesn't have a precise nature, it never will. All I know is, I don't know how I've done without him." This positive scene in the film, in which a transsexual literally takes the stand and openly denounces the brutality of the police force, while at the same time acknowledging her love for the man on trial is remarkable. The post-operative transsexual takes a powerful stance and decides her fate for herself. By standing up for Prentice and, ultimately, for herself, Kim finds a voice that she has never had. The film clearly supports the transsexual as a strong and vital person in society, one who will not be bullied or silenced. *Different for Girls* is cutting edge because of its emphasis on placing the transsexual in a position of power in the film's narrative.[4]

Power, in this film, is not just represented through Kim's decisive actions in support of Prentice, but also through the willingness to show the nude transsexual body. The intense love between Prentice and Kim culminates in the film's one sex scene, but second nude scene, in which Prentice finally comes to understand who Kim is as a woman and to understand his own sexual desires for her. Prentice, always curious about Kim's gender transition, asks point blank whether he can see her naked. His request is punctuated by his assertion that he and Kim are "mates" and "he showed [her his] appendix scar once;" evidently he considers this an even exchange. He claims he is just "curious" to "see everything more clearly" so that he understands her choices and her gender identity completely. Kim removes her clothes slowly for Prentice and for the audience. Spence does not shy away from filming Kim's body from both behind and in front of her. Prentice has the privileged position of viewing Kim's body first, but then the viewer is allowed to look at what Prentice is seeing. In the first nude scene in the showers, Karl seemed to want to wash away his difference and we sensed his alienation and loneliness. Here, in this scene, although Kim declares that "after all this trouble, [she] can barely bring [herself] to turn round," she does in fact show that she loves her body. As a boy, Karl despaired of his body, but here, as an adult woman, Kim rejoices in hers *because* she turns around. Kim's nudity, at this point in the film, is powerful in its openness and real physical beauty. The camera lingers on Kim's body; at first we see just her breasts as she stands in her underwear talking to Prentice. Then we see her in a full frontal pose, as Prentice stands staring at her, visibly aroused and struggling to take in the new person who is before him. In "A New Kind of Tranny," Gary Morris observes "this is a powerful, virtually unprecedented image of the unapologetic transsexual standing naked before us in a narrative film, demanding acknowledgment." As viewers, we see everything that Prentice is seeing; we see Kim's breasts and pubic area, as she stands unabashedly showing her naked, new body to Prentice.

What Is Woman?

In *Second Skins,* Jay Prosser explores transsexuality "as a passage through space, a journey from one location to another" (5). Kim's "passage" has been both a tangible one, as we have seen her transition from Karl to Kim, and almost a theoretical one because she has merged one perspective of her identity, maleness, with another perspective of her identity, femaleness. Kim, herself, identifies both with her new identity as a woman and with her old identity as the boy, Karl, *because* of Prentice. What Prentice sees as the naked Kim is a subjective view of the body and identity. He sees Karl/Kim as female and is attracted to him/her in a way that he did not allow himself to feel or act on when he was younger. However, he sees Kim's new body and he understands her "passage through [a] space [ial]" reconfiguration of self. Prosser argues that:

> [T]ranssexuality is precisely a phenomenon of the body's surface. In the cultural imagination that figure of the body as costume is surely welded most firmly to the transsexual . . . sex reassignment surgery is considered the hinge upon which the transsexual's "transsex" turns: the magical moment of "sex change." (63)

Kim's new body is not just about changing her shape, adding breasts, and surgically removing and reshaping her penis, but about how Prentice

remembers Karl's body. Kim states that "no one has ever asked" to see
her transformed body, but it is Prentice who needs to rationalize the
memory of Karl's body with his new knowledge of Kim's body and the
new person he knows as "Kim". To understand himself and his desires, he
must be able to merge the knowledge and memory of the male identity
with the knowledge and new experience of the female identity.   For
Prentice, Kim, her body, and her identity are more than the "magical . . .
sex change." These aspects of Kim are the merging of memories of the
past with new experiences of the present. When Prentice gazes on Kim's
body, touching it and declaring that her body "is nothing like [his]" and
that it is "so soft," he is harkening back not only to his own maleness but
to the person he once knew as Karl. It is as if he almost expected Kim's
body to be like his own, and he is pleasantly surprised by Kim's softness
and femaleness.

Prentice's sexual arousal for Kim is coupled with a relinquishing of
physical restraint on his part. He states to Kim: "you say your mind could
never accept your body before, but I don't want to struggle with it either."
By saying this to Kim he accepts his own desire for her, although he is
wary to make the first move and is caught off guard when Kim asks for his
hand so that they may be physically closer. Again, Spence is unafraid to
leave the camera on these two shy, but curious lovers; as they explore each
other's bodies, we are there to witness the exchange. The transsexual
body, moreover, is clearly sensual and inviting.

There is no brutality in this moment and no rejection of Kim on
Prentice's part. There is simply the sexual desire that two people feel for
each other. Although Kim's body is naked and exposed, which we also
saw when we first viewed Karl's naked body in the shower, she is no
longer vulnerable or alienated. As viewers, we are asked to embrace her
female body as she stands in front of us, and we are asked to believe in her
femaleness. In taking Prentice's hand and drawing him to her, Kim is
clearly in control of her own sexual experience. We see this later, too,
when she moves to be on top of Prentice and looks down on him.

The evolution in subjectivity that has taken place over the course of the
film allows this moment of physical exposure to be seen and experienced
as revolutionary. The transsexual woman has finally found a place in
society, and as Surya Monro points out "'fitting in' does in itself widen the
mainstream" perspective of gender and individuality (166). Certainly,
Kim has widened Prentice's and the viewer's perspectives about female

identity. Nowhere is this more evident than when Kim and Prentice ponder and caress one another's respective bodies, prior to having sexual intercourse. The detail that is given to this moment in terms of the way that these two people kiss and touch underscores the emphasis in the film on the power of lived subjectivity. To Prentice, Kim is a woman; therefore, the physical act of touching one another's bodies and experiencing sexual intimacy is a cathartic experience for both Prentice and Kim. This is a moment for Prentice and Kim to revel in their sexual desire for each other, but also for the film viewer to accept the male to female transsexual as just another "ordinary woman."[3] When Kim and Prentice finally have sexual intercourse, Prentice's interesting response is that "it fits, it bloody fits!" Prentice's surprise at being able to fit his penis inside of Kim, again harkens back to Prentice's need to rationalize and to understand the identity of this person whom he once knew as Karl with the person whom he now sees as a woman. To say that his penis "fits" is to not only accept Kim for who she is, but also to accept himself and his desires for her. However, the final part of this scene does not leave us with Prentice's striking comment, but with Kim's face and her obvious physical and emotional pleasure. This is more than a sexual moment for Kim; it is a moment that is also about freedom, power, and experiencing desire as a woman. By allowing the camera to stay on Kim's face here, Spence gives the transsexual woman an identity that is as much about individuality as it is about gender.

The truly remarkable aspect of the sex scene between Prentice and Kim is that we are not left to wonder what happened to these two people. In the final part of the movie, we get to see this couple move forward, stay together, and actually remain happy. The idea that a heterosexual man and a transsexual woman could actually be suited for each other is what this film suggests and even what this film seems to support and encourage. In light of this, the final part of the film focuses on Kim's and Prentice's domestic settling in with each other. Prentice even asks Kim whether having sex means that "[they] have to get [their] own habitat together and buy salad bowls." Prentice's question seems initially trivial; however, the question is actually quite provocative because it suggests a way to envision a rather mainstream domestic future for these two people.

Spence lingers on this moment of Prentice and Kim lying together in bed after having sex. Initially, the camera view is high above them, but slowly the camera moves in for a close-up. There is nothing forced about this quiet moment between Prentice and Kim; they cuddle and enjoy each other, reveling in the ability to touch one another. Lying together so closely emphasizes the intimacy that they share together. This moment also gives Kim a chance to take the lead in the relationship, a role that is new for her. Prentice has lost his job, his motorcycle, and can no longer afford to live on his own. Kim comes to his rescue by offering him a place to stay and an opportunity to sell their story to a tabloid to make some money.

Satisfaction and Domesticity

When the story does come out, however, it is Kim who believes she will lose her job because her "face is splashed all over the newspapers." Prior to these new events, Kim had led such a quiet life, desiring to simply fade into the background and to be anonymous. In one of the final scenes in the film, Kim arrives at her job wearing a bright red suit, something that she would have never worn prior to this when she only wanted to be a good verse writer for the greeting card company she works for, and nothing more. This change of suit color from dull gray to vibrant red suggests the kind of changes that Kim, herself, has gone through and the kind of control she now has in her life. She is a strong woman, who believes in herself, so much so that when asked by her boss "what happened?" Kim replies, "Well, after they removed my penis they created a hole in my perineum. They inverted the remaining penile skin and scrotum into the opening and made a vagina." This response to a question that could have referenced anything in Kim's life, suggests the emergence of a "new" Kim. She steps outside of her role as demure, fragile, quiet female to embrace a new voice, a new identity, and a new life for herself with Prentice. Moreover, the entire issue of Kim's sex change and her transsexual identity takes a backseat to the more pressing focus of showing Prentice and Kim as a successful couple.

As viewers, we follow Prentice and Kim into the domestic space of Kim's apartment and into their new lives together. However, Spence does not portray their relationship or their exchanges as pure bliss and rapture. Prentice still retains some of his slovenly ways, his clothes are strewn around the bedroom, and he demands of Kim to "make [him] some breakfast" when they are getting up in the morning. However, Kim, ever the doer in her new role in the relationship replies, "I might have changed a lot, but I can't manage becoming your mother as well!" Here, there is a play of words focusing on change; Kim has certainly changed, we have seen this throughout the film beginning with the first shower scenes with

Karl and leaving viewers with her relationship with Prentice. However, the change may be in the viewer as well. The viewer has had a change in perspective; we see and believe in this new woman and in her relationship with this new man, Prentice. This line of Kim's also preempts the next and final scene in the film where we see Prentice and Kim dressed all in black leather and walking toward their brand new Ducati 916 motorcycle. It does not seem like a coincidence that the motorcycle is the same red color as Kim's striking red suit we saw her in earlier.

The evolution has taken place in Prentice and Kim's relationship by the final scene in the film. Walking towards the motorcycle, we hear them bickering about work, running errands, and who is going to cook dinner. Their final exchange has to do with who is "riding pillion". Kim wins out in the end with the assertion that it was she who convinced Prentice to go to the tabloids with their unique story, and therefore, it is she who gets to drive the bike and, of course, be in control. The blending of Prentice and Kim's body on the motorcycle suggests how well they have come to blend together in life. This might be the ending of any mainstream romantic comedy; two people are drawn together and form a solid relationship. However, their history as two young boys together in school and the radical changes that have taken place after their meeting so many years later, make this film entirely different from a traditional romantic comedy. However, the emphasis at the end of this film is on just how much control Kim shows when handling the motorcycle. The narrative of the ability to ride has mirrored the narrative of her relationship with Prentice. At first, she was apprehensive about even getting on a motorcycle, and later when Prentice taught her how to ride, she lacked real confidence in herself as a driver. But at the end of the movie, she shows herself to be entirely at ease on a bike, obviously relishing in her ability to handle this machine. No longer is Kim holding on to Prentice on a bike, but it is Prentice who is holding on to Kim, as she whips around corners, through gates, and out onto the open road. This final image of Kim and Prentice emphasizes Richard Spence's clear interest in showing an extraordinarily positive representation of the transsexual in film.

Works Cited

A Soldier's Girl. Dir. Frank Pierson. Perf. Troy Garrity and Lee Pace. 2003. DVD. Showtime Entertainment, 2004.

Adventures of Priscilla, Queen of the Desert, The. Dir. Stephen Elliot.
    Perf. Terence Stamp, Hugo Weaving, Guy Pearce, and Bill Hunter.
    1994. DVD. MGM Home Entertainment, 2000.
Berardinelli, James. Rev. of Different for Girls. *Reel Views*, 1997.
    <http://www.reelviews.net/movies/d/different.html>.
Boys Don't Cry. Dir. Kimberly Pierce. Perf. Hillary Swank, Jeanetta
    Arnette, and Matt McGrath. 1999. DVD. 20th Century Fox, 2000.
Crying Game, The. Dir. Neil Jordan. Perf. Forest Whitaker, Miranda
    Richardson, Jaye Davidson. 1992. DVD. Live/Artison. 1998.
Different for Girls. Dir. Richard Spence. Perf. Steven Mackintosh and
    Rupert Graves. 1996. DVD. First Look Pictures, 2000.
Gritten, David. "A Change for the Good." *Los Angeles Times* 18 Sept.
    1997, Special to the Times, Home ed.: F-13.
Halberstam, Judith. *In a Queer Time & Place: Transgender Bodies,
    Subcultural Lives*. New York: New York University Press, 2005.
Morris, Gary. "A New Kind of Tranny." *Bright Lights Film Journal*. Vol.
    19. July 1997.
    <http://www.brightlightsfilm.com/19/19_different.html>.
Orlando. Dir. Sally Potter. Perf. Tilda Swinton, Quentin Crisp, and Jimmy
    Somerville. 1993. DVD. Sony Pictures, 1999.
Prosser, Jay. *Second Skins: The Body Narratives of Transsexuality*. New
    York: Columbia University Press, 1998.
Queen, Carol and Lawrence Schimel, eds. *Pomosexuals: Challenging
    Assumptions about Gender and Sexuality*. San Francisco: Cleis Press,
    1997.
Monro, Surya. *Gender Politics: Citizenship, Activism, and Sexual
    Diversity*. London: Pluto Press, 2005.
Rev. of Different for Girls. *Queer View*. May 15, 1997.
    <http://home.snafu.de/fablab/queerview/226differentforgirls/english226.htm>.
Rigoulot, Leslie. Interview with Richard Spence. *Film Scouts Interviews*.
    January 23, 1996.
    <http://www.filmscouts.com/SCRIPTs/interview.cfm?File=ric-spe>.
Russo, Vito. *The Celluloid Closet: Homosexuality in the Movies*. New
    York: Harper & Row Publishers, 1987.
Silence of the Lambs. Dir. Jonathan Demme. Perf. Jodie Foster, Anthony
    Hopkins, and Scott Glenn. 1991. DVD. MGM Studios, 2001.
Sylvia Scarlett. Dir. George Cukor. Perf. Katherine Hepburn and Cary
    Grant. 1936. DVD. Warner Home Video. 2007.
Whittle, Stephen. Foreword. *Finding the Real Me: True Tales of Sex and
    Gender Diversity*. Ed. Tracie O'Keefe and Katrina Fox. San Francisco:
    Jossey-Bass, 2003. ix – xi.

Woolf, Virginia. *Orlando*. San Diego: Harcourt Inc., 1956.

Notes

[1] There are films that exist that deal with both the cross-dressing person and his/her sexuality. Two important examples of the cross/dressing homosexual are Edouard Molinaro's *La Cage aux Folles* (1978) and *La Cage aux Folles II* (1980). Mike Nichols's American remake, *The Birdcage* (1996) also deals with the homosexual man who dresses like a woman and takes on feminine and woman-like characteristics. In all three of these films, a male character dresses as a woman and is a homosexual. However, passing as female in these films is not ultimately about being a woman. These men embody feminine characteristics, but do not desire to *be* female. Also, Beeban Kidron's *To Wong Foo, Thanks for Everything, Julie Newmar* (1995) presents three men who all dress as women, but who do not just define themselves as drag queens, but also as definitely homosexual. These films deal with cross dressing men and none of the men in these films wants to be a woman or says that they are in any way transsexual. They appropriate women's clothes, a more feminine persona, and take on mostly submissive characteristics in their relationships with other men to create the masculine/feminine dichotomy, such as might be seen in a stereotypical heterosexual marriage.

[2] I refer to Rupert Grave's character as Prentice and Steven Mackintosh's character as Kim because this is how these two characters refer to each other in the film. Prentice is rarely called Paul except by Angela, his girlfriend, in the first part of the film. Kim is called by her first name, and only very occasionally is she called Ms. Foyle. Prentice also refers to Kim as Karl very early in the film.

[3] When interviewed about his performance in *Different for Girls*, Steven Mackintosh explains that he didn't want his performance of Kim to be about camp and drag. He states "[a] lot of transsexuals don't have surgery in order to be glamorous. Some of them have a taste in clothes bordering on the boring. For them [the operation] is just about becoming an ordinary woman" (David Gritten, *Los Angeles Times* 1997).

[4] The film reviews of *Different for Girls* listed in the IMDB database that are written by American reviewers regard the film in a negative light, criticizing the plot as narrow and shallow and the transsexual representation as unconvincing. However, almost all foreign reviewers listed in the IMDB database see the film as unique and an important contribution to a very small group of films devoted to positive representations of the transsexual. Although this is a relatively small group of film reviews, it does seem to suggest a higher level of tolerance for sexual difference outside of the US. Perhaps, it is no surprise then that *Different for Girls* is a British creation and won the Grand Prix of The Americas at the Montreal World Film Festival.

Richard Spence, the director of *Different for Girls*, had the following exchange with Leslie Rigoulot during an interview at the Sundance Film Festival where the film was shown in 1997.

Rigoulot: There seems to be a different attitude towards sex in England.

Spence: We are fascinated with the borders of gender and sexuality. In America, there are more movies with 200 dead bodies, but let's not have someone's dick hanging out! In the UK, they have a less conservative view of sexuality.

CHAPTER FOUR

MODERNIZING THE ENEMY: STEVEN SPIELBERG UPDATES WELLS'S *WAR OF THE WORLDS* TO REFLECT THE CURRENT TERRORIST THREAT

THOMAS C. RENZI

Most people would agree that one measure of the artistic genius of a literary work is its durability, its capacity to maintain, generation after generation, wide critical and popular appeal. Another measure of this genius, probably not so commonly appreciated, is the extent to which a compelling, creative story lends itself to adaptations that can suit a different audience at different times and under different circumstances. That is, rooted in the plot or characters of a work are facets that plumb our primal core and serve as basic blueprints from which future writers can draw inspiration and reshape the original material to satisfy the tastes of a changing world. Told properly, the story never loses its power and influence, regardless of time and place. *The Tempest* can be vivisected and transformed into H.G. Wells's *The Island of Doctor Moreau* (1896), then launched into outer space as Wilcox's *Forbidden Planet* (1956), and later brought back to earth as Mazursky's *Tempest* (1982). Hamlet can wear black leotards and sulk about the corridors of a medieval Danish castle, or don a knit cap and stroll the streets of modern-day New York, or undergo a reincarnation as a lion king in the African jungle. Similarly, Odysseus can become Twain's Huck Finn or Conrad's Marlow or the Coen brothers' Everett Ulysses McGill; Faust can become Shelley's *Dr. Frankenstein* or Stevenson's Dr. Jekyll or Cronenberg's Seth Brundle. Critical appraisal from this standpoint depends not only on the intrinsic aesthetic merits of the original work, but also on the versatility and malleability of its material, its potential for translation and metamorphosis into a new, albeit fundamentally related, story.

Such adaptability is clearly inherent in the early science fiction of Herbert George Wells, as Jorge Luis Borges acknowledges in his eulogy for the influential author:

> Not only do [Wells's first novels] tell an ingenious story; but they tell a story symbolic of the processes that are somehow inherent in all human destinies. The harassed invisible man who has to sleep as though his eyes were wide open because his eyelids do not exclude light is our solitude and our terror; the conventicle of seated monsters who mouth a servile creed in their night is the Vatican and is Lhasa. Work that endures is always capable of an infinite and plastic ambiguity; it is all things for all men, like the Apostle; it is a mirror that reflects the reader's own traits and it is also a map of the world.[1]

Before writing his *fin-de-siècle* novel about a Martian invasion (1898), Wells had already treated then-current issues in three published novels, what he called his scientific romances: *The Time Machine* (evolution and socialism), *The Island of Dr. Moreau* (evolution, science, and religion), and *The Invisible Man* (the seductive nature and illusion of absolute power.) These stories share allegorical qualities that enhance their "infinite and plastic ambiguity," give their themes universality, and allow for a variety of interpretations. These same allegorical traits in *The War of the Worlds* make it most suitable for its subsequent adaptations, which, over the years, have reshaped the story to reflect the issues and concerns of a particular era.

Figure 4.1 Wells's Martian emerging from the space capsule—Wells created his tentacled aliens according to then-known living conditions on Mars and his ideas on where human evolution was heading. Spielberg's aliens appear as the dark side of his earlier E.T.

Frank McConnell, in his comprehensive examination of Wells's science fiction, tells us that rumors of war in Europe were rampant during the 1880s when most countries were expanding their armies and making technological strides by updating their arsenals and improving their weapons' destructive capacities: "...any number of relatively minor conflicts, particularly the Franco-Prussian War of 1870, had indicated as strongly as possible that a worldwide conflagration was not far off, and that it would be fought, when it came, with ferocity and with machines of destructive efficiency—and indiscriminacy—hitherto unknown." McConnell credits I. F. Clarke, author of Voices Prophesying War, with cataloguing a great many of these stories, among them The Battle of Dorking, one of the early seminal versions of these "invasion tales" illustrating the dire effects of countries collapsing into chaos.[2]

Wells, a man constantly immersed in issues related to social interaction and the human condition, did not forge The War of the Worlds in a vacuum. Under the constant influence of circulating "invasion tales," and specifically with fears of a German invasion on the minds of many English (World War II will explode a mere sixteen years later), he created a Martian blitzkrieg to symbolize the actual menace lurking on that front. He simply codified his story, composing an allegorical tale in which the enemy is depicted as a cipher that could stand for any overpowering aggressor.

Besides monitoring the escalating tensions among nations, Wells would have also been mindful of the hegemonic practices raging worldwide during the nineteenth century's Age of Imperialism: Europeans vying for footholds in newly colonized Africa; Britain clinging possessively to India and the Suez; America seeking expansion in the Pacific region. Each grasping nation espoused a firm belief in its own manifest destiny. In *The War of the Worlds*, Wells's narrator notes the parallel between the Martian invasion and the European extermination of the dodo and the Tasmanians: the technologically superior civilization carelessly and casually annihilates a docile species or a less developed culture that is defenseless against its onslaught.

Forty years later, in 1938, Orson Welles and the Mercury Theater adapted Wells's novel to the now infamous radio play that stunned listeners and drew international attention. Welles had prompted writer Howard Koch to update their predecessor's story, which he did, moving the central setting from London to Grover's Mill, New Jersey. Once again,

Martians were substituted for a very real earthly threat, the Axis Powers, and particularly the Germans who had brought the world closer to war after instigating the Munich Crisis earlier that year.

Figure 4.2   Orson Welles broadcasting his 1938 *War of the Worlds*—the radio broadcast exploited the real fears of an anxious America.

Orson Welles's perceptive treatment of H. G. Wells's material opened others' eyes to the story's potentials for adaptation. Since then, numerous alien-invasion films have surfaced, imitating Wells's original story even if they failed to admit their indebtedness to it. This particular group of films exploits our fear of the unknown and presents the aliens as warmongering demagogues who intend to conquer Earth and, in most cases, annihilate the human race. Among these quasi-adaptations are *Earth vs. the Flying Saucers* (Fred F. Sears, 1956), *Independence Day* (Roland Emmerich, 1996), *Mars Attacks!* (Tim Burton, 1996), and *Signs* (M. Night Shyamalan, 2002, which does openly allude to Wells's novel).[3]

In 1953, producer George Pal and director Byron Haskin released their film version of Wells's *The War of the Worlds* while the superpowers were in the throes of the Cold War. The film updates the original story, relocating central events around a modern Los Angeles and pitting the American atom bomb against Martian technology. As an adaptation, the film implies a link between the alien invasion and the Red scare. Hence, the Martians come, appropriately enough, from the "red" planet. Also, when a sequence of shots late in the film shows the devastation wrought upon the world's familiar landmarks and monuments, no damage is reported in Russia or its satellites. The disguised masterminds behind the worldwide holocaust would not, of course, wreak destruction on their own property

Figure 4.3   Dr. Clayton Forrester (Gene Barry) and Sylvia van Buren (Ann Robinson) in the devastated farmhouse—the scene is a loose adaptation of Wells's story where the narrator is trapped in a house with the military man. In Spielberg's film, Ray Ferrier (Tom Cruise) and Harlan Ogilvy (Tim Robbins) more closely parallel Wells's characters but with necessary modifications.

There was a *War of the Worlds* television series (1988-1990) developed as a sequel to the 1953 film and based on the premise that Earth's bacteria had not killed the Martians as was thought, but merely placed them in suspended animation. Decades later, environmental radiation destroys the offending microbes, and the Martians revive, becoming a menace to humanity all over again. Their unique ability to usurp human bodies and assume an individual's identity is reminiscent of the stolen identities in 1950s' sf films, such as *Invaders from Mars* (William Cameron Menzies, 1953), *Creature with the Atom Brain* (Edward L. Cahn, 1955), and *Invasion of the Body Snatchers* (Don Siegel, 1956), which planted in us vague apprehensions about our neighbors, unsettling suspicions that we could never truly know who was our enemy or friend. These films allegorized the fears instilled in Americans when McCarthyism confirmed and perpetuated the fiction that there existed an underground communist plot to take over our country. Now, after 9-11, a comparable paranoia exists today, the fear that anyone living in the most typical of American homes and neighborhoods can be a potential terrorist. These stolen-identity films of the 1950s and afterwards could easily be reinterpreted with implications related to this modern anxiety.

This is precisely the case, in 2005, when Wells's imperialistic Martians achieved a high watermark by coincidentally becoming the subject of three separate film projects. Although two of these films tried to distinguish themselves by including the English author's name in their titles, they both went directly to DVD, meekly yielding the major movie market to their competitor, the big-budget extravaganza directed by Steven Spielberg.[4]

The first of these two modestly budgeted entries, H. G. Wells's *The War of the Worlds*, was ambitiously directed, filmed, edited, and co-scripted (with Susan Goforth) by Timothy Hines. Its tagline alleged that it was "the first authentic movie adaptation of the 1898 H. G. Wells's classic novel," and the film justified this claim by setting the story in Wells's time period and following the novel with a high degree of fidelity—creditable qualities that come at the expense of dramatic tension and skilled filmmaking. Audience reaction was divided but keenly defined. About two-thirds of those who submitted comments to the Internet Movie Database, possibly disappointed that they were deprived of non-stop action and eye-popping spectacle, complained that the film suffered from mediocre special effects, stodgy acting, and near-stagnant pacing. Meanwhile, the other third, more tolerant in their tastes, praised it for treating themes and issues with some maturity and depth. This latter group is most likely the science fiction aficionados who are often willing to overlook abysmal production standards if a story's ideas are developed competently and logically.[5]

The second film that year, H. G. Wells' "War of the Worlds" (minus the definite article) was directed and co-scripted (with Carlos De Los Rios) by David Michael Latt. Like the Hines film, it had simplistic special effects and low production values (Producers at The Asylum boasted that it cost only a million dollars.) Like the Hines film, it subordinated spectacle to intimate scenes where characters bared their emotions and debated their philosophies. And like the Hines film, it endured reviews that, as might be expected, were divided in the extremes: those looking for extravagant visual effects were disappointed; those more interested in the development of substantial ideas gave it a satisfactory grade. However, Latt did enjoy more of a fifty-fifty split between defenders and detractors, possibly because his actors were more convincing.

So now we come to the most significant of the recent adaptations of Wells's masterpiece, Steven Spielberg's 2005 summer blockbuster. There is the temptation to call his *War of the Worlds* "the most ambitious effort to date" because of the grandiose and nearly seamless CGI (computer generated imaging) effects that create an impressive virtual reality. However, we have to remember that, in 1953, the Pal-Haskin production used state-of-the-art special effects for that time (and which, in some respects, still hold up today), and the film was no less painstakingly assembled. Spielberg's adaptation is prompted by the new crisis facing our world, a global threat from terrorists, as marked by the tragic events of 9-11. The film addresses issues related to that catastrophe while maintaining a remarkably close connection to Wells's original story. (The Hines and Latt productions also imply the consequences of a terrorist attack; however, this paper will focus on the Spielberg entry and save these other two for future discussion.)

That the film is an allegory on the threat of terrorism is obvious from the many relevant allusions interspersed throughout the story. The first occurs after Mary Ann (Miranda Otto) and her new husband Tim (David Alan Basche), preparing to visit her parents in Boston, drop off her two children, Robbie (Justin Chatwin) and Rachel (Dakota Fanning), at the home of their father, Ray Ferrier (Tom Cruise). Mary Ann reminds her son that he has to finish writing his school assignment on the French occupation of Algeria, a subtle foreshadowing of the alien invasion and occupation of Earth.

Little Rachel follows this with a comment that encapsulates the central irony of the film. Nursing her finger after picking up a sliver from the porch railing, she reluctantly, from across the room, displays her hand for her father. Ray is sitting in an armchair. He coughs and says the sliver needs to come out so the wound won't get infected. She refuses and, with her mature, grown-up outlook on such commonplace matters, replies, "When it's ready, my body'll just push it out." Ray's coughing and his reference to an infection are reminders of the presence of viruses and germs that, mundane concerns for humans, will prove lethal for the aliens. Coincidentally, Rachel's sliver is a microcosmic symbol for the aliens who, having invaded and occupied foreign territory, will, when Earth is ready, be "pushed out."

The scene that calls attention to an explicit parallel between terrorism and the alien invasion occurs shortly after the initial resurrection of the giant Tripod in Ray's neighborhood: both Ferrier children question whether terrorists are responsible for the attack. After the Tripod's appearance, Ray, looking for a way to escape the siege on his neighborhood, commandeers a van from his mechanic friend Manny (Lenny Venito). While Ray speeds away, barely in time to avoid the destruction and mayhem, a frightened Rachel, lying in the back seat, screams, "Is it the terrorists?" Ray gets on the expressway and starts to explain to his son what he saw minutes before. Robbie asks, "Is it terrorists?" Ray, of course, says no, but the association is clearly intimated, the children's questions voicing what should be our interpretation of the symbolic event.

Other ironic allusions emerge from the diatribe spouted later by Harlan Ogilvy (Tim Robbins, adopting, for no apparent reason, the surname of the astronomer in Wells's novel but playing the role of the military man.) While fleeing a firestorm wrought by the giant alien Tripods, Ray spots Ogilvy holding a rifle in the air and beckoning him and Rachel toward the entrance to his storm cellar. Ray takes his daughter into what he believes is a providential safe haven. Ogilvy soon unveils his overzealous and maniacal plan to overthrow the invading horde and Ray realizes that his savior is demented. While shoveling frantically in one of his dead-end tunnels, Ogilvy lets fly a string of wild assertions:

We're the resistance, Ray. They can't occupy this country. Occupations always fail. History's taught us that a thousand times. This is our land. We eat it, we breathe it, only we can live on it. They can't survive here, Ray. They weren't built for it.

Meanwhile, the aliens are conquering and destroying at will. They do occupy our land, they do eat on it—literally, for they drain the blood and bodily fluids from humans—and they do live on it. They are the survivors, while humans, totally helpless and vulnerable, appear to be the endangered species.[6]

The irony in Ogilvy's words is multi-layered. First, for all his fanatic ranting, he is totally accurate in predicting the outcome of the aliens' illegal claim on our planet. His perceptiveness is not evident until the end of the film, when we hear his words echoed in the words of the narrator (Morgan Freeman), who explains that we, as human beings, have earned the right to cohabitate with the microbes of this world because of our longstanding symbiotic relationship.

Then, too, with the alien assault symbolizing a terrorist attack, we, as Americans, can only concur with Ogilvy that we will fight ferociously to repel any invasion that threatens our way of life. That said, there is still another irony related to current political events. For whatever reasons the United States had attacked Iraq, and whether people agree that our motives were noble or ignoble, valid or ill-founded, the Iraqis must in turn view us as the alien invaders bent on destroying their culture and institutions. From the Iraqis' perspective, Ogilvy's outburst identifies Americans as the arrogant aliens arrogating Iraqi land, and Iraqis must see themselves as "the resistance," believing that Americans "can't occupy this country" because history has repeatedly shown that "occupations always fail." With all the patriotic fervor that we Americans feel for our country, we must appreciate that Iraqis feel the same for theirs and will stubbornly insist that Iraq belongs to them: "We eat it; we breathe it, only we can live on it. The Americans can't survive here, Abdullah. They weren't built for it."

In respect to Iraq, this last irony may remind us a little of Mark Twain's "The War Prayer," in which a ragged stranger steps up to the church podium and warns the congregation about the true consequences of their prayer calling for the destruction of their enemy. While we think of ourselves as the guardian of right and our foe as the personification of evil, we may fail to realize that our opponents are people who will have to endure all the hardships, suffering, and pain that comes with warfare— which ultimately makes them no different from us. Yet this is not the way we (or any bonded community or group or clique) approach a conflict. To avoid this moral dilemma, Spielberg's *War of the Worlds* follows Wells's novel and Haskins' 1953 film and portrays the invading aliens as visibly repulsive and irredeemably malevolent. Both aspects are important, because their ugly, inhuman appearance prevents us from identifying with them, and their unprovoked attack and wanton killing make them unequivocally monstrous and unforgivably wicked. In an odd way, this is gratifying because it confirms our perception of our enemy: whether Germans or Communists or terrorists, they must be heartless beasts with no iota of human compassion in them.[7]

The first appearance of the alien machine is a fabulously harrowing moment in the film. The effectiveness of this segment depends on the skillful merging of CGI with reality to create a scene of dreadful wonder and terrifying spectacle. Ironically, the emergence of the gigantic Tripod from beneath the ground inspires in the audience the same emotions felt by the characters in the story, the conflicting ambivalence of awe and terror. The local crowd mills about the site where lightning bolts had struck, curious about the inexplicable weather phenomena and waiting for something to happen; they should instead be running for safety. When the Tripod finally does surface from its subterranean retreat, the people stand and gawk, hypnotized by its monstrous magnificence yet fearful because of its eerie, foreboding presence.

The Tripod's resurrection comes at the expense of the nearby church, which not only collapses because of the shifting ground and tremors, but bears the brunt of the machine's supreme symbolic insult. After the steeple teeters and crashes into the square, after the machine pokes its head out of the ground and the church's cross tumbles off a mound of earth clumped on its "head," the alien Tripod raises itself to its full height. It emits a deafening bellow, a loud foghorn-like yawp that represents its birthing cry, but also imitates a burst of flatulence. In that moment, more earth streams from its groin area onto the spot where the church had lately stood, blatantly mimicking a defecation. Unlike Lemuel Gulliver, who urinated on the Lilliputians' Royal Palace with the sincere intent of putting out a fire, the Tripod's defecation is the deliberate desecration of a revered and sacred human institution. The sacrilegious act has a precedent in Haskin's 1953 film, where one alien machine's destructive rays shatter the stained glass window of a church, and seconds later, machines begin to fail all over the world. The post-hoc-propter-hoc inference is that killing humans is one thing, but in defiling God's house, the aliens have gone too far and God punishes them. In Spielberg's film, the cause-effect relationship is still implied in this emergence scene, although the distance between this moment and the realized fate of the aliens is so remote that the immediate connection may be obscured.

Figure 4.4: The alien tripod defecating on the church—the sacrilege appears earlier here than in the final climactic scene of Pal's 1953 film. Pal linked religion to his resolution of the alien invasion, whereas Spielberg converted the outcome into something more naturalistic, even atheistic.

We should interject a question here: If the Christian church stands on the side of humans, the supposed side of right and justice, then what religion, if any, supports the aliens? We never discover enough about the invaders to learn whether they believe in some deity or in a God or gods, but it makes no difference, because historically, no matter which and how many religions worship God, be they Christian, Muslim, Jew, or whatever else, each one will insist that, from its own defined theocentric point of view, the others cannot possibly be worshiping the same one true God. As symbols of terrorists, the extraterrestrials are alien not only in their ethnicity but also in their theology.

This scene in which we first see the emergence of the Tripod further reinforces the notion that the aliens represent terrorists. The characters' consensus in the film is that the alien invaders had planted their giant machines deep in the ground millennia ago and activated them now because they have decided that Earth is ripe for plundering. The buried machines symbolize dormant terrorist cells entrenched in the very foundations of our society, slumbering patiently for many years until they receive orders to galvanize their brethren and wreak who-knows-what kind of havoc on our innocent and unsuspecting communities.

This premise creates a plot gap for the film: how Ray, the female news producer, and Harlan Ogilvy deduce the full extent of this information is beyond the logic of the story. From his one initial run-in with the alien machine, Ray could not have garnered enough evidence to draw all of his startling hypotheses, which he delivers so authoritatively to Robbie, making them sound more like definite facts; and with all communications systems inoperable, the female reporter—and especially Ogilvy, isolated in his cellar—could not have had access to such complete knowledge of the enemy. (How does the reporter know that the bulge in the lightning bolt is an alien? How does anyone know that the machines were planted in the ground even before humans evolved?) The film needed to provide additional evidence to help us understand how these three could have obtained their information.

One reason for this lapse in logic is that the story is told from the limited perspective of the main protagonist—which, as a narrative viewpoint, is still in all a good choice by the filmmakers: it effectively enhances the tension and terror of the story and it remains faithful to the novel, which is also told from the viewpoint of a single, ordinary man caught up in the struggle for survival. The difference is that Wells, facing similar obstacles in his storytelling, had the advantage of the novel form: he could insert events and information unknown to the narrator by employing several literary devices, such as the flashback and alternate anecdotes filtered through the narrator. An interesting thing about Wells's novel, one that is easy to overlook, is that the entire story is told in retrospect after the invasion and demise of the Martians have already occurred. This enables the narrator to include information that was not available at the onset of the assault and was learned only after the crisis had ended. At one point, he actually deviates from his personal account and reports events witnessed by his brother. Also, he occasionally inserts information provided by scientists who, with the event passed, have made discoveries about the Martians, their physiology, their weaponry, and their red weed.

The scenes that take place in the two basements, Tim's in suburbia and Ogilvy's in rural America, contain allusions that further reinforce the film's allegory of a potential terrorist attack. When Ray and his children first arrive at stepfather Tim's house in an affluent neighborhood, all appears peaceful and safe. Highlighting this mood is the family photograph with Rachel and Robbie sitting cozily and securely beneath a blanket alongside their mother and stepfather. However, while Ray snoozes with the children in the basement, a plane suddenly crashes into their house, and they are saved only because they get to the separate furnace room just in time to escape the impact and the flames.

The scene is one of many that strain our ability to maintain a suspension of disbelief. If an airplane crashed directly on a house, it hardly seems likely that any person would survive unscathed, let alone three. When Ray ascends the basement stairs the next morning and comes upon the sight of the disaster, the hull of the plane is torn open, yet we see no dead bodies (a couple of bulging blankets on the seats may hide corpses)—only a lone cameraman scavenges the wreckage for food and water. This man is one of three people from a television news crew who happened by in their van. Why their van and Ray's and a variety of other military vehicles and cars still function is not very clear, since the aliens were able to render inoperable every appliance and machine that depends on batteries and electricity. Then, too, when Ray gathers his children into the van to leave their stepfather's house, the vehicle, despite its proximity to the crash site, appears untouched—and Ray casually backs it up and negotiates through a narrow path conveniently provided by the scattered debris.

Figure 4.5 Conflagration on the countryside—an example of an event that strains credibility is that Robbie, after winning his independence from his father, rushes headlong into the battlefront, yet survives the flaming holocaust that inundates the hillside.

Although our common sense says that logic has at times deserted the plot for parts south and beyond, our intellect may be able to overlook these "flaws" if we emphasize allegory over verisimilitude, if we minimize the implausibility of these moments and accept them as symbolic events. (Of course, this is not always easy to do, and for some of us, impossible.) To illustrate, in the scene just described, Ray is carrying a handgun for protection. After getting comfortable in the basement of Tim's house, he falls asleep at a time when he should have been most vigilant. The danger that threatens him and his family, however, requires far greater defensive measures than a paltry handgun. The plane's crashing into a house where normalcy appears still intact is a reminder of 9-11, when two planes had crashed into the World Trade Center on a peaceful, ordinary day. America's defense floundered—in effect, slept—at the moment we needed it most. Despite having the most sophisticated defensive system in the world, the United States failed miserably against the heinous, coordinated scheme of conspirators who used our own planes to destroy a symbol of American economic preeminence. Likewise, in causing a plane to crash into Tim's house, the aliens destroy a symbol of the American family. Spielberg has no bodies on the plane because he needs no bodies to indicate the parallel. The added carnage may have contributed to the realism, but it is not required to relay the implications of the symbolic catastrophe.

The ramifications of an alien culture overrunning our nation are symbolized in how Tim's spacious, well-lighted modern basement contrasts with the dank, dirty, rat-infested storm cellar of Harlan Ogilvy. The lavish life style of many Americans before the alien invasion has degenerated into an austere, primitive existence. To further underline this deterioration of our once highly civilized society, Ray is forced into a situation where he must kill Ogilvy if he and his daughter are to live. Their altercation in hand-to-hand combat represents survival of the fittest at the most primal level. The contest between the two men was established earlier when an alien probe snaked its way into the cellar and each man had a different opinion of how to deal with it: Ogilvy was ready to confront it (a hawkish, militant attitude); Ray preferred to use a wait-and-see method (a conservative, tactful approach.) In current world politics, debate on how to deal with terrorists tends often to fall into these two extreme camps.

One thing offered on modern DVDs that I've come to value immensely is the special features, which frequently contain a history of the film's production, interviews with the actors and film crew, discussions about camera techniques and special effects, and out-takes and deleted scenes. Sometimes, this behind-the-scenes approach can enhance our understanding and appreciation of the film. However, at other times the information can be trivial, superficial. Most of the special features that accompany Steven Spielberg's War of the Worlds may satisfy general viewer curiosity about the production, but they offer few meaningful insights about the film's themes and the creative decisions that determined the construction of the story. As one example, costume designer Joanna Johnston claims that the reason she clothed Ray Ferrier (Cruise) in a dark brown leather jacket instead of a black one was to deviate from the conventional look and make him appear more distinctive.

Nonsense!

She gave him a dark brown leather jacket because it was important to code him in some (excuse the pun) fashion. And this she does.

The reason for the brown leather jacket becomes more evident when we examine the implications of three particular scenes that involve reflected images. (There are at least six important scenes involving reflections; for the purpose of this essay, however, we're only concerned with the following three.) The first one shows Ray reflected in the television screen after he turns it off; he then tosses a baseball mitt to Robbie, coaxing him to join him in the backyard for a game of catch. A little later, two mirrored images occur in succession when the alien machine, newly risen from beneath the street, is reflected first in a store window with people standing behind the pane, and then in a car windshield while Ray stands alongside the vehicle. The third scene occurs after Ray brings Robbie and Rachel to Tim's house and he tries to fix them peanut butter sandwiches. He makes an effort to feign normalcy in the face of the alien attack, but when his children refuse to eat, he erupts in a rage, throwing one slice of buttered bread against the window. In a kind of "over-the-shoulder" shot taken from behind Ray, we see his reflection in the pane, standing to the left, while the slice of bread, on the right, sticks to the glass and starts to slide grotesquely downward.

These three scenes involving reflections work on multiple levels where the combination of elements in each tableau suggests relationships between humans and technology and between Ray and his children. The reflection of the giant Tripod appearing in juxtaposition with several onlookers and then with Ray suggests a momentary stasis between humans and this sinister alien technology, a stasis that in several seconds will be shattered when the machine begins to shoot green disintegration rays (laser beams?) at its human quarry. When Ray's figure is reflected in the television screen (the low-angle shot gives him a looming presence), he, in effect, replaces the television program that he just shut off. Symbolically, he substitutes himself for technology to introduce a moment of play that does not require anything mechanical. Robbie, however, retaliates against this gesture by deliberately missing the ball and letting it smash a hole through one of the house windows. Later, when Ray's reflection appears in the kitchen window at Tim's house, he has tried again to bond with his children by performing one of the simplest of ordinary tasks, to make peanut butter sandwiches for them. Yet Rachel declares she has a peanut allergy and Robbie says he is not hungry. Both of Ray's efforts are, from his point of view, genuine attempts to show paternal concern for his son and daughter, and both times he is rebuffed.

Further, when Ray is reflected in the television, he wears a light brown jacket (not the leather one yet) and a green hooded sweatshirt. Later, when he is reflected in the kitchen window, he is finally wearing his brown leather jacket (over the same green sweatshirt); outside the window, an evergreen shrub is visible and appears to blend with his mirrored image. Thus, Ray is associated with browns and greens, earth tones, while the alien Tripods, sleek metal machines, appear ominous in the cold, hard colors of silver and black. On one level, the War of the Worlds refers to humans against aliens, but as these reflected images suggest, it is also nature (earth tones, evergreen) against machine. Because human technology appears so helplessly inferior to the Tripods, the supposed contest is, as Harlan Ogilvy observes, no more a war "than there's a war between men and maggots." In the end, we discover that the less obvious war, the silent conflict between nature and machine, is the more critical war, the one in which David slays Goliath and preserves Earth for human habitation. This is the irony of Wells's title, and it is the same irony carried into Haskin's and Spielberg's films. Spielberg's creative and innovative use of iconography to convey these thematic ideas is especially noteworthy.

Another of these images that work effectively is the red weed that proliferates over the countryside. A product of Wells's imagination, the weed does not appear in Haskin's film, but Spielberg, with some modifications, chose to retain it. In Wells, the plant spreads everywhere, and then like its sowers, dies off, unsustainable in Earth's atmosphere. In Spielberg's film, the red weed is fertilized with human blood—at least that is what Ogilvy asserts, although it is never validated from an official or secondary source. Supposedly, Ogilvy has seen the machines siphon blood from humans and then spray it on the spreading vines. If so, the blood may be the reason that the weed is red, not that the aliens originate from the red planet Mars, a point never quite confirmed in the film.[8] Spielberg, like Wells, uses the weed as a symbol of occupation and domination—the insidious infiltration of a foreign culture into every facet of life of the defeated peoples. One of the most dynamic images of the film occurs when Ray leaves Ogilvy's house and climbs the ridge that overlooks a valley. For miles and miles in all directions, the red weed radiates like a crimson carpet over the landscape, a cosmetic makeover indicating that the new alien dynasty has replaced our familiar world. It is also symbolic of the violence and bloodshed the aliens have inflicted to achieve this. Even after the weed decays, it leaves unsightly traces, disturbing reminders of the former presence of the conquerors and their devastation.

A substantial number of reviews sent to the Internet Movie Database by the movie-going public issued strong criticism about the scene in the Boston street at the end of the story. With the world waylaid and flattened all around, this major American city still has its brownstones standing at attention in snobbish defiance. However, if we consider this as another instance where allegory overshadows logic, we can accept it as contributing to the thematic design of the story. The alien invasion decimated our civilization and undermined our humanity, as symbolized by Ray's descent from Tim's affluent suburban home to Ogilvy's squalid farmhouse and by his having to resort to murder in order to survive. This ending, contrived as it seems, hints that our former way of life is not utterly destroyed. Ray and Rachel have witnessed the end of the monster machines, and their triumph in reaching their destination, the home of her grandparents where the family unit is restored, represents a return to the way of life that Americans knew before they were displaced by war. With renewed hope and communal effort, people can resurrect everything they once had.

Related to this is the question of why Ray undertook to return Robbie and Rachel to their mother in the first place. In Wells's original story, the narrator is on a desperate quest to reunite with his wife—a goal we may easily discount while envisioning the horrific series of events that he endures. In a world gone berserk, however, we should find it very natural to want to cling to the things that provide us with some semblance of normalcy, and what better to signify that than to seek out those closest to us. And so Ray, estranged father and husband, feeling perhaps that his ex-wife is more competent than he to take care of the children, chooses to return them to her. His quest to reunite his children with their mother in Boston parallels the quest of Wells's narrator striving to reunite with his wife, and the success of that mission, coming just after the first signs of the alien defeat, suggests something indomitable and persistent about the human spirit.

Ray's role as an intermediary between his children and his ex-wife is suggested by his surname, Ferrier. He is a ferrier, a ferryman, in the sense that he is "ferrying" his children to their mother. (He succeeds where the ferry that tries to cross the Hudson River fails.) Homophonically, his name is also linked to "farrier," a person who shoes horses, which affiliates him with Rachel's toy horses. While Ray and Robbie are throwing the baseball back and forth, Rachel sits at a table, playing with two toy horses, one of which has a green blanket on it. If the pun on his name enables us to associate Ray with horses, then the colors of brown (horses) and green (blanket) reinforce his connection to the earth-tones motif.[9]

One unfortunate shortcoming that I do have difficulty condoning is the fact that Ray Ferrier is transformed from Everyman into Superman. The film deliberately—and effectively—introduces him as a blue-collar dockworker whose simple life style is punctuated by his singular interest in car engines and his one self-indulgent amenity, his super-charged Mustang (another subtle suggestion of his association with horses.) This cursory reference to his knowledge of cars explains why he can tell Manny to change the solenoid when the van won't start. His station in life parallels that of Wells's narrator, a "speculative philosopher" who leads a quiet, uncomplicated existence. Suddenly, however, when pressed into action, Ray single-handedly destroys a Tripod, a feat that raises him from an everyday Joe scratching out a living to a lofty hero of Mission: Impossible, smoothly and competently eradicating the bad guys. Of course, dad had to get himself and his daughter out of the Tripod's gunnysack. It might have been more logical, however, if the soldier who yelled "Everybody down!" had been given that task—then ol' dad could have preserved his integrity as an everyday Everyman, the way the film initially portrayed him. (Wells's narrator performs no such deed, retaining his Everyman status to the end.)

Figure 4.6 Tripod attack on the ferry—the literal ferry reminds us that Ray Ferrier, as implied in his name, is a figurative "ferrier," conveying his children back to their mother.

Throughout the picture, with realism frequently subordinated to allegory, Spielberg still captures some of the genuine aura of actual wartime situations, scenarios that could come to pass if terrorism achieved even a limited and temporary success. This is depicted primarily in the scenes showing mass evacuations, such as when Robbie drives past the lines of refugees making their way along the road. They lug their most treasured belongings, choices they had to make before fleeing their homes. After Ray loses his van to the mob, he and his children become refugees themselves, wandering among the bands dispersed across the countryside and heading blindly in the same direction toward some vague, indefinite place of safety and refuge.

The ferry scene, when the Tripods abruptly appear and attack, contains a number of realistic elements demonstrating how mass hysteria affects behavior and reason. The significance of this depends on its comparison with the previous scene where Ray loses his van to the mob. Ray had let Robbie drive the van while he slept, warning him to avoid crowds because, if people see he has a working vehicle, they will try to take it from him. Robbie inadvertently drives into the middle of a throng of refugees. Ray takes the wheel, and as he inches along, one man yells, "You can carry twenty people in there." Ray knows the unpredictable nature of mob mentality, that people will act out of sheer desperation and that, because he cannot help everyone, he had better help only his immediate family. He rejects their pleas. Despite this resolution, the mob stops him and seizes the van. At the ferry crossing, his role is reversed: Ray and his children become the ones in need of a ride. In the frenzy of the Tripod assault, the ferry captain limits the number of people who can ride his boat. After being refused the chance to board along with others on the dock, Ray manages to force his way onto the ferry with his children and yells at the guards, "There's plenty of room. There's room for hundreds more." His words iterate those of the man who shouted at him while he was driving his van. Ray demonstrates an ambiguous quality in human nature. As long as a person can satisfy his own needs (such as when Ray has the van), he can remain aloof to the needs of others. However, when that same person is deprived of certain needs (such as when Ray and others are kept from boarding the ferry), he will demand that others supply him with his wants. In a moment of crisis, fear breeds desperation, and desperation can spawn irrational, inhuman behavior.[10]

Steven Spielberg appears in a 2005 science fiction documentary that examines alien invasions in general and the 1953 and 2005 *The War of the Worlds* adaptations in particular.[11] In his interview, he admits that, in making his film, his creative decisions were influenced by the cataclysmic event in September 2001: "I certainly would have made this *War of the Worlds* differently pre-9-11. It would have been a little more of the Hollywood science fiction." He acknowledges the allegorical nature of Wells's story and that he refigured it to depict the unthinkable outcome of a successful terrorist invasion: "My movie is more about the American refugee experience.... My movie is what happens when Americans are put on the run...heading away from the eastern seaboard—that is an image that is evocative for me and my generation post-9-11." Admittedly familiar with countless images of Parisians fleeing their city during World War II, Spielberg depicts in his film a grim scenario that Americans would find impossible to conceive, that war could be fought on our own land—such as during a terrorist invasion—and that we could be displaced from our homes and have our families torn violently asunder.

Figure 4.7 Refugees on the march—Spielberg inserts realism into his film, based on his familiarity with documentary war films showing people fleeing areas of conflict.

The Internet Movie Database provides 2,561 reviews of Spielberg's film, more people claiming they "hated" it (1,242) and giving it substandard ratings than those saying they "loved it" (1,211).[12] Except for Robbie's miraculous escape from the hillside conflagration and Ray's jarring evolution from Everyman to hero, I feel more kindly disposed toward the film and am willing to give it more latitude for its illogical moments. Because it fails to contend with those ideologies, paradoxes, and speculations that make science fiction so intriguing, it may fail to appeal to the staunchest of sf connoisseurs. However, presented as an allegory that emphasizes symbolism over realism and plausibility, the film succeeds very well. Spielberg's expertise in layering his iconography with rich connotations and ironies and in telling much of his story through visual, cinematic means is what makes *War of the Worlds* a thoughtful and intelligently constructed film. Suspenseful and spectacular, it is highly entertaining, well-designed, and meaningful, a creative reworking of

Wells's original story, and a competent allegorical treatment of the potential threat of terrorism.

Notes

[1] Jorge Luis Borges, "The First Wells," H. G. Wells: The Critical Heritage, ed. Patrick Parrinder (London: Routledge and Kegan Paul, 1972) 331.

[2] Frank McConnell, The Science Fiction of H. G. Wells (Oxford University Press, Oxford, 1981) 131-132.

[3] The Day the Earth Stood Still (Robert Wise, 1951) is an anomaly that deserves mentioning here. Sure, Klaatu (Michael Rennie) appears as a benevolent ambassador who encourages warmongering earthlings to find a compromise for the sake of peace, but his warning is delivered like an ultimatum with no alternative: humans must conform to the dictates of the intergalactic community or face annihilation at the hands of the technologically superior extraterrestrials. Although it may sound irrational, people would rather endure war and conflict within their own group, whether within families or within nations, than have some outside authority intervene and impose its will on them. Klaatu's message, then, noble on the surface, can be construed as a kind of demagoguery not very far removed from that of Wells's Martians.

[4] Although Spielberg scheduled his film for release in Japan and Europe in mid-June 2005, it did not debut in America until June 23 (premiering in New York), nine days after Hines's and five days before Latt's were released on DVD. That three feature films based on the same story should be released at virtually the same time gives rise to numerous speculations. One is that the producers of the Hines and Latt films hoped to capitalize on the hype surrounding the Spielberg production, so that the title, through name recognition, would automatically attract an audience. At the same time, they may not have believed they could compete against Spielberg in the theaters, and so went immediately to DVD to capture the home market as quickly as possible.

[5] The Internet Movie Database (http://www.imdb.com) invites viewers to submit comments on any film. Reading some of the reviews of War of the Worlds, one is amazed at how observant and sagacious—and highly critical—the general public can be about film.

[6] Wells's Martians are clearly vampiric in that they suck the blood from humans for their own sustenance. Spielberg's aliens, according to Ogilvy, siphon human blood to fertilize their red weed. Both are symbolic in their own way. Wells suggests that humans, as mere creatures subject to all the laws of nature, can become food for a dominant species just as easily as humans use subordinate species for food. In a clever variation on this idea, Spielberg links the human bloodletting to the red weed, thereby suggesting that the loss of our familiar landscape, gradually evolving into an environment that suits our conquerors, occurs at the loss of our own blood.

[7] Although Wells, Pal, and Spielberg have different conceptions of the aliens' appearance, they all depict them as thoroughly gruesome and repulsive beings.

Wells's aliens still hold up as the most authentic and impressive because they are the least anthropomorphic and because he bases their biological makeup on scientific and evolutionary possibilities which he describes in detail.

[8] At the beginning of Spielberg's film, during the narrator's exposition, we follow a sequence of images: a round droplet of water on a leaf converts to the blue orb of earth as seen from outer space, and this in turn converts to the red circle of a stop light suspended above rush-hour traffic. The fact that the red disc obliterates the blue one foreshadows the alien devastation of our world. This, coupled with the growth of the red weed that overtakes the countryside, suggests that the aliens are indeed from Mars, the red planet, but other than these couple of visual allusions, their origin remains ambiguous, leaving open our interpretation of what they may symbolize.

[9] Through all their adversity, Rachel totes around two significant objects, a third-place ribbon she won in a horse riding competition and a small stuffed horse, both indicating her deep love of horses. Since Rachel finds security in her plush toy, and since we can associate Ray with horses, then subliminally, she either seeks solace and reassurance from her father or already feels that he provides these necessary comforts. This consideration almost excuses his turnabout from Everyman to hero (my ensuing complaint about Ray's heroics that contradict his status as a common man) because he fulfills what may be her most sensational fantasy of him as a father.

[10] We can't forget that Ray, in desperation, had already appropriated the van from Manny as if he were entitled to it. He knew it was the only working vehicle in the area and the sole means of a quick escape. This parallels the scene in Wells's novel (Book I: Chapter 9) where the narrator, in a conscious deception, "borrows" a dogcart from a tavern owner without alerting him of the imminent danger. The narrator conveniently rationalizes that his own need is greater than that of the other man.

[11] Watch the Skies! Science Fiction, the 1950s and Us was produced, written, and directed by Richard Schickel and released in 2005. Although the documentary contains references to many sf films and their different attitudes toward extraterrestrial life, the discussion frequently returns to *The War of the Worlds* and Pal's and Spielberg's adaptations.

[12] This was the total as of January 2, 2007, when I last accessed the web site for this article. The loved-it and hated-it figures do not total 2,561. Into what category the other eight reviewers fit is not clear.

CHAPTER FIVE

"MEN IS WHAT WE ARE":
FIGHT CLUB, THE AUTHENTIC MASCULINE,
AND THE POLITICS OF STYLE

STEPHEN BRAUER

About one third of the way through *Fight Club* (2000), director David
Fincher manages to dramatize the key themes of the film in one brief set
piece. [1] As Jack and Tyler step onto a city bus, Jack tries to summarize in a
voiceover what happens for the men once they join fight club, in which
men fight one another *mano a mano* with only a few rules guiding their
manners during the fight.[2] As Jack thinks about the change that happens
for the men in fight club as they come to either fight or watch night after
night, he says, "We all started seeing things differently. Everywhere we
went, we were sizing things up." They become alert to what might hurt
them, who might pose a threat. While standing on the bus, Jack spies a
Gucci underwear advertisement picturing two men, one facing forward
wearing only bikini briefs and the other facing away from the camera,
naked and holding the underwear. Both men are in fabulous shape, with
tight chest, abdominal, and gluteal muscles posed appealingly for the
camera. The cropping of the image, though, leaves both bodies without a
head, and the image seems therefore to stand not for a particular man but
for any man wearing Gucci underwear. As Jack looks at the ad, he
continues his voiceover, "I felt sorry for guys packed into gyms, trying to
look like how Calvin Klein or Tommy Hilfiger said they should." At that
moment Jack turns to Tyler and asks smirkingly, "Is that what a man looks
like?" Tyler laughs and says, "Self-improvement is masturbation. Now
self-destruction..." Jack smiles at the appeal of this last phrase and the
scene ends.

Barbara Creed, in an essay examining male stars of the 1980s, notes
the ways in which images of such heavily muscled men as Arnold

Schwarzenegger and Sylvester Stallone in action films "play[ed] with the notion of manhood" by "performing the masculine" (65). On one hand, their overwhelming musculature served to emblematize their gender status; on the other hand, the way in which they exhibited their bodies undercut that status by revealing an anxiety that led them to equate muscles with manhood, manufactured bodies with masculinity and potency.[3] Fight *Club* is a film that is interested in action and, as its central focus, the film explores the representation of masculinity and manhood in contemporary culture. In the Gucci ad in this scene, we find one of the more prevalent images of manhood that we can locate in our culture. In the image we find two highly aestheticized male bodies: hairless, lacking any flab, blemishes, or noticeable flaws. They seem to have been airbrushed clean not only of imperfections but of the reality of what most male bodies look like. When Jack and Tyler confront this image, they instinctually spurn the treatment of the male body as a product to sell, and in turn show a disdain for advertising and consumer culture. They immediately reject the image as having anything to do with what "a man" looks like. Indeed, they recognize the way in which not only the image but the bodies in the image have been manufactured. Jack notes how men pack into gyms to engineer new bodies, and Tyler labels the desire to improve how one looks to be nothing more than masturbation. Both of them reject these bodies as emblems of masculinity – for Jack it is somehow unnatural and for Tyler it is narcissistic; moreover, they both reject the aestheticization of the male body that the advertisement represents. The scene on the bus ends with a guttural scream, as Fincher bleeds the audio of the next scene into this one. That next scene is a brutal fight between Tyler and another man in the fight club, and both men punch, grapple, and tear at one another until they are pulled apart. As Tyler stands, triumphant in this fight, his arm, chest, and abdominal muscles are rippled and tight, just as in the advertisement. But Tyler is sweating and bleeding profusely from his nose, and the inclusion of his head in the image both individuates him from the men in the Gucci ad and signal that this is not the picture of male beauty but of male violence. Here is something closer to the self-destruction he advocated on the bus.

Fight Club traces the story of a young man, Jack, (played by Edward Norton) who works as a recall coordinator at an insurance agency. Jack is slipping into spiritual or psychic ennui, and he begins to attend support group meetings for a number of diseases and afflictions he does not have. These meetings provide him with emotional connections to others that he does not seem to locate elsewhere in his life. After meeting a charismatic new friend, Tyler Durden, (played by Brad Pitt), however, he stops attending these meetings and initiates a fight club, which serves as a place where he and other men can voluntarily fight one another and enjoy the rush of aggression and structured violence. Before long, the fight club grows into a popular underground scene for scores of men. Eventually, though, Tyler takes it in a new direction of mischief and public pranks that ultimately evolve into mayhem, anarchy, and terrorism, as he hatches a reactionary plan to blow up a number of buildings that he believes will destroy the credit system, destabilize the economy, and free people from their enslavement to consumer culture.

As exemplified by the scene on the bus, the film takes on representations of masculinity in contemporary culture, and explores the anxieties concerning male social roles within a culture that purportedly feminizes men by seducing them into an interest in consumer culture. In the case of the Gucci ad, the advertisement both seeks to make men beautiful, essentially feminizing them, but also seeks to appeal to men to both transform their bodies into the type seen in the advertisement and to buy Gucci underwear to better accentuate the appeal of that physical stature. The film opens with Jack suffering from doubts about his masculinity, dramatized first by his deep interest in his home furnishings and then by his participation in a support group for men dealing with the effects of testicular cancer. Figuratively, he is emasculated. The overt physicality of the fight club, though – represented in the image of the sweaty, bloody, and victorious Tyler after his fight – seemingly restores his lost masculinity. Jack embraces fight club as empowering in its own right until he comes to recognize that Tyler's desire for destruction ultimately proves to be much more of a threat to his well being than any interest he might take in duvets, glassware, or coffee tables.

Henry Giroux has argued that the film is "reactionary", for while attempting to reject Late Capitalism and consumerism, it fails to actually engage with all the elements of consumer culture and ultimately reinscribes and reproduces what it aims to critique. Giroux writes that Fincher fails to engage with the pathology of the male violence at hand in the film and that "*Fight Club* becomes complicitous with the very system of commodification it denounces since both rely upon a notion of agency largely constructed within the immediacy of pleasure, the cult of hypercompetitiveness, and the market-driven desire of winning and exercising power over others" (15).[4]   I would take issue with Giroux, for the film does not portray the men's desire to win so much as it shows their desire to move out of passivity. For the men in fight club, the point is not to win: the point is to participate, to fight, to experience life directly. Moreover, I would argue, while the film seemingly critiques the consumer culture of the late twentieth century that sends Jack into a spiritual funk at the beginning of the film, and which he seems to reject when he smirkingly repudiates the authenticity of masculinity in the Gucci advertisement, *Fight Club* ultimately operates as a sophisticated satire of the anxiety concerning male social roles within a contemporary culture that apparently emasculates men. After all, the image of Tyler, bloodied but triumphant over his opponent, is in its own way just as aestheticized as the images of the men in the Gucci ad – anyone viewing this scene will be seeing Brad Pitt and his sculpted, naked upper body, which has been built and engineered just as much as the bodies of the men in the ad. The film, in other words, subverts its own apparent critique through how it works as a film and Fincher undercuts his own representation of male violence as revelatory and liberating. In this article, I will first explore how the film moves in this direction narratively, and then I will examine how the function of fashion in the film itself complements this narrative movement.

Authentic Masculinity

Fincher offers a compelling representation of consumerism early in the film, in a *montage* in which the home furnishings from the IKEA catalogue, along with the written copy from the catalogue itself, materialize in the narrator's apartment as he speaks to an IKEA customer service representative on the phone. In a clever digital editing sequence, Fincher shows the showroom photographed in the catalogue materializing in the narrator's apartment as his actual furniture and furnishings, with the price included. Recognizing that something is amiss when his home is merely a reconstruction of a showroom, the narrator remarks in the voiceover that, in his life, "everything is a copy of a copy of a copy." This serves as a central articulation of the narrator's crisis. He has already told the audience that he is suffering from insomnia, but we have not yet seen the underlying cause of that insomnia. This moment marks the first moment of clarity about what is wrong. From the inside of a consumption-based model of contemporary living, he offers what is now often a frequent lament in the age of late capitalism: the inability to locate any sense of authenticity in his experience. What is original, what has validity, he seems to say, in a postmodern world that privileges *pastiche* and in which he cannot locate authentic experience? Moreover, this scene seems to ask, what happens to the individual in a consumption-based model of living? While one way of viewing the scene is to focus on how the catalogue seems to "come to life" in the narrator's apartment, another way of viewing it is to recognize how he is visually ensnared within the frame by the furnishings that materialize all of a sudden in his apartment as he moves across it. It is as if the products themselves are imprisoning him and denying him any means of escape. Not only, then, does this scene signal that he is struggling to locate authenticity in his daily environment, it reveals that he is struggling to locate an authentic self.

Jack visits a series of support groups as a means to forge connections with other individuals and as a path to what he believes will be authentic experience. The experience of pain, he seems to believe, will surely be something he can identify as authentic, and will provide a way for him to share his suffering with others, even if his pain will be a misrepresentation - after all, although he has a type of psychic pain, he does not in fact have any of the terminal illnesses for which the groups meet. Nonetheless, he is searching for community, and he locates it in "Remaining Men Together," a support group for men with testicular cancer. His embrace of this group reveals how issues of masculinity are also implicit in his postmodern *malaise*. The men in this group suffer from a deep cultural anxiety about their manhood, dramatized most clearly by Bob, who has developed large breasts as a result of the hormone therapy he has undergone to treat his cancer. Jack derisively identifies them as "bitch tits," which would seem to signal his own issues with masculinity that he masks underneath a vitriolic misogyny. But at the same time, Jack comes to relish his opportunity to fold himself into Bob's maternal arms and to weep. Bob gives voice to the central dilemma facing the group, which, because of the physical results of the cancer and the treatment, has to do both with emasculation and feminization. As Bob hugs him, he says, both as a statement and a question, "We're still men." Jack answers in a deadpan, "Yes we're men. Men is what we are." This repeated assertion of manhood identifies what these men need the most support for – their conception of their own masculinity. The repetition is telling, for the gentleman, it seems, doth assert too much.

This dynamic is later complicated by Tyler, who explicitly links the anxiety concerning manhood with consumption. Tyler asks Jack, "Do you know what a duvet is?" "A comforter," he answers. "It's a blanket, just a blanket," says Tyler. "Why do guys like you and me know what a duvet is? Is it essential to our survival – in the hunter/gatherer sense of the word? No. What are we?" Although we might expect his answer to be "men," echoing his earlier response to Bob that "Men is what we are," the narrator's answer to Tyler is "Consumers." In this equation, I would argue, we can recognize that consumption is treated as a threat to essential masculinity, to what we might call an authentic masculine experience. (The film's deep concern with male roles is solidified by an almost-exclusive male cast, with the single prominent female role that of Marla, a woman that Jack meets in a couple of support groups and with whom he and Tyler form a complex triangular friendship/sexual relationship.) Tyler says that men like Jack and him, men in general, should not be concerned with duvets, with home furnishings that we locate in an IKEA catalogue. Tyler links consumption with the feminine, and suggests that when men see themselves as consumers, they are in a crisis concerning their own masculinity.

Such a suggestion was not new ground in the 1990s, of course; such a crisis had recurred in the culture for decades, as noted by many critics. Susan Faludi argues in *Stiffed*, her 1999 social history of "the betrayal of the American Man," that "[b]oth the feminist and the antifeminist views are rooted in a peculiarly modern American perception that to be a man means to be at the controls and at all times to feel yourself in control" (9). However, Faludi reports of her encounters with men, "The men I got to know...had without exception lost their compass in the world...Their strongest desire was to be dutiful and to belong, to adhere with precision to the roles society had set out for them as men" (9). While the typical 1990's man was taught that he should be in control of the helm, he in fact found himself "lost at sea" and unable to locate his proper social role. Faludi locates the roots of the crisis in "the economic transition from industry to service, or from production to consumption" and claimed that this "is symbolically a move from the traditional masculine to the traditional feminine" (38). Yvonne Tasker notes that through the 1980s men became "more overtly targeted as consumers of lifestyle" and consequently that the "invitation...to define themselves through consumption [brought] with it a consequent fabrication of identity" (110). Tasker focuses on the action cinema of the 1980s and early 1990s, the dominant commercial films of the time, which were centered on buff, pumped-up, and hypermasculinized male movie stars such as Arnold Schwarzenegger, Sylvester Stallone, Jean-Claude Van Damme, and others. She sees in these films an exploration of masculinity or masculinities, arguing that the action cinema of that time portrayed "male figures [who] offer a parodic performance of 'masculinity,' which both enacts and calls into question the qualities they embody" (111). The early 1990s, with the popular and critical success of such films as *Thelma and Louise* and *Terminator 2*, offered a series of role reversals in terms of gender representation, as powerfully embodied in *Terminator 2*, with the buffed, physically imposing, and aggressive mother played by Linda Hamilton and a nurturing, maternal cyborg played ironically by the former champion bodybuilder Schwarzenegger. This portrayal coincided with what Faludi claims to see operating in the culture of late twentieth-century America, in that men were operating in new social roles but were not well equipped to do so. Faludi argues that the older American male paradigm of labor, as opposed to service, failed to provide a viable model for the contemporary male in crisis because, she says, that paradigm "defined manhood by character, by the inner qualities of stoicism, integrity, reliability, the ability to shoulder burdens, the willingness to put others first, the desire to protect and provide and sacrifice. These are the same qualities, recoded to masculine, that society has long recognized in women as the essence of *motherhood*" (38). The resulting gender confusion is paralyzing for men.[5]

Fincher's film operates within this cultural dynamic, tracing the transformation of the protagonist from a consumption-obsessed, spiritually empty office drone into a charismatic anarchist who organizes legions of men to strike out against corporate America. At first, the "Remaining Men Together" support group functions as a space in which he could feel validated. Jack says of his experience there, "Every evening I died and every evening I was born again – resurrected. Bob loved me because he thought I had lost my testicles too. Being there, pressed against his tits, this was my vacation." We might ask what he needs a vacation from – from his job or from the feminizing aspects of the culture? Ironically, the testicular cancer that brings the men there for support only reinforces the emasculated nature of men's social roles. Either because of this or in spite of it, Jack looks for solidarity by choosing a place that bars women from participation. Marla's intrusion into his support groups, most powerfully illustrated by her participation in the testicular cancer group, "ruined everything," as he says in the voiceover. When she asks him later why he hasn't been to any of the groups, he says, "I found a new one – it's for men only." This is indeed the function of the fight club – Tyler and Jack together form a space to act out masculine desire without the presence of women, a space that they can control. In some ways, the fight club echoes what happened in "Remaining Men Together." The language of "resurrection" that Jack found in the support group is echoed in how he describes the fight club – "The hysterical shouting came in tongues like at a Pentecostal church. When the fight was over, nothing was solved but nothing mattered. Afterward we all felt saved." Whereas the bonding in the support group was about loss and emasculation, the bonding in the fight club centers on a notion of masculinity that is linked to violence, power, and endurance.

The feeling of transcendence that the men experience in the fight club – "Afterward we all felt saved" – functions as an act of solidarity that separates them from the rest of society. This is reinforced by the credo of the group: "The first rule of fight club is that you do not talk about fight club. The second rule of fight club is that you do not talk about fight club." Fighting offers them a clear and clean way to nonverbally articulate their masculinity in a safe and controlled space.[6] The club, however, operates as much through exclusion as it does through solidarity. The relationship between the power of the authentic masculine experience and the exclusion of women or of any form of "the feminine" is necessary in Tyler's eyes. Although he is involved in a sexual relationship with Marla, Tyler sees her as just a "silly cooze" and a "predator." He says to Jack, regarding her role in their lives, "We're a generation of men raised by women. I'm wondering if another woman is really the answer we need." In fact, for Tyler, they are the very problem of what ails the culture, in that the ideology of late capitalism is too grounded in a worldview that has failed men. He says in another of his speeches, "Advertising has us chasing cars and clothes, working jobs we hate so we can buy shit we don't need. We're the middle children of history, man, no purpose or place."

A rejection of consumption is crucial to what happens in the fight club, for it offers the potential for release and freedom from the obligations and even shackles of late capitalist culture. This conflict between possessions and freedom is most clearly dramatized when Detective Stern calls Jack to inform him that the explosion that blew up his apartment was not an accident. Tyler tries to cajole him into saying into the phone, "The liberator who destroyed my property has realigned my perceptions...we reject the basic assumptions of civilization, especially the importance of material possessions." However, he ends up saying, "That condo was my life, okay? I loved every stick of furniture in that place. That wasn't just a bunch of stuff that got destroyed – it was me." Jack is pathetically still beholden to those home furnishings straight out of the IKEA catalogue, even if he knows that they lack originality or distinction. In contrast, Tyler offers a radically different ideological vision in the fight club. In speaking to the men who gather in the dank basement of a dive bar for the opportunity to batter one another, Tyler says, "You are not your job; you are not how much money you have in the bank; you are not the car you drive; you are not the contents of your wallet; you are not your fucking khakis." He presents this challenge as a means of liberating others from – as he puts it directly to Jack – "the things that you own [that] end up owning you." To express themselves as men, they need to move away from the hegemonic aspects of consumption – which has been traditionally gendered as feminine – to something that will offer them an authentic masculine experience.

For Tyler, authenticity is linked directly to the presence of physical pain. He is the one who first asks Jack to punch him so that he can experience it, leading to the creation of the fight clubs. Later, he purposefully spills lye on Jack's hand and forces him to accept the pain that comes with the chemical burn. He says, "Stay with the pain, don't shut this out. Don't forget your pain...Without pain, without sacrifice, we would have nothing." In this moment, Tyler figures physical suffering and pain as those elements that are finally and firmly authentic and valid. This moment is clearly meant as a rebuke to Jack's succumbing to the psychic or spiritual ennui that he was suffering from at the beginning of the film, as well as his succumbing to the desire to escape. Tyler implicitly argues that such pain is to be disregarded as not of any real account; moreover, he suggests that the support groups offered a false escape from the pain that debilitated Jack from moving forward and that instead made him rely on the support groups. Instead of trying to escape pain, Tyler argues that Jack should embrace it as the means through which one can achieve a true sense of freedom. When Jack tries to escape what he is feeling by using techniques he learned in his support groups, Tyler slaps him, forcing him back to the present moment of suffering. "Stop it," he says, "this is your pain, this is your burning hand. It's right here...It's the greatest moment of your life, man, and you're off somewhere missing it." In place of seeking refuge from the suffering – as the support groups encouraged him to do – Tyler argues that he surrender to it, accept it, and then use it.[7]

Tyler demonstrates the power (and seduction) of this thinking when the owner of the bar where fight club meets demands that they no longer use the basement of the bar for their fights. In response to Lou – the owner of the bar – Tyler merely says that they'd really like to continue to use the basement because they really like it there. In repeating over and over that they "really like it [t]here," Tyler drives Lou to anger, to the degree that he starts to attack Tyler in order to assert his authority and to teach Tyler a lesson. This backfires on Lou, though, as Tyler refuses to fight back against Lou and his bodyguard and instead embraces the beating and the onslaught of violence as empowering. As he's getting pummeled, his fellow members of fight club watch in admiration and Tyler laughs, apparently enjoying it. He leaps on Lou and drips his blood all over Lou's face, saying, "You don't know where I've been, Lou, you don't know where I've been." Disgusted by this, Lou staggers away with his bodyguard, allowing the group to remain in the basement. The representation of violence in this scene is telling, not so much for its brutality, but for Tyler's willingness to surrender to the pain and not to curb it, which leads to his eventual "victory." While Tyler had been a charismatic leader of the group before, from this point on a cult of personality forms around him as the men in the club come to see him as their inspirational leader and the voice of their frustrations and aspirations. Prior to Lou's arrival he had told the group:

> The men I see in Fight Club are the smartest and strongest men who have ever lived. I see all this potential – and I see it squandered. Goddamnit, an entire generation pumping gas, waiting tables: slaves with white collars…We have no Great War, no Great Depression. *Our* Great War is a spiritual war. *Our* Great Depression is our lives. We've all been raised on television to believe that one day we'd all be millionaires and movie gods and rock starts, but we won't. We're slowly learning that fact and we're very, very pissed off.

In this speech Tyler moves from a frustration with gender roles within the contemporary economy to a more impassioned articulation of generational loss.[8] The power of his resentment takes hold after Lou's beating, after Tyler demonstrates that he can handle the debasement of what others do to him and still maintain autonomy and achieve what he wants. Immediately following Lou's departure, the men gather around Tyler in admiration and the cult of personality truly takes shape. Tyler hands out "homework assignments," small tasks and mischievous pranks for the members to complete. These pranks, though, soon evolve into Project Mayhem, leading to the transformation of fight club from a site of male bonding through the shared experience of pain to fight club as the embodiment of a revolutionary ideology that seeks to transform the culture through a politics of violence.

By the end of the film, when Tyler's intentions (the anarchic annihilation of the credit system) have become clear and the undercurrent of destruction that is fundamental to his vision has become obvious, he seems less charismatic than unhinged. The hypermasculinity that he represents – the misogyny, the embracing of violence and pain as both cathartic and transcendent, the resentment over what consumer culture has led him to become – is superseded by the shot of Jack and Marla hand in hand, alone in the frame facing away from the camera, at the end of the film. Together as a couple, in what is figured as a moment of intimacy between them, they watch out the window as a series of skyscrapers implode and collapse, and the horror of the destruction of Project Mayhem makes clear that there are other alternatives to Tyler's unleashing of anarchy.

The Politics of Style

Henry Giroux has denigrated *Fight Club* because "No space exists within the film for appropriations that might offer critical engagements, political understanding, and enlightened forms of social change" (15). I would argue, however, that the filmmakers' representation of style manifests a politics that pushes viewers to engage critically with the logic of acquisition that is at the heart of late capitalism. Of special interest to me in this argument is a little-seen document that is part of the press kit issued by the film studio as part of its publicity material for the film.[9] This press kit is nothing more than a catalogue made up of items from the film, including clothes worn by Jack, Tyler, and Marla, and housewares and home furnishings from the film.[10]

Everything in the catalogue is priced as if it was a real item for sale; the clothes and other items are captured in stills from the film, arranged in a compellingly frenetic design, and packaged with type that mimics typical catalogue diction. The catalogue, although it appears much like others one might receive in the mail, is actually a devastating parody of the form, as encapsulated in its boldface and all-capitalized opening message: "Every item in our Fall line is guaranteed to satisfy and impress. Having trouble defining yourself? Can't quite gauge where you stand in society? At fight club we eliminate the guess work so you have more time to leaf through this season's answer to pornography…catalogues." The language here echoes Jack's from early in the film, when he waits on the phone for a customer service representative to help him and says in his voiceover narration, "I'd flip through catalogues and wonder, 'What kind of dining set defines me as a person?'" The catalogue from the press kit mocks this mindset in the very descriptions of what it offers for sale. For a colorfully patterned tie like the one Tyler wears while selling soap at Barney's, the catalogue reads, "We realize that your only motivation for working is so you can afford to furnish your condo with sensible living solutions that double as your only measure of self worth. If you can admit to this critical character flaw, then we've got the neckwear for you. Pointless, contrived and colorful, these eyesores are guaranteed to brighten any office." For a dress shirt, the sales pitch goes, "The companion piece to our Latch Tie, this classic shirt can also be worn with a traditional tie. It can also be worn without a tie. And on occasion, it has been worn with no tie, unbuttoned and untucked. We are not in the business of telling you how to wear your shirt or live your life. Lord knows you've got it all figured out. Why else would you be wasting valuable time on this catalog?" The tone of the catalogue is aggressive in its sarcasm, challenging in how it presents clothing as a solution to one's unhappiness. The text reads at one point, "Let us know how you think you measure up in society. Our take is that if you actually feel the need to purchase any of this crap, you don't think you measure up to society's standards very well at all." In this way, the catalogue copy seems to echo Tyler's rejection of consumer culture as a space in which men can locate themselves.

The film's position on style is not as neat as this might suggest, however. The filmmakers complement the story's interest in consumer goods through close attention to the characters' clothing in the film. Jack mainly wears gray or beige button-down shirts and drab, earth-toned clothes that signal both his place in a conformist corporate structure and his spiritual *malaise*, while Tyler sports what we would have to identify as an array of fabulously stylized retrochic shirts, suits, and sunglasses. His clothes are consistently vibrant, colorful, and surprising, especially in the context of how Jack dresses. In a commentary on the film, costume designer Michael Kaplan and cinematographer Jeff Cronenweth discuss the stylistic contrast between Tyler and Jack:

> Michael Kaplan: "After reading the script, I knew that Tyler Durden was going to be pretty out there wardrobe-wise, to go with how out there he was as a character...I asked Fincher how far he could go colorwise and he said you can't go too far with Tyler Durden. I was amazed at how far he let me go."

> Jeff Cronenweth: "He's primarily the only person who wears anything like that, right?"

> MK: "Brad's side of the wardrobe trailer was vibrant and Edward's was grays and beiges and so boring. You couldn't believe those two characters were in the same movie."

JC: "That right there defines the personalities of the two characters perfectly."[11]

The clothing in *Fight Club* certainly does serve to reveal the personalities of the two main characters, but it also underscores how Tyler's charisma, through a type of bedazzlement, shields his thinking. First with Jack, and then with the other men in the fight club, Tyler attracts other characters with his looks and his actions, and he slowly works to change their thinking about how contemporary society works and how it should work.   And he's a charming and good-looking seducer. Nonetheless, the filmmakers nicely undercut Tyler's ideas.   While his reactionary politics become clear by the end of the film, the filmmakers all along have subtly undermined his ideas through the visual cues embodied in his clothes.   Although Tyler verbally critiques men's interest in consumer goods and their corresponding emasculation in the age of late capitalism, and although he seeks to reestablish some semblance of authentic masculinity through the fight club and Project Mayhem that grows out the club, Tyler's fabulous threads – and their connotation of a deep commitment to style – subvert his message and reveal a hypocrisy in the anxiety with contemporary male social roles.

Fashion and style are crucial components in how David Fincher and the other filmmakers construct their characterizations of the figures in *Fight Club*. In dressing the people in the support groups, for instance, Michael Kaplan put them in mundane, somber tones and clothes that mirror their sober lifestyles. The visuals in these scenes – like the stories of the men and women in the support groups – purposefully lack vivacity and color. The one time that Fincher injects spirit into the support-group sequences is when Chloe asks that someone in the group have sex with her.   The green paisley scarf that she wears as a sort of bandanna camouflages the effects of chemotherapy on her hair, along with her red blouse, symbolize her free spirit and – ironically – her liveliness. Marla's entrance into the support groups, of course, changes the nature of the space for Jack. Like Jack, Marla is "a tourist" who comes to the meetings to garner some semblance of spiritual peace but who does not actually suffer from the diseases that the others do; in sharp contrast to Jack, though, Marla dresses the part of the outsider. Kaplan puts her in an array of secondhand, vintage dresses, jackets, and shoes that harken back to an earlier era and that bespeak an individual style. Jack, on the other hand, dresses to blend into the background, with clothes that feature predominantly drab, earthtone colors that seem to symbolize the state of his *psyche*. In deciding on the color of Jack's shirts, Kaplan chose a "pale, grayish beige," in contrast to white, because a white shirt might "pop" visually onscreen and call attention to itself. The point, for Kaplan, was to ensure that Jack's clothes never drew the viewer's eyes.

Other than for Marla, clothing, in both the workplace and in the support group settings, serves to identify individuals as likeminded and almost literally of the same stripe. There is a clear dichotomy between those who work inside corporate culture and those who do not. The men in the insurance company, for instance, as with many of the men in the film who work as bankers, police officers, waiters, and politicians, dress like one another and thereby form an ideological community that is articulated through their fashion choices.   This becomes especially apparent after fight club takes off, as Jack comes to work wearing the same type of outfits that he has before, but now with something incongruous in his corporate uniform: cuts and bruises on his face and head.   Standing at a urinal next to him, Jack's boss stares incomprehensibly at him. They are dressed similarly but Jack has a large purple bruise around his eye. A few scenes later, Jack sits in on a meeting in a conference room, dressed in suits like the other men, but with cuts, bruises.   As the men discuss icons they can use in their PowerPoint presentations, Jack smiles, revealing a mouth full of blood. The others are horrified. Jack no longer fits the image of the corporate drone. To stand out in the workplace, it would seem, connotes idiosyncrasy, a desire for independence, and even something dangerously different. These men form a type of army and their drab-colored suits with their patterned shirts are their uniforms, both serving to protect them and to allow them to maintain anonymity.

The young men who follow Tyler beyond fight club into Project Mayhem are an even fuller evocation of an army, though, and their clothes manifestly denote uniformity. As a way to test them and their loyalty to his endeavor, Tyler forces them into an initiation during which they must endure all manner of verbal insults and rejections and even physical abuse. After passing the test, they can then move into the dilapidated Paper Street house where he and Jack live, leaving behind all of their belongings, except for some light bedding and some very specific clothes. The first thing Tyler says to the first recruit upon allowing him to enter is, "Got two black shirts? Two pair black pants? One pair black boots? Two pair black socks? One black jacket?" Fashion and style, what the men will look like during Project Mayhem, even ahead of what they will do, is of primary concern to Tyler. He has the same recruit shave his hair into a tight crewcut, and he says admiringly of the new look, "Like a monkey ready to be shot into space. A space monkey, ready to sacrifice himself for the greater good." He calls his recruits space monkeys: hailing them as pioneers, in that monkeys were the first animals to enter space, while simultaneously denigrating them as subhuman. Tyler salutes their willingness to give up their allegiance to consumer capitalism and to challenge it through acts of vandalism and ultimately terrorism; at the same time, he is willing to risk their lives to bring his vision to fruition. They are anonymous, without any identity beyond their purpose in Tyler's vision. As one of the men says, "Sir, in Project Mayhem we have no names." Lacking names, lacking any semblance of distinctive identity in their black clothes and crewcuts, they are a fascist army blindly following their dictator – a frightening mirror image of the corporate men dressed in drab suits and "pale, pale grayish beige" shirts. All of these men seem to be following a similar manual as to "what a man looks like." This image is one of uniformity, silence, and discipline. The space monkeys embody a stoic masculinity that endures and toils, without complaint. A man, in this way of thinking, does not try to stand out as different or as an individual. Along with the other men who efficiently go about doing their jobs, he is merely a single cog in a larger machine. Tyler says to them, "You are not special. You are not a beautiful or unique snowflake." They believe him, and dress – and act – accordingly.

Tyler's fashion choices, on the other hand, bespeak nonconformity, individuality, and a direct challenge to the status quo. Unlike the corporate drones or the space monkeys, Tyler is not interested in stoic masculinity. He speaks openly about what bothers him about modern culture and he has no interest in enduring it. He wants to change it. His clothes likewise are the opposite of Jack's, in that what he wears quite clearly calls attention to him. When Jack first meets Tyler, they are sitting on an airplane next to one another. Jack is wearing a gabardine suit, an off-white button-down shirt, a loosened patterned tie to match the suit, and black dress shoes. His hair, not surprisingly, is neatly groomed in what we might call a businessman's cut. He has clever sayings and ways of thinking about situations – as when he calls Tyler a "single-serving friend" – but he never really puts himself into opposition with how things work. Sitting next to him, Tyler is dressed nothing like Jack; even though he has the exact same briefcase as Jack, Tyler is dressed nothing like him. He wears a crimson blazer with exaggerated white stitching and exposed pockets, a white patterned shirt opened at the neck and with the collar folded on top of the jacket, brown-accented houndstooth pants and patent-leather cordovan

Gucci shoes that Michael Kaplan "found in a junk shop in Palm Springs." His hair is gelled into a spiky coif, and he sports sunglasses with red-tinted lenses. His outfit is both ridiculous and fabulous. He is dressed like no one else on the plane, and especially stands out seated next to Jack. Immediately upon meeting Jack, Tyler asks him to view situations from an alternative perspective, as when he suggests the illustrated passengers on the airplane safety card have been anaesthetized with high levels of oxygen so that they accept their fate calmly as the plane crashes. Tyler may have the same briefcase as Jack, but he does not think like him.

When we next see him, later that same night, he has changed into a vintage, brown leather jacket, with the same shirt as before, but now unbuttoned at the top and bottom, and black athletic pants and boots. Jack, on the other hand, wears what he had on earlier, though he has loosened his tie further and exposed his white undershirt. For the most part, he maintains the same look even outside of work. His corporate identity is his overall identity marker. Tyler is radically different, both in what he wears and at work and in how he goes about that work. As a projectionist, he wears a black t-shirt with white stars and loose-fitting maroon pants. As a waiter at a luxurious restaurant, he wears the waiter's uniform but accessorizes it with a walkman and headphones. In both of these jobs, moreover, he is a subversive presence. He splices in single frames of pornography into family films at the movie theater and urinates into the cream of mushroom soup at the restaurant. Whereas Jack sits at a desk and completes reports, Tyler acts as the "guerilla terrorist of the food-service industry." As part of his job as a soap salesman, Tyler sells his soap to department stores for $20 a bar. Tyler is dressed in what Michael Kaplan identifies as Tyler's "idea of business attire" – which is a white linen seersucker suit, with a short yellow-and-gold striped polo shirt that leaves much of his lower midriff exposed, and boldly patterned white, yellow, and blue tie. As on the plane, his hair is gelled into spikes, he sports a goatee, and he wears his red-tinted sunglasses. If this is his idea of business attire, he is clearly operating from a different set of principles than the other men in the film. The women who buy his soap, as well as the woman in Barney's who tells Tyler that "This is the best soap," are oblivious to the fact that Tyler's key ingredient in the soap is human fat he has procured from the garbage bins outside a liposuction clinic. The irony and subversion are bold, just like Tyler's outfit. As Jack says in his voiceover, "It was beautiful. We were selling rich women their own fat asses back to them." Tyler succeeds through his very iconoclasm, and his style is both central to that vision and an embodiment of it.

Tyler always retains his individuality. Even during Project Mayhem, as he limits the space monkeys to black clothes and anonymity, he chooses to maintain his own clothes, and he keeps his name preeminent in the planning of the work in the project. While Robert Paulson is only afforded a name in death, Tyler Durden is a name that is virtually mythological to everyone involved in fight clubs and in Project Mayhem. As Jack's clothes become more drab as the film proceeds – a button-down shirt, usually untucked, a light gray t-shirt, khaki pants, either a tan or blue windbreaker or a charcoal gray overcoat – Tyler's seem to become more outrageous. Michael Kaplan says of the challenge of dressing Brad Pitt in his role as Tyler:

> The difficult things about Tyler's clothes being flamboyant was that I'm so used to trying to have the clothes remain in the background and just kind of aid the character but also remain in place. Some of these clothes are a little more attention-getting than I'm used to doing and I kind of got nervous because whenever I'm too aware of the clothes the actors are wearing I feel like I'm not doing my job. It's almost like upstaging. But Tyler was this character that needed that kind of a presence and so it was necessary for me to kind of stay on it and push the character, push the colors, and the humor of what he was wearing.

The flamboyance, as well as the humor, reaches its apex when Jack finally confronts Tyler – that is, the alter ego that Jack has conjured up for himself and who goes by the name of Tyler Durden. As Tyler reveals that Jack has conjured him up, he wears a faux fur coat over a mesh t-shirt that is cut just below the chest. In forcing Jack to accept the fact that he has been the one who has created fight club and Project Mayhem, he says that he is the man that Jack would like to imagine himself to be, claiming, "I look like you want to look." Tyler is, then, the embodiment of Jack's wish to be independent, to break out of his corporate uniformity and stoic masculinity.

Michael Kaplan says of Jack, his life, and his conjuring of Tyler, that "it's so mundane and boring you understand the motivation for it and the need to get out of it. And Tyler is so effervescent and so colorful you can understand the attraction." Jack wants to break out of the limitations of his environment, which he sees as both emasculating and feminizing. Unlike the men at work and in Remaining Men Together, Tyler, the man Jack would like to be, does not simply endure what is happening to him, but instead fights back against it, rejecting everything about the broader culture. This is where we can see the subversion and irony at play in how Fincher and Kaplan use fashion in the film; however, for Tyler does not represent Jack's best or only alternative. A central concern of Tyler's is his expression of style. Although he claims to have no interest in appearances, his fashion choices belie that claim. Style, in fact, becomes the film's manifestation of the critique of Tyler, one of the central signs that Tyler is not everything he claims to be. For example, while he browbeats the space monkeys into black, anonymous uniforms because not one of them is a "unique snowflake," he dresses as someone who does see himself as one of a kind. His clothes suggest that he is quite conscious of what he is wearing and how it looks, and that he takes pride in the idiosyncrasy of his style.

Tyler's hypocrisy complements the subversion of how the film explores male anxiety about social roles in the age of late capitalism. Most of the men in the film seem to want to fade into the background, dressing similarly – in drab, colorless clothes – and embodying a stoic masculinity. Tyler, however, dresses like a rock star. He wants to show his difference, even while claiming others are not special or distinct. Whereas others speak of him in mythological terms, he forces them to be nameless. Tyler forces others to do what he himself does not need to, and his very sense of style is the sign of his hypocrisy. The filmmakers subvert Tyler's message through how they dress him. We should recognize the irony of someone telling us that we need to evolve beyond consumer culture – that "the things we own end up owning us" – when so many of his clothes come from chic vintage stores.

Space Monkeys, Lads, and Metrosexuals: Men and Style in the New Century

The men in Remaining Men Together claim, "Men is what we are." But in a room full of men with testicular cancer, who are losing one of the central biological attributes of their sex, what does "men" mean? *Fight Club* examines the cultural constructions of men at the end of the 20th century. What does a man look like? This is been a fair question to consider as the 1990s have shifted into the 2000s. The film offers a number of competing images in its portrayal of the male body: buff Tyler; slim and reedy Jack; Bob, with his bulk and his "bitch tits"; the comely Angel Face, played by Jared Leto, who Jack beats mercilessly, ultimately disfiguring his face, because he "wanted to destroy something beautiful." The film does not represent one single vision: Tyler and Jack mock the male bodies in the Gucci ad as emerging from narcissism and then Fincher presents Tyler's body in the next scene in much the same pose seen in the advertisement. Tyler forces the space monkeys to adopt uniformity as their identity, while insisting stylistically on his own singularity. One way of recognizing how the film operates is understanding how its portrayal of men emerges out of an ongoing cultural debate about style and the representation of the male body.

In the last ten years, as we have moved back and forth between lad culture and the metrosexual, men have had to look at a variety of models for the image they wish to portray as their embrace of what it means to be a man. In terms of popular culture, one place to look for constructions of manhood would be men's magazines. In the mid-1990s, publishers launched a number of men's magazines in Britain, including *loaded*, *FHM*, and *Maxim*, that were quickly grouped together in the category of "lad magazines." These magazines tended to focus on the *clichés* of hypermasculine culture – beer, babes, and high-tech gadgets. In contrast to what a number of critics had taken to calling the "new man" of the 1980s and early 1990s, who gave greater attention to clothing, grooming, and style, the lad was much less interested in what he looked like and much more invested in what he could consume (including images of, and the corresponding fantasies about, scantily clad women.) The success of these magazines in Britain was virtually immediate, and in April 1997, Dennis Publishing brought *Maxim* to the United States, with FHM joining it in the spring of 2000. By 2001, each magazine was a major success, with circulation figures for *Maxim* at 2.5 million and 750,000 for *FHM*.[12] These numbers made each magazine a major player in the American publishing scene. In 2003, even with a 7% drop in newsstand sales that year, *Maxim*'s circulation was more than twice than those of the much-more established *Esquire*, *GQ*, and *Details* combined; moreover, Dennis Publishing's *Stuff*, another lad magazine, outsold all three as well.[13]

These magazines have become in the past ten years a commercially powerful force in American culture. Their covers, almost always featuring a young woman in the entertainment business dressed alluringly and revealing much of her body, dominate most newsstands. The emphasis that these magazines place on the consumption of goods, and of women, seeks to situate men as powerful and in control of their lives. James Davis sees in this positioning, though, a frustration with what men have in their lives, as opposed to what they receive in and through the magazine. He argues, "Ostensibly a celebration of unexamined, untheorized, unselfconscious pleasure in the joys of 'natural' manhood, *Maxim* magazine is a kaleidoscope of omnidirectional contempt and anger"

(1016). The lad magazines, with their emphasis on the rampant articulation of male desire, channel that anger through the objectification of women as sexual objects and the depiction of them as subservient. Davis's use of "omnidirectional," though, does more than point out the misogyny in these magazines, for it suggests that male anger is not only directed at women, but at other men. This is an important element to consider.

Throughout the 1980s and 1990s, more and more men paid attention to style and appearances, and the term the "new man" took prominence in Britain, and to a lesser extent in America. In 2002, though, Mark Simpson coined the term "metrosexual" to identify men who pay attention to issues of style, and this term has taken hold in the cultural marketplace.[14] Metrosexuals, according to critic Toby Miller, are straight, middle-class "feminized males who blur the visual style of straight and gay" (112). These men pay serious attention to issues of style in terms of their clothes and their grooming choices, while trying to negate the implications of homosexuality such attention stereotypically creates by striving to maintain the look of the straight male.[15] This is a delicate line to tread, of course. In the Bravo Network's reality program *Queer Eye for the Straight Guy*, five gay men tutor straight men about cooking, grooming, interior design, and fashion. Although the gay men often comment on the attractiveness of the straight male, they are careful to never go too far in creating the sense that there is any real attraction between them. Instead, the focus of the show is to help the men be better mates, or more appropriate matches for their heterosexual partners. So while the "teachers" relay advice on clothes, haircuts, and color coordinating a room, thereby demonstrating their superior knowledge of elements that make heterosexual men more attractive to their partners, they never subvert or challenge their pupils' heterosexuality, not do they seek to feminize them. They do try to change them, however, and this might account for the "anger" that Davis perceives in the lad magazines.

The commercial success of *Queer Eye for the Straight Guy*, which debuted in 2003, has coincided with the rise of the metrosexual in the marketplace. In 2002, 15 percent of all beauty products sold were for men's grooming products, and the combined sales of men's fashion and grooming combined for nearly $65 billion in 2004.[16] Citing numerous studies, Toby Miller points to a series of statistics that suggest that, by the late 1990s, men had become much more conscious of their looks: an increase of 34 percent in male cosmetic surgery between 1996 and 1998 and a 316 percent increase in hair transplants between 1999 and 2001.[17] Miller, in much the same vein as Susan Faludi, identifies the emergence of the metrosexual as a result of the shifting economic conditions for men following World War II and the rising economic power of women. Paying attention to appearances, in Miller's view, became a way for men to battle age and wage discrimination for position in the workplace (113-114). If, as Simpson and Miller imply, metrosexuality as a style functions as a means through which straight men can change in socially acceptable ways, then the lad magazines represent a reactionary pull away from such change and attempt to revert to pre-feminist times when men could be men and women were objects. When we see these two images of manhood in these terms – metrosexuals as a response to economic anxiety and its concomitant implication of failure and the lads as a response the new man and the implicit claim that men need to change for the better – we can recognize that these two images are little more than two sides of the same coin. After all, the lad magazines are telling men what to pay attention to, what to buy, and how to act, much the same way that the "Fab Five" on *Queer Eye* instruct their charges. As Mark Simpson suggests, the metrosexual and the lad are both "in fact manifestations of male narcissism and selfishness and isolation: That is, after all, what consumer culture faithfully delivers to us" (Lindsay 43).

In an article published in 2005 in *Advertising Age*, Greg Lindsay argues, "The metrosexual and the *Maxim* reader are as schizoid in their own way as Jack and Tyler in *Fight Club*. Portrayed in the media...as the battling claimants to the empty throne of manhood, they're actually the same man, reassembled in slightly different configurations where one set of brands is swapped out for another" (43). The tension between these two images of manhood and their coexistence in the culture mirrors that at the heart of *Fight Club*. The film dramatizes the battle over the representation of the male body, and as I argued in the beginning of this article, Fincher compactly illustrates it in the scene between Jack and Tyler on the bus as they view with scorn the men in the Gucci underwear advertisement. Toby Miller writes, "The male body is up for grabs as sexual icon, commodity consumer, and worker" (112). As Tyler and Jack view the ad, they confront what it means to treat the barely dressed male body as a product to sell, or the means through which to sell. They reject the aestheticization of the male body, the manufactured nature of the bodies in the ad, and label it narcissism and masturbation. But at what point does their fight club, to which Fincher immediately cuts after Tyler smirkingly extols "self-destruction," embrace just such a narcissism? The violence that begins in fight club and is transformed into Project Mayhem is not liberating, nor particularly revelatory. It may be authentic, of a kind, but Fincher asks us to interrogate why that type of experience is inherently more masculine than any other type of experience, including shopping for clothes, duvets, and dining room tables through catalogues.

Works Cited

Butler, Judith. *Bodies That Matter: On the Discursive Limits of Sex*. NY: Routledge, 1993.

—. *Gender Trouble: Feminism and the Subversion of Identity*. NY: Routledge, 1990.

Creed, Barbara. "From Here to Modernity: Feminism and Postmodernism," *Screen* 28 (2) 1987: 47-67.

Clark, J. Michael. "Faludi, *Fight Club*, and Phallic Masculinity: Exploring the Emasculating Economics of Patriarchy," *The Journal of Men's Studies* 11 (1) Fall 2002: 65-76.

Clark, Suzanne. "*Fight Club*: Historicizing the Rhetoric of Masculinity, Violence, and Sentimentality," *Journal of American Culture* 21 (2) Spring 2001: 411-420.

Crowdus, Gary. "Getting Exercised Over *Fight Club*," *Cineaste* 25 (4) 2000: 46-48.

Davis, James P. "Maxim Magazine and the Management of Contempt," The Journal of Popular Culture 38 (6) 2005: 1011-1021.

Faludi, Susan. *Stiffed: The Betrayal of the American Man*. NY: William Morrow and Company, 1999.

Fight Club. Dir. David Fincher. Perf. Edward Norton, Helena Bonham Carter, and Brad Pitt. DVD. Fox, 2000.

Friday, Kirster. "'A Generation of Men without History'": *Fight Club*, Masculinity, and the Historical Symptom," *Postmodern Culture* 13 (3) May 2003: 38-62.

Gilmore, David. *Manhood in the Making: Cultural Concepts of Masculinity*. New Haven: Yale University Press, 1990.

Giroux, Henry. "Private Satisfactions and Public Disorders: *Fight Club*, Patriarchy, and the Politics of Masculine Violence," *Journal of American Culture* 21 (1) Winter 2001: 1-31.

Grønstad, Asbjørn. "One-Dimensional Men: Fight Club and the Poetics of the Body," *Film Criticism* 28 (1) 2003: 1-23.

"The Lads are Coming!" *MediaWeek* 5 March 2001: 9

Lee, Terry. *"Virtual Violence* in *Fight Club*: This is What Transformation of Masculine Ego *Feels* Like," *Journal of American and Comparative Cultures* 25 (3/4) Fall 2002: 418-423.

Leonard, Devin. *"Maxim* Has a Midlife Crisis," *Fortune* December 8, 2003: 56.

Lindsay, Greg. "Man vs. Man," *Advertising Age*, June 13, 2005: 1, 42-43.

Miller, Toby. "A Metrosexual Eye on *Queer Guy*," *GLQ* 11 (1) 2005: 112-117.

Penley, Constance and Sharon Willis, eds., *Male Trouble*. Minneapolis: University of Minnesota Press, 1993.

Rehling, Nicola. *"Fight Club* Takes a Beating: Masculinity, Masochism, and the Politics of Disavowal," *Gramma* 9 (2001): 187-203.

Savran, David. *Taking It like a Man: White Masculinity, Masochism, and Contemporary American Culture*. Princeton: Princeton University Press, 1998.

Tasker, Yvonne. *Spectacular Bodies: Gender, Genre, and the Action Cinema*. NY: Routledge, 1993.

Wike, Scott and Barbara Pickering, "The Search for Male Identity within Modern Society: A Rhetorical Analysis of David Fincher's *Fight Club*," *Popular Culture Review* 2 (2004): 63-76.

Notes

[1] I would like to thank Stephanie Sorg and Joan Saab for their assistance in preparing this article.

[2] Although he is never named "Jack" in the film and is even identified as "Narrator" in the film credits in honor of his voiceover narration, critics often refer to this character as "Jack" because as the film proceeds he begins to refer to himself with this name during his narration. For clarity's sake in this essay, I am adopting this name for the character.

[3] Creed was one of many critics interested in configurations of gender, identity, and performativity in the late 1980s and early 1990s. Judith Butler's work at the time, especially *Bodies That Matter* and *Gender Trouble*, was at the forefront of this scholarship and continues to be influential today. Other valuable texts include David Gilmore's *Manhood in the Making: Cultural Concepts of Masculinity* and *Male Trouble*, edited by Constance Penley and Sharon Willis.

[4] Suzanne Clark has offered a thoughtful response to Giroux in which she concurs with his notion that the film's expression of hypermasculinity as liberating is problematic, and in which she worries that "the film simply underscores an increasingly dangerous antipathy to any public order" (418). At the same time, however, Clark suggests that the film may be less didactic than Giroux suggests and that it can play "a rhetorical function" in the culture that might lead to a more nuanced critique and understanding of gender and violence.

[5] Many critics have seen connections between Faludi's book and Fincher's film. Michael Clark, for instance, argues that while the film seems almost to take up exactly Faludi's argument, it ultimately parts ways with its "failed" ending, as it turns away from the type of community and communal thinking that Faludi encourages.

[6] Terry Lee sees the film's violence as "a projected picture of the 'virtual violence' that one can enact within the psyche to destroy harmful gender-role paradigms to make room for healthier masculinities" (422).

[7] Nicola Rehling argues that "the film is structured around masochism at both the diegetic level of men claiming mastery through physical pain and abuse, and more figuratively, in the film's disavowal of white heterosexual privilege" (188). Conversely, Kirster Friday asks, "Is the masochistic, male violence that informs the practices of the fight clubs a palliative, a vehicle to a new identity…or is it merely another symptom of the powerlessness and crisis of identity it is supposed to redeem?" (46). For more on men and masochism in American culture in the late twentieth century, see David Savran, *Taking It Like a Man: White Masculinity, Masochism, and Contemporary American Culture.*

[8] In "The Search for Male Identity within Modern Society: A Rhetorical Analysis of David Fincher's *Fight Club,*" Scott Wike and Barbara Pickering offer a rhetorical analysis of Tyler's speech, and of the film itself, ultimately focusing on the film's evocation of the failure of the American Dream for men.

[9] This catalogue is also part of the website for the film. The extent of the catalogue, as well as the text itself, differs slightly from the press kit. For clarity's sake, I will reference the press kit material in this essay.

[10] I am indebted to Gary Crowdus for mentioning this press kit in his review of the film after its release on video. See "Getting Exercised Over *Fight Club,*" *Cineaste* 25 (4) 2000: 46-48.

[11] This commentary, as well as the comments from Kaplan, I quote later in this essay, comes directly from the commentary on the *Fight Club* DVD.

[12] "The Lads are Coming!" *MediaWeek* 5 March 2001: 9

[13] Devin Leonard, "*Maxim* Has a Midlife Crisis," *Fortune* December 8, 2003: 56.

[14] "Meet the Metrosexual," Salon.com, July 22, 2002.

[15] Simpson has a slightly different take, writing, "The typical metrosexual is a young man with money to spend, living in or within easy reach of a metropolis…He might be officially gay, straight, or bisexual, but this is utterly immaterial because he has clearly taken himself as his own love object and pleasure as his sexual preference."

[16] Miller 113-114; Lindsay 43.

[17] *Marketplace,* National Public Radio, June 3 1999; American Academy of Facial Plastic and Reconstructive Surgery, *2001 Membership Survey: Trends in Plastic Surgery* (2002): qtd in Miller 114.

CHAPTER SIX

FASHIONABLE *FEMMES FATALES*: CUTTING THE EDGE OF CUSTOMARY MORALITY IN PAUL VERHOEVEN'S *BASIC INSTINCT*

ANTHONY D. HUGHES

Daemonic archetypes of woman filling world mythology represent the uncontrollable nearness of nature. Their tradition passes nearly unbroken from prehistoric idols through literature and art to modern movies. The primary image is the *femme fatale*, the woman fatal to man. (Paglia 13)

As Camille Paglia notes, the archetypal *femme fatale* has a long history that has evolved from her earliest prehistoric incarnations to her most recent representations in modern cinema. Along with other mythic figures, such as, for example, the male Hero, *femmes fatales* have a remarkable history indeed. These iconic figures have haunted and enchanted mankind from the dawn of time. As Leslie Fieldler has insightfully noted, their enduring presence is partly due to the fact that "Mythology is psychology in the profoundest sense of the word" (24). As long as human beings have created art to explore the eternal human themes of love, death, power, and gender difference, they have needed iconic figures which allow them to externalize, explore, and reconfigure a seemingly infinite variety of masculine and feminine subject positions and psychological states. Paul Verhoeven's *Basic Instinct* (1992) is a cutting edge, postmodern film that continues this long line of mythical incarnations of the *femme fatale*. To achieve this visionary reconfiguration of the *femme fatale*, Verhoeven and screenwriter, Joe Eszterhas, subvert the entire range of the *femme fatale* film's classic U.S. cinematic tropes.

The *Femme Fatale* Film: a Film Type or a Bonafide *Genre*?

In his analysis of Hollywood film *genre*s, Thomas Schatz argues that all film *genre*s demonstrate a specific iconography, characters, and themes that audiences recognize as unique to that *genre*. For example, the typical western is often set in a mid-west location, has cowboys wearing western clothes and gun belts, often passive women who are variously idealized, and western themes (such as reinforcing the law of mid-western culture.) To be considered a bonafide *genre*, each *genre* must have these elements. The war *genre*, sci-fi *genre*, or romance *genre* each has its representative iconography, characters types, and themes. Moreover, Schatz argues (after Focillion's, *The Life Forms of Art*), most art movements or philosophies go through four distinct periods in their evolutionary cycle: 1) an Experimental stage in which the *genre*'s basic conventions are established and taught to the audience; 2) a Classical period in which these conventions are repeated and expected by the mass audience; 3) a Refinement stage in which "certain formal and stylistic details embellish the form" (34), allowing it to move from "transparency to opacity: to explain itself, to address and examine its status as a popular form" (34); and lastly, 4) all movements, including film *genre*s, reach a Baroque period in which the *genre* deconstructs itself. At this stage, Schatz says:

> The formal or stylistic elements become so mannered, self-reflexive and accented that they become the substance of the work itself. We no longer look through the form (into a mirror to glimpse an idealized cultural image) as at the form itself to examine and appreciate its structure and cultural appeal. During this stage, the *genre* becomes self-reflexive, begins to value and justify itself. (34)

With Focillion's model in mind, we can take a Western *genre* and track its development through its various stages: *The Great Train Robbery* (1903); *The Searchers* (*The Wild Ones*) (1969); and *Unforgiven* (1992). By tracking this *genre* across the century, we can see that it continued to evolve because audiences continued to say, "Yes, we can believe this is reality or truth. We can suspend our disbelief." Moreover, the great *auteurs* often push film *genre*s from one stage to another. Stanley Kubrick's *2001: A Space Odyssey* (1968) is an excellent example of a visionary director moving the sci-fi *genre* forward from its Experimental and rather primitive 1950's stage into a new Classical phase, which was then imitated by later directors. When we look across the history of film *genre*s in any culture, we can see that cutting edge films are often on the cusp between these developmental stages. Such films and their *auteurs* trim away the old unusable aspects of the *genre* with which the audience has become "saturated" (Schatz 12), and add either new filmic technologies and/or *genre* reconfigurations that move the *genre* forward. Viewed from this perspective, *genre* films also function as cultural mirrors, reflecting a culture's current customary morality or belief system. Furthermore, films often become "blockbusters" because they strongly reinforce the culture's current mythology.

To understand why *Basic Instinct* is such a remarkable cutting edge film, it is first important to understand that the "*femme fatale* film" is a bonafide film *genre* because it meets all the basic *genre* requirements defined by Schatz. Briefly, B*asic Instinct* exhibits the standard cast of characters, traditional plot line with traditional themes, as well as traditional settings and symbols that are unique to the *femme fatale* film and thus, qualify it as a film *genre*. Moreover, the *femme fatale* film has progressed through all the standard stages of a *genre's* evolution as outlined by Schatz, with its Refinement stage incarnated in Verhoeven's *Basic Instinct.*

After providing a brief overview of the history of the *femme fatale genre* with its classical cast of characters, thematic elements, visual symbols and iconography, it will become evident *that Basic Instinct* stands notably at the end of a long line of *femme fatale* films. In many respects, *Basic Instinct* not only moves the *genre* into its fully realized Refinement stage, but it is also a penultimate example of how a cutting edge film can both move and not move audiences to accept a radically new customary morality.

An Overview of the *Femme Fatale Genre*

Since the dawn of cinema at the turn of the 19th century, a dazzling parade of *femmes fatales* and male heroes have strutted across the silver screen. In the Silent Period (1900-1927), films—such as Monta Bell's *Man, Woman, and Sin* (1927) and Clarence Brown's *Flesh and the Devil* (1927)—represented the *femme fatale genre* in its Experimental stage. As their titles suggest, these films were strongly imbued with a Puritanical, American, customary morality; typically, they followed an Adam/Eve paradigm in which the central male hero is depicted as a romanticized figure innocently lured by the *femme fatale's* seductive wiles. At the climax of most silent films, the *femme fatale* becomes a scapegoat figure and is killed off in retribution for the male "sin" of defying customary morality (of straying from the male fold), and thereby, the *femme fatale* restores patriarchy with her sacrificial death. Like Eve, the *femme fatale* becomes the scapegoat for the male's loss of control, desire, and his repudiation of the "father" or customary morality. Once she is eradicated at the climax of these early films, the male hero can return to his "Manhood Act" (Stoltenberg 5).

During the Golden Age of Hollywood (1930-1950), numerous *noir* films—such as Billy Wilder's classic *Double Indemnity* (1944), and Robert Sidomack's *Out of the Past* (1947)—reflect the *femme fatale genre* in its Classical phase. Audiences recognized the *genre* at this point with its Classical characters, themes, and iconography. As soon as Phyllis Dietrichson clomps down the stairs in Wilder's *Double Indemnity* (1944) in her high heel shoes and her daring anklet (which even shocked the French!), audiences knew Walter Neff was in deep trouble. With the advent of the *noir* world's darker, fatalistic view of human nature (male and female alike), which was rooted in German Expressionism, two key shifts occur in the *femme fatale genre's* traditional representations of masculine and feminine subjectivity. Many *noir femmes fatales*—such as Kathy Moffet in *Out of the Past* and Phyllis Deitrichson in Wilder's *Double Indemnity*—wield more power; they are more overtly seductive, strong, determined, clever, manipulative, and revealing in both their dress and attitudes. Moreover, in keeping with their evolution across the century, they begin to adopt more "masculine" aggressive attributes and start wielding phallic weapons such as guns and using them. Conversely, the male figures' heroic qualities and power (which were always re-stabilized during the *denouement* of most silent films) begin to erode. Although *noir* males' tragic falls are still generally romanticized, their macho edges begin to crack because the *femme fatale* has become a far more daunting and unmanageable antagonist. Moreover, in the typically, spiritually bankrupt *noir* world, the silent film's male journey of desire, sin, atonement, and redemption simply becomes a journey of poor ethical—not necessarily moral—decisions; the Christian overtones of the silent era disappear into the morally murky worlds of the *noir* nightmare. Part of this erosion is also caused by more prominently acknowledged subterranean psychological forces of which the male hero seems only dimly aware. The *noir* male's narrative journey parallels a journey into his own subconscious; many a Jekyll meets his Hyde. The implicit sense in silent films that the *femme fatale* and her "Good Good Girl" (Fiedler 259) double are projections of a split male *psyche* becomes far more explicit in film *noir*. As discussed later in this essay, the central male protagonists in all *femme fatale* films are not battling "real" women at all, but projections of a conflicted psychological make-up.

Although *femmes fatales* are generally still killed at the climax of forties' *noir* as a symbol of a restored patriarchy, they prove to be far tougher and deadlier antagonists than their distant cousins from The Silent Period. In many respects, although the *femme fatale* has not reached the remarkable heights of power she eventually wields in the postmodern era, the *noir* period's dark, anti-romantic German Expressionistic sensibility represents a major step forward for the growth of this figure. *Noir femmes fatales* find a welcome home and a golden opportunity to "ply their trades" in the liminal night worlds of the *noir* period. Although U.S. films from the first two major films periods were censored by the Hollywood Production Code instituted in 1934, the ultimate strength of the customary morality was firmly in place. Indeed, the Hollywood Production Code assured that it remained embedded in and reinforced mainstream Hollywood's traditional representations of masculine and feminine subjectivity. Despite these political and social forces, the general erosion of male power before the *femme fatale* steadily continues through the modern period (1950-1980). Among other political and culture shifts in popular U.S. culture (for example, the 60s Feminist Movement), this progressive loss of male power continued steadily through the Modern Period. The slow demise of the Hollywood Production Code in the 1960s and the introduction of the rating system in 1968 opened the floodgates for an increase in graphic violence and adult sexual situations beginning in the late 60s with films such as Arthur Penn's *Bonnie and Clyde* (1967) and Mike Nichols' *The Graduate* (1968). The seeds of the far more graphic violence and sex depicted in postmodern films (such as *Basic Instinct*) were planted in the late 60s via films such as these.

Although there was a lull in the production of *femme fatale* films during the Modern Period, during the Postmodern Age (1980-present), the *femme fatale genre* made a remarkable resurgence that parallels its growth during the *noir* era. A short list of these films includes: *Body Heat* (1981), *Fatal Attraction* (1987), *Black Widow* (1987), *Femme Fatale* (1991), *Basic Instinct* (1992), *Romeo Is Bleeding* (1993), and *The Last Seduction* (1994). The primary development during this period is a startling shift in a whole host of the *femme fatale* film's previous conventions, including a major shift regarding masculine and feminine power relations and subject positions. The once alluring and dangerous but ultimately impotent *femmes fatales* from the first half of the century evolve into highly powerful and seemingly invincible deadly, erotic forces which culminate in many ways in Verhoeven's *Basic Instinct*. Additionally, the once romanticized and ultimately victorious male heroes of the Silent and Classical periods devolve into the new postmodern fallen male figures or anti-heroes of the *fin-de-siecle*. Essentially, the male's psychological fear of the mythic *femme fatale*—that she will, figuratively or literally castrate him and appropriate his power becomes fully realized in the postmodern era. The most spectacular example is Verhoeven's vision of the *femme fatale* as "Satan" (Verhoeven) in the guise of Catherine Tramell, played hauntingly by Sharon Stone in the most "audacious" (Verhoeven) performance of her career.[1]

Verhoeven's *Auteur* Habits of Mind

In many respects, *Basic Instinct's* psychosocial richness is allowed to unfold due to Verhoeven's own audacious directorial style. His blockbuster U.S. films are characterized by a notable technical prowess and visual gymnastics. Often described as "stylish" and "flashy" (Maltin 413), they offer a "violent, action-packed assault on the sensibilities..." and demonstrate a "...penchant for startling visuals, explicit sex, graphic violence, although his intelligent directing is anything but careless or irresponsible" (Monaco 877). Verhoeven's "unremittingly bleak and ugly" (Maltin 1025) and "ultra-violent"(Monaco 877) vision of *fin-de-siecle* life is one of the major reasons that *Basic Instinct* is so representative of the postmodern American *femme fatale*. *Basic Instinct's* subtle surrealism; its intentionally confusing, disturbing gender delineations; and its profound sense of a decadent, randomly violent world typifies the paranoid, nightmarish subjectivity of the postmodern *femme fatale*, and by association, of the postmodern, ultra-Kafkaesque world itself. *Basic Instinct* reflects U.S. culture at the end of gender evolution whose major thematic and psychological conflicts first flowered in silent films such as Clarence Brown's *Flesh and the Devil* (1927) and Monta Bell's *Man, Woman, and Sin* (1927).[2]

Like many European directors, Verhoeven's work has distinct European and U.S. phases. His major Hollywood breakthrough came with *RoboCop* (1987), a film that showed he knew the U.S. adolescent pulse. Moreover, *RoboCop* shows Verhoeven's penchant for mocking and playing up to mainstream American customary morality which was ..."Puritan from the start" (Duncan 145). During his early years in the Netherlands, Verhoeven made several fllms, each of which was progressively more sexually and violently graphic: *Turkish Delight* (1973),

Keetje Tipple (1975), *Soldier of Orange* (1979), *The Fourth Man* (1979), and *Spetters (*1980). Even given a relatively more liberal European sensibility, many protested that his films were misogynistic and/or depicted derogatory views of people with disabilities. As Verhoeven has said, however, "I always push the limits. I try to do things that I have not done before, that are dangerous, overwhelming and challenging. I like controversy" (Duncan 179). Although *Keetje Tipple* reflects a "superficial social commentary on working class life," (Maltin 632) *Soldier of Orange* is considered" an exceptional character study" and an impressively directed work (Monaco 867). His first U.S. film, *Flesh and Blood* (1985), is a fairly sophisticated and grizzly romantic adventure set in plague-ridden, sixteenth century Europe. When we view the overall development of Verhoeven from his earliest art-house efforts to recent works (such as the admittedly horrendous *Showgirls* (1995), he appears to have become swept up in a Hollywood whirlwind of glitz and glamour, opting for the immediate gratification of the shiny surface rather than a lasting depth. However, Verhoeven's love of glitz and glorification of decadence is an intentional desire to hold up the mirror of our age to itself. Whether he is making a socially conscientious work (such as *Soldier of Orange* (1979) or reveling in the sci-fi flights of fancy of *Total Recall* (1990), his work is always marked by a concerted effort to shock his viewers with graphic violence, sex, and a disturbing vision of modern life.

Via a similar desire for "shock and awe," *Basic Instinct* (1992) embellishes all the narrative and thematic tropes of the traditional *femme fatale genre* and takes them to their ultimate extremes, moving this *genre* into a highly embellished Refinement stage. As in many postmodern works, the *femme fatale* is now a super killer; she is ultra-sexual, cunning, and irresistible. The male protagonist is now hyper-angry, anarchistic, and self-destructive. The corrupt moral order that first blossoms in the *noir* period reaches new, Kafkaesque realms of backstabbing, double-dealing, and mystery—all of which provide the central male protagonist with greater fodder for his anarchistic tendencies. Lastly, even the *femme fatale genre's* traditional male bond between the two central male characters—what Leslie Fiedler calls the "holy marriage of males" (350) is questioned as one of the last vestiges of chivalric male subjectivity. Throughout the film, the male bond is subtly mourned and parodied via Curran and his partner, Gus, who refer to one another as "Cowboy" and "Haus"—echoing the lost, chivalric realm of the heroic cowboy. Like Haus in the Bonanza television series, Gus Moran has a beer belly that hangs over the cowboy belt buckle that he wears wherever he goes. In traditional *femme fatale* films, this male bond is always tested by the *femme fatale* but is triumphant in the end, especially during this *genre*'s Experimental and Classical stages. However, in *Basic Instinct*, which subverts all this *genre*'s previous patterns, it is the *femme fatale* herself who eradicates Curran's male buddy, Gus, in a horrific murder during the film's climax.

The *Femme Fatale Genre*'s Traditional Cast of Characters

Below its slick, slippery surface, *Basic Instinct* is a film of remarkable psychological depth. Like numerous *femme fatale* films (such as *Flesh and the Devil* (1927) and *Double Indemnity* (1944), *Basic Instinct*'s cast of characters includes numerous sets of "doubles". These doubles include a major dynamic protagonist who is seduced and nearly destroyed by the *femme fatale*. This protagonist usually has a male "buddy" or "Good Boy" who is his best friend and who constantly warns him to beware of the *femme fatale*. This Good Boy functions like a conscience figure and represents one aspect of the central male's *psyche*, in Freudian terms, his super-ego. Moreover, in all *femme fatale* films, it is the male bond between these two figures that, when healthy and whole, represents a sound patriarchal world, a world the *femme fatale* always threatens and invades. Secondly, the *femme fatale* herself is usually mirrored by a "Good Good Girl" (Fiedler 259); she's the *femme fatale's* double and represents the customary morality. Again, if read psychoanalytically, *femmes fatales* and their doubles—as well as many of major and minor male figures—are all projections of the male *psyche*, similar to the way in which some dream interpreters believe that all the figures who appear in our dreams are manifestations of our various selves. In Freudian terms, these figures represent a psychic split which Freud delineates in his essay, *The Most Prevalent Form of Degradation in Everyday Erotic Life*" In that essay, Freud argues that some males may develop a Madonna/Whore split in their *psyche*; their lustful desires are only aroused by a "lower" woman, and their feelings of love and tenderness are split off onto a pure woman or mother figure. This is one of the major psychological undercurrents played out in all *femme fatale* films. For example, in *Double Indemnity,* Walter Neff must choose between Phyllis Dietrichson and her daughter, Lola. In *Flesh and the Devil* (1927), Leo, the central male protagonist, must choose between Felicitas, the *femme fatale*, and Hertha, the "Good Good Girl" (Fiedler 259) who ultimately saves the day with her fervent prayers to God. In *Basic Instinct*, Curran must choose between Catherine Tramell and Dr. Beth Garner. Moreover, most *femme fatale* films include a punishing father figure who also represents the customary morality; this figure often dogs the central male protagonist throughout the film. In *Flesh and the Devil* (1927), he is played by Pastor Voss, and in *Double Indemnity,* Barton Keyes doubles not only as Neff's male buddy but also his father figure. (Near the climax of Wilder's film, Keyes tells Neff, "Papa has it all figured out".) Also, in some *femme fatale* films, there is an archetypal mother figure, representing patriarchal womanhood in all her glory. A notable example of this figure from the early postmodern period is Ann Archer, the mother in *Fatal Attraction (1987).* She saves the day and her family, another key symbol of a sound patriarchy, at the climax by shooting Glenn Close, the psychopathic *femme fatale,* who rises up out of the bathtub like a monster coming back to life in a classic horror film. Lastly, in many *femme fatale* films, there is often a third male party— often a father figure or husband, from whom the male hero must steal the *femme fatale*. In *noir femme fatale* films, this older male is often killed in an interesting replay of the oedipal drama. This love triangle can be seen in *The Postman Always Rings Twice* (1946) and in *Double Indemnity,* among numerous films. In summery, these are the central characters and psychological undercurrents found in the traditional *femme fatale* genre. Read psychologically, all these figures represent aspects of the male protagonist's disturbed *psyche*. If read as modern American mythology, they represent either guardians or enemies of the status quo.

Verhoeven's *Basic Instinct,* scripted by Joe Eszterhas, takes this traditional cast and subverts it to a great extent. First, *Basic Instinct* certainly sports the traditional male protagonist, Nick "Shooter" Curran (Michael Douglas), who becomes obsessed with a *femme fatale,* Catherine Tramell (Sharon Stone). As her name suggests, Tramell does indeed "Trammell" and viciously murder numerous characters who cross her path. In typical American style, Curran's masculinity is partly defined by his relationship with his male buddy, Gus Moran, (George Dzundza) or "Cowboy," the "Good Boy," as well as Dr. Beth Garner (Jeanne Tripplehorn), the requisite "Good Girl". In an amusing twist to the Good Girl's typical function as redeemer/savior, Garner is cast as Curran's personal psychologist. By the advent of the *fin-de-siecle,* the male protagonist in *femme fatale* films is so angst-ridden that he now requires professional help! In *Basic Instinct,* Curran is provided with a Good Girl who is professionally trained to lead him back to a central societal position. Moreover, in another Verhoevian twist on the traditional *femme fatale* narrative in which there is a third "male" figure from whom the male hero steals the *femme fatale, Basic Instinct* offers Roxie (Leilani Sarelle) or "Rocky" as Curran condescendingly calls her, Tramell's female lover with whom Curran competes for the affections of Tramell. Lastly, following the *femme fatale* film's standard cast, Curran's world is populated by punishing father figures such as Captain Talcott, his stereotypically badgering and sometimes understanding boss, and Lt. Nielsen, the Internal Affairs investigator, who antagonizes Curran throughout the first third of the film—until Tramell kills him to frame Curran and have him suspended from the force. Via this traditional cast of key figures, Curran experiences a Verhoevian nightmare version of the classic *femme fatale* "fantasy" that is light years away from the romanticized, chivalric world of Brown's *Flesh and the Devil* (1927) and the progressively darker *noir* world of Wilder's *Double Indemnity*. Indeed, in *Basic Instinct*, the *noir* world of this *genre*'s Classical period becomes pitch black in its highly embellished Refinement stage.

Although *Basic Instinct* includes this standard cast of morally and psychologically symbolic characters, they are not the clear cut figures of good and evil that they were in previous decades.[3] For example, Beth Garner, the "Good Good Girl" (Fiedler 259) is a red herring throughout the film and is an intentionally ambiguous and multi-layered figure. Beth has experimented with bisexuality in college with Tramell, and we aren't sure if she isn't still obsessed with Tramell and actually is a murderer till near the climax of the film. Moreover, Hazel Dobkins, a minor figure, appears to be a quiet archetypal mother who floats around throughout the film and is apparently a "friend" of Tramell, who she studies for psychological interest. However, Dobkins is no pure Earth Mother; she's a reformed madwoman who went crazy and murdered her entire family. Similarly, after Roxy's death, we learn that she flipped out in early childhood, murdering her brothers in a peak of fury. Moreover, Lt. Neilson, the standard Father figure who dogs Curran, turns out to be a sleazy policeman on the take who sells Curran's dossier to Tramell for $50,000. (As is typical of the *femme fatale genre's* traditional narrative structure, as the plot unfolds, we continue to delve into the history of the major characters—especially the *femme fatale*—and we slowly learn the true "evil" or pathological nature of their hidden selves.) Verhoeven notes in the director's commentary on the re-released director's cut of *Basic Instinct* that he wanted all these characters to be ambiguous; this intentional confusion about the "good" or "evil" nature of key characters is another major embellishment Verhoeven makes which moves the *genre* into its Refinement stage. Lastly, Verhoeven inverts and takes to their ultimate extremes, the two central figures of Catherine Tramell and Nick "Shooter" Curran, both of whom I will discuss in the following sections of this analysis.

The Postmodern *Femme Fatale*: Marriage
of the *Femme Fatale* and Horror *Genre*s

Basic Instinct's exposition establishes Verhoeven's intentionally disturbing film-making style and his graphically violent, dark vision of the postmodern mythic *femme fatale* and the disintegrating state of masculine subjectivity. It also establishes Verhoeven's overtly manipulative, effective directorial style. Following the "big bang" approach, that is, starting a film with a dramatic kickoff, the opening murder sequence of Johnny Boz (a prize fighter Tramell is dating at the start of the film) is designed to shock the audience and to create a glorified, mythological aura surrounding Tramell's horrific, pathological castrating power. Verhoeven initially lulls the audience into a false repose. The credits roll while melodically seductive new-age music soothes the viewer as geometric prism shapes meld hieroglyphically in soft earth tones and sensuous lighting. These elusive shapes are actually highly blurred shots of the slowly gyrating bodies of Johnny Boz and Catherine Tramell "making love" in the opening scene. Verhoeven avoids the predictably sultry saxophone soundtracks that introduce countless modern *femme fatale* films, such as *Body Heat* (1987). This is another example of the *clichés* from the *genre*'s Classical period with which audiences had become "saturated" (Schatz 34). His choice of a synthesized new-age treatment by Jerry Goldsmith (a seductively elusive theme that Verhoeven spent countless hours developing) adds to the film's stylish modernity, and the elusive musical motif suggests the postmodern *femme fatale*'s mysterious, brooding, and barely contained sexual power. As Jan De Bont, the cinema photographer says, "The music is Catherine Tramell" (Bont, DVD commentary).

As Verhoeven continues to lull the audience into a serene mood, a languorous opening pan shot sets up a central trope that runs throughout the film, namely the dislocation of direction and space. The camera pans into what appears to be the real world, which turns into a mirror image in the mirror on the ceiling of Boz's bedroom. Mirrors are key visual symbols in *femme fatale* films, often expressing the *femme fatale's* duplicity, narcissism, and ambiguity about her true self. As the camera slowly pans down to the real lovers on the bed, the audience is already unsure—as it will be throughout the film—of what is up or down, reflection or reality, killer or red herring. The opening sequence with its mirrored ceiling and decadent decor not only establishes the theme of inversion but also extends the traditional *femme fatale* film's melding of sex, money, and death. As James Agee notes when discussing Walter Neff and Phyllis Dietrichson from Wilder's *Double Indemnity* "...among these somewhat representative Americans, money and sex and a readiness to kill are as inseparably interdependent as the Holy Trinity" (Agee 119). *Femme fatale* films from the silent period partially associate the *femme fatale's* "evil" with sexual and monetary greed, and *noir* works extend this association; however, in the postmodern period, this motif is embellished to its extreme in the *genre's* Refinement stage. Part of the *femme fatale's* newfound power—and the male's desire for her—includes her hyper-wealth and hyper-sexual prowess. Unlike many *femme fatale* figures from the Silent and Golden ages who need to seduce men to appropriate their masculine power, in *Basic Instinct*, Tramell does not need Curran to help her either commit murder (a point graphically made in the opening scene) or gain wealth. Before she ever meets him, Tramell has a net worth of 110 million dollars—a fact which impresses Curran tremendously—and as Gus, Curran's partner quips, "She {even} has a degree in fucking with people's heads." The overall sense of Tramell's motivation to become involved with Curran is not due to an "evil" sexual wantonness on her part—as in *Flesh and the Devil* (1927)—or a practical desire to free herself from a deadening marriage—as in *Double Indemnity* —but primarily due to a desire to play power games with Curran. As Verhoeven says, "She wants to commit murder merely to see if she can get away with it" (Verhoeven DVD commentary.) Curran is simply another interesting case study for Tramell's next book and just another in a long line of males with whom she becomes involved for her pleasure and amusement. She does not need him for money or murder. In fact, during the opening murder scene in which Tramell bludgeons Boz to death with an ice-pick, we see the *femme fatale* figure transformed into a penultimate killing machine, a highly symbolic murder that embodies the essential male fear of and self-destructive desire to be consumed by the *femme fatale* in "the ecstasy of death" (Verhoeven, DVD commentary.) Along with the diversionary sense of Tramell's involvement with Curran, the opening murder scene shockingly demonstrates that Tramell possesses a deep-seated, pathological drive to "trammel" every male who crosses her path. Indeed, Verhoeven's vision of the *femme fatale* as "the devil" (Verhoeven, DVD commentary) becomes the penultimate incarnation in the postmodern era of this archetypal figure, a pathological killer disguised as an all-American blonde beauty.

Along with her hyper-wealth and taboo breaking bisexuality, Tramell reflects other radical departures from previous directorial visions of the classic *femme fatale*. Although she is overtly sexual and often seductively dressed in highly provocative, expensive clothes, she is also the most androgynous example of a postmodern *femme fatale.* (This androgynous quality is later one-upped by Lena Olin's over the top performance in *Romeo is Bleeding* (1993). Along with her hyper-feminine appearance, she also appropriates the traditional "masculine" character traits that in previous films were only allowed to be wielded by male protagonists. These traits include her incredible intelligence; (as Beth Garner yells to Curran: "She's evil; she's brilliant!.) Indeed, the entire film is a testament to her "diabolical plan" (Verhoeven, DVD commentary.) The audience struggles along with Curran and the LA Police Department to make sense of the maze of complications she concocts a web of deceptions which ultimately, Curran and the police never clearly decipher. In one telling scene when she visits Curran in his apartment and he's ineptly attempting to break up a block of ice for drinks with an ice-pick, she takes over the job, flips the phallic pick in mid-air, grabs it with authority, and begins breaking up the ice with great *panache.* One other example of her masculine prowess is the car chase scene during the rising action in which Curran attempts to tail her along a precarious stretch of Highway 1. Tramell weaves in and out of traffic with the finesse of an experienced race car driver in her expensive Ferrari, while Curran ineptly attempts to keep up with her in his dumpy brown Ford Fairlane, and after several near cashes in his pursuit of her, he eventually loses her in traffic. These voyeuristic tracking scenes are reminiscent of Scotty's surveillance of Madeline in Hitchcock's *Vertigo (1958),* a film on which Verhoeven based much of *Basic Instinct.* In that film, however, Scotty (Jimmy Stewart) is clearly a man in command of his car and surveillance; although, like Curran, he slowly becomes obsessed with his quarry. Eventually, Curran does catch up with Tramell as she visits Hazel Dobkins, the ex-murderess. In his pursuit of Tramell on her trip home, Tramell adds insult to injury and again loses Curran in traffic.

One last opening scene, which establishes the postmodern *femme fatale*'s ascent to power in a seemingly crumbling masculine world, is Tramell's multi-million dollar villa that overlooks the ocean, (a real villa shot on location in Carmel, California.) Tramell's county estate with its richly furnished, lush interior décor, replete with Picassos, underscores the new heights of power that the postmodern *femme fatale* has attained. When Gus and Curran go to the house to interrogate her, they find Tramell sitting on a chair perched on the edge of a cliff overlooking the ocean, gazing out like a queen in command of her kingdom. When they first round the corner, the establishing shot of Tramell has her finishing a cigarette (a classic *femme fatale* symbol) which she flicks into the ocean in a masculine gesture, reflecting how she treats all things, including lovers, when she's through with them. She's wrapped in a $4,000 Armani shawl, which Sharon Stone bought when clothing designer Ellen Mirojnick let her go on a shopping spree on Rodeo drive, "So I knew how it felt to be a person who could shop like that" (Stone, DVD interview.) Throughout this scene, she emanates utter confidence and sexual bluntness, and constantly throws Gus and Curran off balance with her whip sharp responses and chutzpah. The males constantly look to each another for reassurance and direction. This perch on the edge of the cliff will the first of many precipitous places that she leads Curran with her toying manipulation of him. Also, in true mythic fashion, Tramell is associated with the power and mystery of the sea and sunlight. In the reverse shots of her with the house behind her, Jan De Bont, the cinema photographer, placed small mirrors to reflect a white glistening sun behind her, a small slightly mesmerizing visual touch that adds to her mystery and connection with the powers of nature. Moreover, throughout the film, Tramell's wardrobe primarily consists of expensive, gray, beige, and brown, billowy outfits, "earth tones" as Jan De Bont, the cinema photographer, describes them; these colors express her connection with nature and the mystery of her physical "earthy" power. Although her outfits are often sensuous and seductive, they also have a certain masculine edge—as do her manners and body language, adding to Tramell's androgynous quality; in short, she possesses the beauty of a woman but the power of a man. In many scenes, she appropriates traditional male behaviors; for example, in a later scene, when she is being taken off to the police station by Gus and Curran for questioning, it is she, not the men, who leads the way out the front door of her villa.

Lastly, the most powerful and horrifically shocking introduction to the androgynous power of the *femme fatale* occurs at the climax of the opening love-making scene. When Tramell pulls out the ice-pick and viciously bludgeons Johnny Boz to death in a series of montage shots, echoing Hitchcock's shower scene in *Psycho* (1961), Verhoeven truly shocks the viewer with his horrifically graphic murder in which her bound male victim is stabbed to death at the height of the *femme fatale's* orgasm. One symbolic shot (which had to be edited out of the U.S. version in order for it to get an R rating) is that of the ice-pick going through Johnny Boz's nose, an obvious image of the castrated male. With this opening murder scene, Verhoeven, in a sense is saying, whereas all the earlier *femmes fatales* in film history may take ninety minutes to arrive at some point even mildly like this or not at all, for this *femme fatale*, this horrific murder is just an introduction to her power. The exposition to *Basic Instinct* establishes all the major postmodern qualities of the new *femme fatale* for the 90s. She is super wealthy, super smart, super deadly, super seductive, super feminine and masculine, and (probably most dangerous of all, and like the "Satan" figure Verhoeven intends her to be), highly deceptive about owning and wielding these powers. In terms of *Basic Instinct's* central female figure, these are some of the major embellishments Verhoeven makes to her classical character that moves the *femme fatale genre* into its stage of Refinement.

The Fallen Male Figures in *Femme Fatale* Films

Curiously, an in-depth study of the male figures in *femme fatale* films has never been conducted. Important insights have been made concerning some of the psychological tendencies of the central male protagonists—primarily by feminist critics—but these comments have generally been made in passing and with the assumption that *the femmes fatales* are these films' central characters. Throughout their history, these films have been referred to as *"femme fatale,"* not, for example, "fallen male" films. Understandably, feminist scholars have been drawn to examine these films' haunting and uniquely powerful females. For example, Janey Place notes that when we recall *femme fatale* films, "we retain the image of the erotic, strong, unrepressed (if destructive) woman" (36). And indeed, the male figures are often overshadowed as much in memory as they literally are on screen—especially if they share the screen with a *femme fatale*. This tendency to overlook the males is curious, however, because a majority of these films' on camera time is devoted to tracking the males' labyrinthine journeys of obsession. Despite this tendency to overlook the males as minor figures, a major premise of this analysis is that precisely the opposite view better reflects the major mythological concerns of these films. *"Femme fatale"* films would be far more accurately termed "fallen male" (or perhaps, "fools for love") films because it is the males' dynamic journeys that comprise their central focus. The *femmes fatales* are essentially static characters who function primarily as catalysts for the males, female initiators who instigate and drive the male journey of desire, discovery, and sometimes, self-destruction. However, this deceptive focusing on the *femme fatale* in these films is one of this *genre's* most subtly subversive aspects. Under the guise of being swept away by "the uncontrollable nearness of nature" (Paglia 13), the male figures "sneak in" a "perverse scenario" (Kaplan 16) a series of subversive longings to overthrow the customary morality. This pattern is similar to what Molly Haskell says of woman's films of the 1920s, although appearing to be cautionary tales, they allow their viewers "to indulge....vicariously, in those peccancies which they were simultaneously made to feel noble in resisting (Haskell 15). It is precisely this scenario that we see played out by the male figures in these films. By distracting the audience (via the camera's focus on woman as object of the gaze), the males and females too—both on and "outside" the silver screen—can indulge in a variety of hidden, anarchistic longings.

One of the major reasons that a study of the male figures in *femme fatale* films has not been conducted is that until recently phallocentric culture has had a marked tendency to avoid examining masculine subjectivity at all. However, during the postmodern era, the imaging of masculinity in film has drawn more attention in light of ongoing gender studies; until then, looking too closely at male subjectivity was shunned— almost as if culture itself were suffering from an unconscious fear of what it might discover. In many ways, as Laura Mulvey first pointed out in her seminal essay, *Visual Pleasure and Narrative Cinema*, classic Hollywood film can be read as a neurotic attempt by phallocentric culture to maintain its structures of power by objectifying and containing woman via the psychosocial apparatus implied by the camera's "male" gaze. What recent studies have discovered, however, is precisely what has been unconsciously feared all along—that masculine subjectivity has never been as monolithically indestructible as phallocentric culture hoped it was. Although postmodern film still clutches to an ongoing stream of idealized hyper-masculine and feminine representations, (male and female Gods and Goddesses), it also now has its share of iconic figures who are androgynous, blending the best of both masculine and feminine characteristics. Although these figures retain their primary sexual essence as masculine or feminine, they are still markedly reconfigured. For example, Laura Croft, "Tomb Raider" is a hyper-feminized figure, but she clearly demonstrates a good supply of "masculine" attributes that are acceptable to and believed by mass audiences. Postmodern customary morality has evolved to the point where it can "suspend its disbelief" that such figures can exist. Similarly, Arnold Swartzenager in *Terminator 2: Judgment Day* (1991) is undoubtedly a hyper-masculine hero (least we forget!), but he assumes the role of a "motherly" nurturing relationship with Conner, the boy he is programmed to protect. Similarly, Sarah Conner, a once archetypal mother, evolves across the first two films from a mild-mannered waitress to a muscular, machine gun totting camouflage wearing soldier.

The Psychodynamics of *Femme Fatale* Films

While I am often leery of psychological models, I do find them fascinating and feel that they are useful for partially understanding the psychological undercurrents in *femme fatale* films. However, I also feel that that the discipline of psychology is still in its infancy even 100 years after Freud began his brilliant forays into the workings of the human mind. In general, however, I feel that the discipline is light years from truly understanding the mind and therefore, many of our current models and analyses are certainly tentative. Regardless, I would like to discuss several key psychological patterns that one finds in these films since they do help one understand some of the major subconscious forces which drive their male protagonists.

An important trend in film criticism that began in the postmodern period is an interest by many film scholars—male and female—to take a new look at masculine subjectivity. Kaja Silverman's, *Male Subjectivity at the Margins,* Sharon Willis' and Constance Penley's, *Male Trouble,* and Peter Lehman's, *Running Scared. Masculinity and the Representation of the Male Body* are a few early examples of this trend that reflect a fresh understanding that below its apparently monolithic surface, male subjectivity is highly unstable. Although this is not surprising news, the descriptions of male pathology are revealing when applied to the *femme fatale genre*. In summarizing their research, Willis and Penley note that the new "...emphasis here on understanding masculinity through hysteria, masochism, and narcissism represents a move away from a sometimes narrow view of masculinity as structured primarily around voyeurism and fetishism" (Willis, Penley ix). Willis and Penley stress that such gender studies are not merely taking up psychoanalytic categories commonly associated with "feminine" positions and applying them to studies of masculine subjectivity, but rather "...what we see here is a continuation of a move begun by Freud and renewed by Lacan to understand these psychical positions or states as descriptive of subjectivity itself, rather than characterizing a uniquely feminine subject position" (Willis, Penley ix). In other words, "masculine" and "feminine" subjectivity are no longer viewed as two lines of study on separate continuums, but rather subjectivity itself is seen as a single continuum possessing various *psychic* states that are neither "feminine" or "masculine," simply human. In classic Hollywood cinema, voyeurism and fetishism have always been central to the imaging of masculine subjectivity—as demonstrated by almost any Hitchcock film (such as *Vertigo* (1956) or *Rear Window* (1954). Not surprisingly, in *Basic Instinct*, Verhoeven (who models much of his film on *Vertigo*) shows Curran voyeuristically and fetishistically spying on Tramell as she dresses and undresses. Much of the camera work, as in *Vertigo* (1956) emphasizes Curran locking his male gaze (via Verhoeven's conspiring subjective camera shots) on Tramell for scopophilic pleasure and idealizing her as a fetish object. Such behaviors are not new to the *femme fatale genre* or the central male's acting out of them; they are a "basic instinct" that unconsciously drive their obsession and fascination with the archetypal *femme fatale*. In this sense, the *femme fatale* does represent "the uncontrollable nearness of nature" (13) described by Paglia in the opening quote of this essay.

Although insightful psychoanalytic readings have been conducted regarding the male figures in *femme fatale* films, such as Claire Johnston's "*Double Indemnity*," these readings primarily discuss these film's oedipal trajectories. On one level, as Johnston notes, the *femme fatale genre*'s standard narrative structure, with its triangle of husband/wife/lover (or father/mother/son) and its doubling of male and female figures into "Good Good," or "Good Bad" Boys and Girls, can be read as a replay of an Oedipal drama that attempts to resolve the male psychic split identified by Freud in *The Most Prevalent Form of Degradation in Everyday Erotic Life*. Clearly, these films have this built in psychological structure, yet it is only the tip of the iceberg and has been pursued at length. However, as noted in Penley's and Willis's descriptions, other psychological "feminine" psychic states also drive Curran's journey of desire. One of the major additions to the male figures' psychological *repertoire* is an anarchistic agenda that involves inversions of "masculine" and "feminine" subject positions, and it is these more interesting and less discussed hidden agendas that I will examine in the next section.

Anarchistic Agendas and Gender Inversions

As noted earlier, several key patterns emerge when we examines the evolution of masculine and feminine subjectivity in the U.S. *femme fatale genre*. During the Silent Experimental period, the *genre* tends to romanticize the central male protagonist. He is imaged as a Good Boy victimized by an "evil" *femme fatale*. After indulging in his "fortunate fall," he ultimately chooses Masculine Duty over Desire, and the *femme fatale* is scapegoated for his "sins" in a happy ever after ending that restores difference and customary morality. However, the subtexts of many silent *femme fatales* films—such as *Flesh and the Devil* (1927) and *Man, Woman, and Sin* (1927)—belie their simplistic Adam/Eve paradigms, suggesting that the male's repudiation of the protective male fold is a "cover story" (Kaplan 218) that conceals a complex of anarchistic longings that actually defy difference and customary morality. Moreover, these longings become more intense, open, and defiant as the *femme fatale genre* evolves into the postmodern period. Verhoeven brings this progression to its ultimate extreme, and it is one of the major embellishments he makes to the classical *femme fatale* film, moving the *genre* into its Refinement stage.

One of the most revealing and subversive aspects of the *femme fatale genre* that goes beyond Freud's paradigm of the male split *psyche* is a secondary set of hidden agendas. As with many Hollywood *genres*, the *femme fatale* film exploits gender stereotypes—both physical and symbolic—as part of the storyline. These exaggerated images of masculinity and femininity are one example of what Louise Kaplan discusses in her study, *Female Perversions: The Temptations of Emma Bovary*. Kaplan notes that all sexual perversions are deceptive in nature and use "...one or another stereotype of masculinity and femininity in a way that deceives the onlooker about the unconscious meanings of the behaviors he or she is observing" (Kaplan 9). Although Kaplan was not referring to onlookers in a movie theater, traditional Hollywood cinema— and the *femme fatale* film in particular—function like a "perverse scenario" (Kaplan 42) in that they evoke hyper-masculine and hyper-feminine stereotypes in a powerful sleight of hand (or eye) to mask the hidden "feminine" and often subconscious longings of the central male protagonist. These are longings normally forbidden by the customary morality. One of these desires is to throw off the shackles of his "Manhood Act" (Stoltenberg 5) and to enjoy a "feminine," passive, or submissive subject position. In her fascinating discussion of Madam Bovary, Kaplan notes that Charles Bovary's submission to Emma's dominance allows him to play out a hidden "feminine" agenda:

> By submitting to Emma's masculine powers, Charles could express forbidden feminine strivings and still be reassured of his masculinity. At the same time, he could adore with impunity the femininities that were forbidden to him. In his enthrallment with her gestures, clothing, hair styles, he could enwrap his soul in femininity and no one would be any the wiser. (Kaplan 235)

A major psychological undercurrent we see in *femme fatale* films are the males enjoying just such an enthrallment. Under the macho guise of being swept away by their overwhelming desire for the *femme fatale*, the male protagonists can experiment with a variety of "feminine" subject positions. A classic example from the Silent period is Josef Von Sternberg's *The Blue Angel* (1930). This film stars Marlene Dietrich as Lola, the *femme fatale*, and Emil Jannings, as Professor Rath, the fool for love who becomes enthralled with Lola and eventually loses every scrap of his dignity and ultimately, his life, to her. During Rath's pathetic decline, many scenes show the Professor working in Lola's make-up room (she's a singer in "The Blue Angel" nightclub) after he has being fired from his professional position due to his "sordid" affair with Lola. In these scenes, Rath prepares her clothes, make-up, and helps her dress before her performances, putting on her stockings for her, eventually becoming her submissive servant. Although *The Blue Angel* (1930) is a remarkably powerful classic example of this hidden agenda being played out, Nick Curran indulges in his own postmodern variety of a hidden "feminine" agenda in *Basic Instinct*.

One key scene in which Curran reveals a hidden longing to submit to Catherine is their first marathon sex scene. After tracking Catherine down at Johnny Boz's bisexual dance club—a postmodern, decadent church that has been redesigned with neo-*noir* neon lighting—and eventually winning Catherine's attentions from an angry Roxie, they retire to Catherine's city home for their first love-making extravaganza. The sex scene is a symbolic dance of power with Curran initially playing the dominant male role; at a climatic moment though, Tramell stops him by scratching his back, sadomasochistically drawing blood, and appropriates the "masculine" on top position, and Curran assumes the submissive, "feminine" position. He then allows himself to be tied to the bedpost with the same fetish object, Tramell's Hermes scarf, from the film's opening love/death sex scene. The tension builds throughout this scene because, like Curran, the audience wonders whether Tramell will suddenly pull out her ice-pick and murder Curran. At the moment of climax, she flings herself on top of him, and as she pulls back, we see Curran is still alive, aware of the close call from which he has been saved, and possibly even aroused by. Regardless, Curran is clearly excited by playing the submissive "feminine" position during the love scene. Moreover, the possibility that it could have been his final love-making scene—because he is aware that Johnny Boz was bound the same way, reflects Curran's unconscious death wish—or psychologically speaking, a wish that the need to play the role of the dominant "man" could be adopted by Tramell, a role she aggressively assumes.

In the next scene, he brags to Roxy, whom he derogatorily calls "Rocky", and says "I think she's the fuck of the century." In terms of

Verhoeven's visionary postmodern recreation of the mythic *femme fatale,* by comparison with previous *femmes fatales* of the 20th century, Tramell is, indeed, "the fuck of the century" on multiple levels. Curran's excited and anxious submission to Tramell's bondage is one of several ways in which the postmodern fallen male more graphically indulges his desire to subvert the customary morality than in earlier *femme fatale* films. This literal, physical submission to the *femme fatale* in the form of bondage "play" is one of the major embellishments that Verhoeven makes to the Classical *femme fatale genre,* moving it into its Refinement stage. Moreover, in keeping with Kaplan's analysis of the hidden agendas behind sexual perversions, through the guise of submitting to the overwhelming power and seductiveness of the *femme fatale,* Curran "sneaks in" his subversive desires—as does Verhoeven via the camera's gaze for the male, and perhaps, female audience.

Social Masochism and Internal Affairs

Another major area in which Verhoeven subverts the *femme fatale genre*'s previous traditions concerns *Basic Instinct*'s inversions of the male's more direct defiance of the customary morality, in particular, as it is embodied in male establishment. In all *femme fatale* films, the *femme fatale* is always a threat to the social order, and in the course of his journey of self-destruction, the male protagonist is slowly drawn into her liminal "feminine" social position, and the implication is that is exactly where he unconsciously wishes to be. During the course of Curran's fall from "grace," he is eventually suspended from the police force. The build up to that moment is orchestrated by Tramell behind the scenes in a brilliantly complicated set of frame ups which reinforce her postmodern, ultra "diabolical" (Verhoeven DVD commentary) powers to deceive and control the male world. She pays Lt. Neilson 50K to see Nick's personal file, an incident which causes Curran to explode at Nielson and be put on leave. Shortly thereafter, Neilson is found murdered, and Curran is put on permanent suspension, being suspected of Neilson's death. It is Tramell, of course, who kills Neilson to frame Curran. After this incident, Curran is off the force and asked to turn in his gun—the ultimate symbol for loss of phallic power.

As he begins his downward spiral via the temptations and sexual frustrations Tramell has aroused in him, Curran reverts to his old addictive behaviors and starts drinking and smoking again, slowly looking more disheveled with every passing scene. Throughout the film, Nick's clothing and demeanor reveal his sadomasochistic fall. At the beginning, he is always neatly dressed in a suit and tie; during the rising action, he starts wearing jeans and sweaters; and by the film's climax, he is smoking constantly, is unshaven, drinking heavily, and wears an old raincoat. Curran's wardrobe changes reflect his slow demise at the hands of Tramell but also reveal his expression of what Kaja Silverman terms "Social Masochism." As Silverman describes it, social masochism is a male pathology, the hidden intent of which is for the male to display his suffering, and anger to the male world and thereby, punish "The Father" with guilt. Although Silverman's and Deleuze's analyses are not specifically described with *femme fatale* films in mind, they delineate a major hidden agenda found in many *femme fatale* films. Following Deleuze, Silverman summarizes the basic nature of social masochism and emphasizes its subversion of difference on multiple levels:

> What is it precisely that the male masochist displays and what are the consequences of this self-exposure? To begin with, he acts out in an insistent and exaggerated way the basic conditions of cultural subjectivity, conditions that are normally disavowed; he loudly proclaims that his meaning comes to him from the other, prostrates himself before the gaze even as he solicits it, exhibits his castration for all to see, and revels in the sacrificial basis of the social contract. The male masochist magnifies the losses and divisions upon which cultural identity is based, refusing to be sutured or recompensed. In short, he radiates negativity inimical to the social order. (Silverman 206)

This is precisely the journey that Nick Curran acts out through *Basic Instinct's* rising action. In light of Kaplan's and Silverman's analyses, it is evident that the sadomasochistic perversion implied by the "Blue-Angel" scenario contains numerous subversive elements whereby under the guise of passionate love, the central male protagonist indulges in not only his hidden feminine longings but also his desires to punish and ultimately overthrow the monolithic male structures of the customary morality. One more quote from Deleuze will underscore this core, subversive desire to overthrow the Law and the Father:

> A contract is established between the hero and the woman, whereby at a precise point in time and for a determinate period she is given every right over him. By this means the masochist tries to exorcise the danger of the father and to ensure that the temporal order of reality and experience will be in conformity with the symbolic order, in which the father has been abolished for all time. Through the contract, the masochist reaches towards the most mythical and most timeless realms, where [the mother} dwells. Finally, he ensures that he will be beaten...what is beaten, humiliated and

ridiculed in him is the image and likeness of the father, and the possibility
of the father's aggressive return. The masochist thus liberates himself in
preparation for a rebirth in which the father will have no part. (Deleuze 58)

During the course of his life-changing exposure to Catherine Tramell,
an antagonist who clearly plays Curran and the entire LA police
department like puppets, Curran gladly meets his match and releases all
the lineaments of his former masculine position within the male
establishment. As the film evolves, Curran exhibits his social masochism
in several scenes, and the primary expression Curran's rebellion takes is
anger. The very first establishing shot of Curran—when he pulls up to
Johnny Boz's house to examine the murder scene—shows Curran's car
screeching to a halt and Curran slamming the door shut when he exits his
car. This expression of his simmering anger is established right from the
opening shot of Curran. The next major scene is his argument with Lt.
Neilson in the local police bar, a scene in which Curran has his first drink
in several months. He blows up at Neilson when Neilson goads him into a
confrontation. This key scene reveals Curran's seething anger against the
establishment as symbolized by Internal Affairs. Immediately following
his confrontation with Nielson, he goes to Beth Garner's apartment, and
Curran violently "makes love" to her, a highly aggressive exchange which
is far closer to a rape than an act of love. There is a clear implication here
that Garner has become a surrogate for Trammel in this scene, with Curran
displacing the frustrated desires he already feels for Tramell onto Garner.
Again, Curran's near rape of Garner is one more expression of his
psychological undercurrent of anger and aggression. As Curran first tells
Garner during their therapy session, "Why don't you just tell them
[Internal Affairs] that I'm just your typical, totally fucked-up cop." And
indeed, in this sense, Curran is an Everyman for the postmodern male in
the *femme fatale genre*.

Other key scenes reflect Curran's slowly blossoming social
masochism. When Tramell lets it slip that she's aware of his personal
history (information which throughout the film she omnisciently has the
power to be privy to) Curran barges into Garner's office demanding to
know why she gave his personal file to Neilson; just after this, Curran has
a physical confrontation with Neilson and must be escorted from the
building. Not long after this blow-up, Curran has to meet with a panel of
psychologists who want to know if he was angry at Neilson because he is
under suspicion for murdering him. After sarcastically describing his
childhood masturbatory habits and toilet training behaviors, he tells them
to "go fuck yourselves." The major scene in which Curran is literally "on

stage" and exhibits his fury with the establishment is the interrogation scene which ironically parallels Tramell's earlier interrogation. In this scene, however, Curran possesses none of Tramell's coolness and is completely defiant, returning all their questions with angry retorts, some of which unconsciously repeat Tramell's own responses, for example, the classic line, "What are you going to do, arrest me for smoking?"

By the film's climax, after Curran has accidentally shot and killed Garner, he has lost all the major symbols of his "Manhood Act" (Stoltenberg 5) and a sound patriarchy due to Tramell's "diabolical" (Verhoeven DVD commentary) plan to systematically eliminate them. He has not only lost but been set-up by Tramell to kill Beth Garner, the film's ambiguously drawn "Good Good Girl" (Fiedler 259); he has also lost his best friend and male buddy, Gus Moran, again, the even more valued symbol of the traditional *femme fatale genre*'s customary morality; and moreover, he has lost his friend due to his own feminization by Tramell as he was "off duty" as Gus tells him, and thus forced to passively wait in the car while Gus walks off to his certain death at the hands of Tramell. At the end of the climactic double murder scene, Curran sits hunched over in the hallway, his shamed, shattered self on exhibition for all to see. His immediate boss, Captain Talcott, comes over and sympathetically tells him to go home and take it easy. Later, after the police have found the evidence that frames Garner for Gus's and Neilson's murderers, evidence which Tramell has planted in her apartment, Curran is congratulated by the man he hates the most, the police chief himself—the ultimate father figure of the Law, who shakes his hand and says "Good work." As the police and Curran follow the trail of planted evidence that Tramell has set up (among other things, pictures of Tramell and Garner from their college days together in Beth's apartment, suggesting that Garner was indeed still obsessed with Tramell), all the evidence slowly comes together to convince the police that Garner was behind all the murders. Curran thinks he still knows better and leaves angrily determined to prove that Tramell set the whole thing up to frame Garner, a final scene during the denouement that I will discuss at the close of this analysis. The primary psychological issue to underscore here, however, is that throughout *Basic Instinct* Curran exhibits a series of behaviors that reflect his fury with the male establishment embodied by the LA police force, via the phenomena of social masochism. Although this hidden agenda can be seen in *femme fatale* films from both the Silent and Classical periods (for example, Walter Neff in *Double Indemnity* telling us he has always dreamed of "crooking the house") it is not until the advent of Postmodern films such as Verhoeven's *Basic Instinct* that this extreme male desire to subvert the status quo is so openly and defiantly displayed. This series of exhibitions by Curran is another major way in which Verhoeven embellishes the *genre*'s Classical stage, moving it into a refined postmodern period.

During the *femme fatale genre's* Experimental and Classical phases, the exposition introduces the protagonist in his pre-*femme fatale* condition. His standard bachelor world is typically replete with the following: a regular, often "macho" job in the work world that establishes his central societal position; a male buddy; an often real or potential Good Girl girlfriend; an antagonizing father figure, and to various degrees, signs and symptoms of certain anarchistic chinks in his male armor; in progressively worsening states, these chinks are respectively seen in *Flesh and the Devil*, *Double Indemnity*, and *Basic Instinct*. Because it takes an anti-hero as its central protagonist, the *femme fatale genre* is unique in that it offers a countercurrent of "weak" males who go against the standard heroic males who have populated Hollywood cinema in an endless stream from Valentino to Clint Eastwood. By allowing its males to "fall", the *femme fatale* film provides a unique opportunity to examine the ways in which our chivalric notions of masculine subjectivity deconstruct themselves from the silent to the modern period. Because each age redefines its customary morality and gender drama, and because cinema reflects and influences these changes, the evolution of the central male protagonist in *femme fatale* film reflects our own age's redefined gender configurations.

Specifically, although silent films posit an Edenic world in which "evil" is outside of man (that is, in woman), *noir* and modern males are imaged as partially or fully "fallen " long before the *femme fatale* ever appears. This change suggests that as the *femme fatale genre* evolves across the century, traditional masculine subjectivity slowly begins to recognize, admit to, and ultimately, even celebrate its potential for and right to "evil," that is, a desire to overthrow customary morality. *Noir* and modern males such as Nick "Shooter" Curran (who suffers from alcohol and coke addiction and who has "accidentally" killed innocent citizens long before he meets Tramell) flaunt their nonconformity and guiltlessly plunge into an abyss that defies traditional masculinity—which is to honor male authority figures; loving and "sticking by" his male brothers; placing the "Good Good Girl" (Fiedler 259) on a pedestal; and most important, resisting the temptations of and eventually vanquishing the *femme fatale* who always threatens the customary morality.) However, in *Basic Instinct* primarily and then in later *femme fatale* films, Verhoeven implodes the Edenic myth of woman as scapegoat for male "sin," and the modern fallen male locates anarchistic desire within himself and *the true "evil" within the customary morality itself.* Like Walter Neff in *Double Indemnity* and other protagonists in *femme fatale* films, Curran strains throughout the film with the "epistemological trouble" (Doane 103) that Tramell represents, but as is characteristic of postmodern male figures, Curran never determines the true "evil" nature of the *femme fatale.* Even during their final lovemaking scene, Curran knows and doesn't know that Tramell is the true killer. This inability on the part of the postmodern male protagonists to determine the *femme fatale's* "evil" nature represents a radical departure from the standard pattern found in films from the Silent and Classical periods. The male bond and customary morality are either fully or partially restored at the end of films from those periods when the *femme fatale* is identified as the site of "evil" and subsequently killed; however, in the modern *femme fatale* film, customary morality is never recovered. Moreover, in works such as *Body Heat* (1987) and *The Last Seduction* (1994), like Tramell, the *femme fatale* is not only not killed; rather, her "evil" genius is glorified as she thoroughly outwits the male world. This glorification serves as a perverse cover-up for the male's hidden anarchistic tendencies. Because she has become a seemingly invincible, hyper-masculine foe, the male's loss of power is somehow more acceptable. He cannot exert masculine control and power over the world because the *femme fatale* has become too formidable, too all-knowing, and too unknown. Occasionally, in a work such as *Romeo is Bleeding* (1994), the *femme fatale* (Lena Olin) is murdered by the central male protagonist but only because she has caused him and the male world so much shame that all he can do is destroy her in a peak of fury just before he attempts to take his own life. In other works—such as *Fatal Attraction* (1978), and *Alien* (1989)—the *femme fatale* is destroyed but not at the hands of an impotent male protagonist but rather at the hands of a mother figure who is allowed to wield "macho" powers only because she is following one of womanhood's primary directives: protecting the sacred, U.S. family and her children.

The Male Gaze Inverted

Another major area in which Verhoeven inverts the traditional Hollywood *femme fatale* film is "the reverse gaze." In her essay on the gaze in Wilder's classic *Double Indemnity*, Claire Johnston claims that Phyllis Deitrichson "stands at the top of the stairs offered to and held in the mastery of Neff's gaze." However, I would argue that a paradigm of a "reverse male gaze" more accurately describes the power structure of the gaze in *femme fatale* films. Mulvey's classic essay, *Visual Pleasure and*

Narrative Cinema, rightly claims that women have been controlled by a male-dominated cinema which historically has presented women as objects of degraded wonder or adoration. As with many other traditions, however, Verhoeven's *Basic Instinct* is also embellished in this regard and Mulvey's paradigm must be reconsidered when examining the male gaze in *femme fatale* films. In this *genre*, the gaze suggests precisely the opposite power structure that feminists have commonly attributed to it. In *femme fatale* films across the century, the gaze symbolizes male powerlessness before the *femme fatale*'s sexual mystery and power. She represents a projection of his unconscious desires and enchantment before the essential otherness of woman and the sexual half of his split male *psyche*. In commenting on the hero's and the camera's involuntary gazing, Janey Place notes that *femmes fatales* are: "overwhelmingly the compositional focus, generally center frame and/or in the foreground, or pulling focus to them in the background. They control the camera movement, seeming to direct the camera (and the hero's gaze, with our own) irresistibly with them as they move" (Place 16). In *femme fatale* films, Mulvey's ubiquitous notion of the classic Hollywood male gaze must be seen as a sign with a different kind of signifier. No longer signifying the generic gaze of a controlling male eye—voyeuristically and fetishistically balancing the problematic of knowledge, difference, and belief—in the *femme fatale* world, the male gaze is a sign of powerlessness, not power over woman.

Verhoeven's "shot heard round the world," that is, the shocking moment in which Sharon Stone reveals her vagina in the infamous interrogation scene, is perhaps one of the most remarkable examples of the *femme fatale's* controlling and simultaneously shocking the male gaze. In an intentionally graphic and shocking replay of the Freudian "moment of horror" (in which the male is reminded of his potential for castration), Verhoeven demonstrates that a major characteristic of any cutting edge mainstream, Hollywood film is to surprise or even shock viewers with sights previously unseen. Throughout this scene, Tramell is clearly in charge and owns all the power. Jan De Bont's lighting is designed to highlight Stone as a queen in white, and the lone chair she sits in with her highly fore-grounded scissor-like legs becomes her throne. Her clothing and hairstyle echo many of Hitchcock's seductive and yet unattainable ice blondes. Her bright white dress and tightly pulled back blonde hairdo with a circular bun in back echo both Grace Kelly in *Rear Window* and Kim Novak in *Vertigo* (a film which Verhoeven's consciously references throughout *Basic Instinct*.) With low floor lighting and set in a single chair on a stage, Van De Bont said he wanted to recreate a "proscenium arch" in which Catherine is center stage. She is brightly and gorgeously lit with luscious white and blue backlighting; however, the men are in the dark, "almost as if they were in prison and she is [the] one who is free" (De Bont DVD commentary.) The low angle shots of Catherine make her appear more dominant, a camera angle that is paralleled by her sharp, confident terse answers to their questions for which Verhoeven often quickly zooms in for assertive close-ups of Tramell's smirking face. She is completely open and unabashed about her sexual escapades, and she continually turns the tables on the interrogators. When asked "Have you ever taken part in any sadomasochistic activity?" she responds with a grin by asking the interrogator what he has in mind? At the climatic moment in this scene, Tramell uncrossed her legs and flashes her vagina. This is a histrionic moment in the *femme fatale genre* because Tramell shocks the male interrogators—and by implication, a mainstream male and female audience—with her most "audacious" response yet. In Freudian terms, she recreates the male child's moment of horror at the discovery of his mother's lack, and the male fear of difference and castration. This fear of the spider woman's castrating potential will eventually be imposed on the entire male world in *Basic Instinct*. Moreover, Verhoeven is obviously displaying his cutting edge sensibility to "shoot it." This image was meant to deeply disturb the "conservative Puritan sensibility" (Verhoeven, DVD commentary) of mainstream, U.S. audiences, an objective which he accomplishes with infamous success. Lastly, this scene is significant in that Tramell's interrogation foreshadows Curran's own interrogation a few scenes later. However, in Curran's interrogation, though he attempts to handle the questions with Tramell's masculine control and assertiveness— even subconsciously repeating some of her answers—he clearly appears nervous and upset, and not at all as cool, calm, collected, and on the offensive as Tramell. This is another example of how the two major dynamic characters mirror one another's *psyches*, although Tramell comes out on top, just as she does during their sex scenes later in the film.

When interviewed about this scene, Sharon Stone claims that she slapped Verhoeven and left the dailies' room, furious that she had been tricked into having this shot taken. Verhoeven makes the opposite claim, stating that all nude shots are specifically stated in any actor's contract before the shooting begins. Regardless of what the truth might be concerning how this scene came to be shot, Stone has said that she realized later that "The shot was necessary for this scene" (Stone, DVD commentary.) Thus, she understood that if Tramell's character was to become the penultimate, cutting edge postmodern *femme fatale*, then it would require her to break one of the penultimate social taboos of the customary morality by ignoring the traditional *genre* boundaries between R and X-rated films. The remarkable controversy and shock waves this one moment in the film sent around the world is a testament to the remarkable rigidity contained in our sexual cultural epistemes. Although it is simply an image of the female anatomy, the incredulous backlash to the scene shows how powerfully this long hidden female genitalia has been fetishized and its existence denied. Although many other embellished elements from *Basic Instinct* have been imitated by later directors working in the *genre*, the vagina image is the only cutting edge element in Verhoeven's film that pushed the customary morality too far; it is an "embellishment" to the *genre* that no other later *auteurs* have ever dared to repeat in any mainstream Hollywood films.[4] In summary then, Verhoeven's *Basic Instinct* and numerous other *femme fatale* films invert the standard male gaze as described by Mulvey. Thus, the classic Hollywood male gaze has become a sign of powerlessness, not power, over the "uncontrollable nearness of nature" (Paglia 13). It is the *femme fatale's* beauty and power that lead and control the camera movement, and Verhoeven's shocking moment during the interrogation scene is the ultimate psychological reversal of the gaze, freezing the male audience and the customary morality in a Medusa-like moment of shock.

Male Bonding in *Femme Fatale* Films

As first coined by Leslie Fiedler in his masterful *Love and Death in the American Novel,* "the holy marriage of males" is a standard trope we see in a great deal of U.S. culture and literature; Fiedler analyzes this adolescent fantasy in Huckleberry Finn via the close friendship that evolves between Huck Finn and Jim, the runaway slave. In Fielder's analysis, this innocent homoerotic bond represents a bulwark against the controlling world of woman as symbolized by the archetypal mother figure, Aunt Polly. Fielder's analysis is highly insightful, however, because it also applies to a great deal of U.S. literature, pop culture, and literally hundreds of male "buddy" films and television shows. U.S. cinema in particular is rampant with "buddy" movies. Indeed, many U.S. films and *genre*s rely almost exclusively on a central male couple who work, play, take road trips together, and often battle some "Other" throughout the film. Certain "macho" *genre*s (such as, The Western, War, and Gangster *genre*s) place a heavy emphasis on the archetypal male bond; however, it can still be found in almost all *genre*s, and the *femme* *fatale genre* is no exception. In fact, because the *femme fatale genre* is essentially about the central male protagonist choosing between the temptations that the *femme fatale* offers and the status quo world his male buddy represents, the male bond is a ubiquitous trope in almost all *femme fatale* films.

In *femme fatale* films, the male bond represents various patriarchal values that reinforce the customary morality. To begin with, the strength of the male bond is a symbol itself of the solidity of the status quo; as long as the male bond remains strong, the *femme fatale*'s lures will not entice or break the central male figure away from his "Manhood Act" (Stoltenberg 5) and the world of work. On a psychological level, the male buddy is like the Dr. Jekyll half of the male psychic split, (the central male's super-ego) who constantly monitors his Hyde side and warns him away from the *femme fatale*. In Stevenson's archetypal novel, there is a double pun at play in Hyde's name; he is a shadow aspect of Jekyll that he must "hide" from the world of customary Victorian morality, and Hyde also represents his sexual sensuous self, his animal "hide," or skin. Throughout the history of the *femme fatale* film, the male buddy is in a constant battle with his friend who tries to steer him back onto the road of righteousness. In silent works (such as, Brown's *Flesh and the Devil* [1927]), the entire film centers around the two main male buddies attempting to keep their friendship alive in spite of Garbo's ever present temptations. In the typical silent film scenario, the central male protagonist repudiates his male friend, then sins, repents, and is reunited; in *Flesh and the Devil* (1927) it is a union that borders on remarriage. Shortly thereafter, Garbo drowns in a lake as punishment for her sinful ways. In most *noir* films, a similar pattern continues, although the sense is that the *femme fatale* figure widens the split in the male *psyche*. As Billy Wilder notes about Neff and Keyes in *Double Indemnity*, "The idea...was to write a love story between two men and a sexual involvement with a woman" (Spiegel 101). Hence, at the close of that film, rather than have Neff march off into the gas chamber (as originally planned by the studio to appease the Hays office Production Code) in a dramatic act of punishment for his sins against the status quo, Wilder choose to have Neff die in Keyes's good graces, in which Keyes lights a final symbolic smoke of friendship for Neff. In this final scene of the denouement, Neff says: "You know why you couldn't figure this one out Keyes, cause the guy you were looking for was sitting right across the desk from you," and Keyes says, "Closer than that Walter."

The "holy marriage of males" (Fiedler 350) is another arena in which Verhoeven's *Basic Instinct* embellishes and subverts this sacred U.S.

model. Typically, he does include a close and important friendship and male bond between Gus and Curran. The film's exposition establishes this bond as warm and friendly. However, throughout the film, the male bond is subtly mourned and parodied via Curran and his partner, Gus, who refer to one another as "Cowboy" and "Haus"—echoing the lost, chivalric realm of the Western *genre*. Like Haus in the Bonanza television series, Gus Moran has a beer belly that hangs over the cowboy belt buckle that he sports wherever he goes, and he likes to hang out in country western bars dressed in cowboy regalia. However, as soon as Curran's obsession with Tramell blossoms, Curran slowly loses his connection with Gus, and in typical fashion, refuses to listen to Gus's warnings to stay away from Tramell. Verhoeven again relishes inverting the *femme fatale genre*'s Classical tropes, because it is Curran's own ineptitude that is responsible for his friend's murder at the hands of none other than Catherine Tramell. In the film's climatic scene, in which Gus is about to be stabbed to death by Tramell, Curran is waiting in his car (because he has been suspended from the force) while Gus goes into an apartment building to follow a false lead that Tramell has lured him into. Curran suddenly realizes that Tramell has set a trap for Gus, because in the previous scene he has just read a description of Gus's murder in Tramell's book proofs called *Shooter*. Curran rushes into the building to save his friend—past the flashing red streetlight outside, but he arrives too late, and finds Gus horribly bludgeoned by Tramell. (She will later leave a platinum blonde wig and LAPD raincoat in the stairwell to frame Beth Garner.)

Verhoeven intentionally has ironic inversions of everything in the Classical *femme fatale* film. For example, it is the *femme fatale* herself who eradicates the sacred male bond (along with everyone else), thereby destroying all the primary symbols of traditional masculine subjectivity. During the film's rising action, Tramell asks, "Why doesn't Gus like me?" when she obviously knows the answer. Once Gus is on her blacklist, it is merely a matter of time before he is also murdered in this shockingly horrific and violently graphic murder scene at the film's climax. Thus, "the holy marriage of males" is destroyed as never before—at the hands of the *femme fatale*. In this final scene, it is the death of his male partner that is depicted as the most horrific loss Curran experiences of all his losses, and it represents his final, climactic tragic loss. With the murder of Gus Moran, Tramell symbolically eradicates the last vestige of the Classical *femme fatale genre*'s sacred male bond. To add insult to injury, Tramell, with her "satanic clairvoyance" (Verhoeven DVD commentary) also has Curran repeat his earlier mistake of shooting some tourists while on duty; thus, when he meets Beth Garner in the hallway just after having found

Gus's dying body, Curran overreacts and kills Garner also (Gus's feminine Good Girl double), subconsciously acting on all the false suspicions about Garner that Tramell has planted in his mind. Curiously, although Curran certainly has a moment when he mourns Garner's death and his own ineptness in killing her, it is Gus's death (he dies slowly and bloodily in front of Curran's guilt ridden, tortured face) that is a greater tragic loss for Curran than Garner's. In death, more loss and value is still placed on the male rather than the female; the "holy marriage of males" (Fiedler 350) is thus still idealized even as Verhoeven subverts it. With these two final murders—both of which Tramell has either executed herself or set-up— her apparently systematic, "diabolical" plan to destroy all the primary symbols of a sound, patriarchal customary morality is complete.

The final scene in *Basic Instinct*, which is both a climax and a denouement simultaneously, brings together all the major embellishments to the *femme fatale genre* that Verhoeven and Eszterhas brilliantly envision. In this scene, Curran returns to his apartment after having experienced the final victory of Tramell over him and the LA police department. He has just left the office where he was congratulated by the chief of police for his "good work" in killing Beth Garner, who all are convinced was the pathological murderer of Boz, Neilson, and Gus Moran. Curran leaves the office still believing that Tramell managed to set up the entire complex trail of evidence to frame Garner but is essentially powerless to prove his theory. After climbing up the winding stairwell that echoes Hitchcock's *Vertigo* (1956), symbolizing the labyrinthine maze of deceptions Tramell has wound around him and perhaps his ascent out of his subconscious, he enters his apartment, and Tramell is waiting for him, as always, seemingly a step ahead of him as she has been throughout the film. Verhoeven notes in the Director's commentary, Tramell, with her "diabolical, clairvoyant" powers, seems to have access to any room she needs to enter, whether it was planting incriminating evidence in Garner's apartment or waiting for Curran when he returns to his own.

When she does confront him, we sense that she is playing yet one last act with him; she cries for only the second time in the film, the first was after Roxy's death, and tells Curran that she looses everyone she loves but doesn't want to lose him also. She has apparently changed her mind from the earlier scene in her villa in which she tells him that her book is finished and thus, so is their affair. After that rejection, Curran leaves furious and that is part of the reason he is unable to save Gus from being murdered; he sits in the car outside the apartment building stewing over Tramell's kiss off. However, in this scene, with her typical *femme fatale* persuasive

powers, she manages to win Curran back again, and they are quite quickly
having their final love scene of the film. This exchange echoes the film's
opening murder of Boz and Curran and Tramell's first love-making scene
during the film's rising action. In a sense, it is the first of Curran's final
series of submissions to Tramell; he has given up on the idea of trying to
prove she is the murderer; her "diabolical" plan has worked too well. Once
again, they make love, and once again, Tramell takes the superior position
on top. Although she does not tie him to the bedpost, he freely reaches
back and grabs it anyway, openly displaying his desire to be bound.
Tramell does her usual back-bending gymnastics as she brings them both
to climax. Again, Curran is willing to risk an ice-pick suddenly appearing,
although at this point, once senses that he does not feel there is any danger
involved. This ignorance on Curran's part of the truth of Tramell again
reflects the *genre*'s postmodern embellishment—that the *femme fatale* has
now become all powerful, invincible, and the "epistemological trouble"
(Doane 103) she represents is now beyond the powers of the male world to
fathom. Curran languishes in bed with her, blissfully ignorant that he is
sleeping and still "in love" with a pathological murderess. Their final talk
about raising a family underscores Curran's blissful ignorance. Tramell
asks, "What do we do now?" and Curran says, "We fuck like minks and
raise rug rats." "I hate rug rats", Tramell says, and we see her arm begin
to move over the edge of the bed, reaching for something. Curran
submissively says, turning to put out his cigarette and exposing his bare
vulnerable back to her, "Ok, we just fuck like minks and forget about the
rug rats." This seems to assuage Tramell, who for a long dramatic moment
appears as if she has a weapon in her hand hidden by her side of the bed.
Suddenly, she reaches around to Curran, grabbing him with her clutching
arm and pulls him towards her for a kiss. This moment amusingly
underscores the central sexual and anti-mother aspect of the *femme fatale*;
she is never associated with motherhood, only the sexual side of the
male's split psyche. Perhaps this is Curran's final submission to Tramell,
the surrender of his "masculine" desire for fatherhood and his willingness
to forgo a happy ever after Hollywood dream of starting a family, of
pursuing probably the primary symbol of a sound patriarchal world. As
Freud says in his essay on the male split *psyche*, Curran cannot love where
he desires and cannot desire where he loves. Along with all the other
lineaments of the romanticized male heroes from this *genre*'s Silent and
Classical periods, Curran's willingness to forgo this last vestige of his
"manhood act" (Stoltenberg 3) is the final nail in the coffin of Tramell's
completed manipulation of him.

In closing, it is important to underscore the remarkable ways in which Verhoeven's film re-envisions the Classical *femme fatale* film for the postmodern period. In applying his extreme inversions and embellishments to the *genre*, he not only moves the *femme fatale* film clearly into its stage of Refinement, but like all cutting edge films, he also sets the style and tenor for future versions of the *genre*. Shortly after *Basic Instinct* appeared, films such as *Romeo is Bleeding* (1993) and *The Last Seduction* (1994) quickly followed. These films clearly stand on the shoulders of Verhoeven's reconfigurations of masculine and feminine subjectivity. In both films, the *femme fatale* figures are even more over the top in terms of their manipulative power, intelligence, sexuality, and androgynous qualities, with the first prize definitely going to Lena Olin's performance in Peter Medak's *Romeo is Bleeding* (1993). Equally fitting, the male figures in these films reach even greater lows of despair, degradation, and ultimately, self-destruction. Finally, in light of Verhoeven's establishment of the *genre*'s Refinement stage, he also paves the way for other director's such as Carl Reiner to begin playing with the *genre*'s Baroque stage possibilities. Reiner's *Fatal Instinct* (1993), starring Armand Assante is a hilarious parody of countless *femme fatale* films, blending many of the Classic *noir* films' tropes with bits and pieces of films from both the Modern and Postmodern periods. The fact that Reiner could make a Baroque style film based on myriad earlier examples of the form is yet one more argument for the notion that the *femme fatale* film is indeed a classic *genre*. One cannot parody and pay homage to non-*genre* films since the Baroque relies heavily upon audience expectation and familiarity with the deep structures of a film form.

Finally, it is important to acknowledge the positive, crucial social influence that Verhoeven's *Basic Instinct* had on the sexual mores of postmodern American culture. As noted earlier, *Basic Instinct*'s graphic depiction and acknowledgement of Lesbian love which received so much controversial backlash from a variety of social quarters was one of the first films daring enough to represent this reality of life. Like many cutting edge films, the touchy subject matter was balked at and attacked when it was first made public, and certain activist groups such as the San Francisco Gay Rights Movement even attempted to halt the shooting of the film, sabotaging the filming of certain street scenes and demanding that the script be revised (Verhoeven DVD commentary); however, to his credit, Verhoeven stuck to his guns and refused to change the script at all, a decision that Eszterhas later agreed was best for the film. As Verhoeven said, "In my country (Holland), gay sexuality is a non-issue, and the mature way to approach it is to deal with it as a non-issue. These protesters have a right to say whatever they want, just as I have the right to make my film the way I want" (Verhoeven DVD commentary.) Whatever one might feel about the negative stereotypes of the gay community that many claim *Basic Instinct* reflected, it clearly broke new ground for the American public to recognize and come to terms with the gay lifestyle as any American's inalienable right. As with many cutting edge films, Verhoeven was ahead of his time in this regard. Now mainstream TV shows such as "Will and Grace" and Ellen DeGeneres's talk show are part of the acceptable norm, a modified customary morality; however, it always seems to take breakthrough films such as *Basic Instinct* which appall some viewers at first to break down these deeply ingrained customary epistemes. Perhaps of all the remarkable embellishments Verhoeven makes in *Basic Instinct* to the *femme fatale genre*, making a film in which he treats the gay issue as a "non-issue" was one of its most invaluable contributions.

Lastly, it is remarkable to consider the *femme fatale genre*'s place in archetypal history. As I quoted from Paglia at the start of this essay, the postmodern *femme fatale* film stands at the furthermost reaches of a "tradition [that] passes nearly unbroken from prehistoric idols through literature and art to modern movies" (13). Seen in this light, the mythic *femme fatale* represents a myriad of social, political, symbolic, and psychological states and subject positions, which reflect, I believe, far more than the just "uncontrollable nearness of nature" (Paglia 13). As a mythopoetic figure, she has grown into a polymorphous vessel into which every age pours its most ancient and most historically particular gender conflicts, queries, desires, and fears surrounding the ever mysterious connections between our most noble and our most unbecoming human propensities for love and violence. From this perspective, *femmes' fatales* films are dizzying indeed. When we watch *Flesh and the Devil* (1927), *Double Indemnity* (1944), or *Basic Instinct* (1992), we connect with mysteries that prompted our earliest ancestors to draw daemonic women on cave walls. The modern man-child and woman still gaze at the *femme fatale*, and thus, at themselves, in the darkened cave of the movie theater, "the daylight dream" space (Tyler 230), and their darkest fears and desires are still projected on a wall before them, but now, through the sublime *photogene* of film, the mythic *femme fatale* moves, speaks, and beckons with a horrible beauty that appears more alive than ever before on the silver screen, and in reality, is alive in our hearts and minds.

Works Cited

Agee, James. *Agee On Film. Volume 1.* New York: Grosset and Dunlap, 1967.

Paglia, Camille. *Sexual Personae: Art and Decadence from Nefertiti to Emily Dickinson.* New York: Viking, 1990.

Deleuze, Gilles. *Masochism: An Interpretation of Coldness and Cruelty,* trans. Jean McNeil. New York: George Braziller, 1971.

Doane, Mary Ann. *Gilda: Epistemology as Striptease, Femmes Fatales: Feminism, Film, and Theory, Psychoanalysis.* New York: Routledge, 1991.

Fiedler, Leslie, *Love and Death in the American Novel,* Revised edition. New York: Delta, 1966.

Focillon, Henri, *Life of Forms in Art.* New York: George Wittenborn, Inc., 1942.

Freud, Sigmund. *A Special Type of Object Choice Made by Men, Sexuality and the Psychology of Love.* Ed. Philip Rieff. New York: Macmillian, 1963.

Johnston, Claire, *"Double Indemnity,"* Women in Film Noir: ed. E. Ann Kaplan. London: British Film Institute, 1980.

Kaplan, E. Ann, ed. *Women in Film Noir.* London: British Film Institute, 1978.

Kaplan, Louise. *Female Perversions: The Temptations of Emma Bovary.* New York: Anchor Books, 1992.

Keesey, Douglas, Duncan, Paul, Eds., *Paul Verhoeven.* London: Tashen, 2005.

Lehman, Peter, *Running Scared: Masculinity and the Representation of the Male* Body. Philadelphia: Temple University Press, 1993.

Maltin, Leonard, *TV Movies and Video Guide, 2007.* New York: Signet, 2007.

Monaco, James. *The Movie Guide.* New York: Perigee, 1992.

Mulvey, Laura, *Visual Pleasure and Narrative Cinema, Visual and Pleasures.* Indiana: Indiana University Press, 1989.

Place, Janey, *"Women in Film Noir* Women in Film *Noir,* ed. E. Ann Kaplan. London: British Film Institute, 1980.

Schatz, Thomas, *Hollywood Genres: Formulas. Filmmakers and the Studio System.* New York: McGraw-Hill, 1981.

Silverman, Kaja, *Male Subjectivity at the Margins.* New York: Routledge, 1992.

Stoltenberg, John. *The End of Manhood. A Book for Men of Conscience.* New York: Plume, 1993.

Spiegel, Alan. *Seeing Triple: Cain, Chandler, and Wilder on Double Indemnity,* Film Literature. Ed. George E. Toles. Winnipeg: University of Manitoba, 1983.

Tyler, Parker. *Myth and Magic in the Movies.* New York: Simon and Schuster, 1946.

—. *The Hollywood Hallucination.* New York: Garland Publishing, 1985.

Willis, Sharon. *Disputed Territories: Masculinity and Social Space,* Constance Penley, Sharon Willis, *Male Trouble.* Minneapolis: University of Minnesota Press, 1993.

Notes

[1] For a complete analysis of the progression of the *femme fatale genre* across the 20th century see: Hughes, Anthony. *The Rise and Fall of Masculine Subjectivity in the American* Femme Fatale *Film.* Doctoral Dissertation, SUNY at Buffalo, 1997.

[2] I am indebted to James Card, author of *Seductive Cinema: The Art of Silent Film.* New York: Knopf, 1994. His screening of silent films such as Bell's *Man, Woman, and Sin* from his own private collection and sharing his wonderful insights about these films from the Silent era was invaluable in my education regarding the evolution of the *femme fatale genre.*

[3] This statement is not meant to imply that films from the silent or classical periods were by any means simplistic in their moral inquiries or psychological richness. Indeed, many films, from both these eras, for example, Monta Bell's *Man, Woman, and Sin* (1927) exhibit a great deal of psychological depth and subtlety.

[4] I thought it remarkable when first seeing this film in a public theatre that the audience barely batted an eye over the incredibly graphic violence, but they gasped and muttered during the interrogation scene and the scene in which Tramell is first seen kissing Roxy.

CHAPTER SEVEN

BATMAN BEGINS:
INSANITY AND THE CUTTING EDGE
OF HEROISM

DOUGLAS L. HOWARD

Riddle me this, riddle me that; look at what has happened to the big black bat. After George Clooney's flawed 1997 romp as the Caped Crusader sent the film series off to the ER, the franchise was resuscitated and revived eight years later under the darker direction of Christopher Nolan, the creative genius behind the innovative memory mystery *Memento* (2000) and the "white night" thriller *Insomnia* (2002). Internet message boards and entertainment columns already started buzzing when Nolan's name was connected to the project in 2003,[1] but the hype among Batman fans began to reach a fever pitch when it was announced that Christian Bale would be next in line to assume the title role.[2] From his sickeningly smarmy portrayal of the sociopathic Walter Wade, Jr. in *Shaft* (2000) to the driven dragon-killer Quinn Abercromby in *Reign of Fire* (2004) to the anorexically unhinged Trevor Reznik in *The Machinist* (2002), Bale, with only a handful of major films to his credit, had already developed a reputation with audiences for his offbeat choice of roles, for his preoccupation with uniquely disturbed characters, and for the extent of his commitment to these performances. As a case in point, "his 63-pound weight loss," according to the *Internet Movie Database*, "is said to be a record for any actor for a movie role" ("Trivia"). But Bale is perhaps best known for his iconic turn as Patrick Bateman in Mary Harron's *American Psycho* (2000), where he convincingly breathed life into Bret Easton Ellis's Wall Street serial killer. In considering Bale for his film, Nolan and his casting directors clearly must have had this role in mind, just as they also must have known that viewers would, as a result, see touches of Bateman in Batman and that Bale's presence would bring a dangerous sense of menace to the dark knight. Even Bale himself has admitted "that Patrick Bateman in *American Psycho* was the character closest to his portrayal of Bruce Wayne" (Darius 23.) In many ways, this "postmodern" reinvention refers and responds to the long, tumultuous history of Batman, a figure alternately of terror, justice, scorn, ridicule, and retribution. And if Batman has adapted with his times and essentially become a reflection of that context, then Nolan and Bale's "cutting edge" (re)creation more dramatically (and disturbingly) speaks to the changing face of heroism in our society.

Nolan's *Batman Begins* (2005) resurrects the hero, both cinematically and culturally, by returning to the dark realism (or, at the very least, to what Batman artist Jerry Robinson has called the "believable fantasy" (7)) that characterized previous portrayals of the figure (in the Tim Burton films as well as in many of the comics and graphic novels) and by mining the pivotal gap in the narrative from the murder of Bruce Wayne's parents to his first appearance in Gotham as the Caped Crusader. Where most of the other "cinematic Batmans" had a better sense of purpose or a more directed conviction from the get-go, Nolan shows us a man in transition, a man who has, as Ducard says when he finds Bruce Wayne practicing on criminals in a seedy Asian prison, "become truly lost" (Nolan). Still stricken by the violent death of his parents, Bruce's personal desire for revenge leads him to plan the murder of their killer, Joe Chill, who has agreed to "testify [against mob boss Carmine Falcone] in exchange for early parole" (Nolan), but Falcone's assassin kills Chill before Bruce ever gets his chance. Wandering the world in an attempt to understand the criminal mind, he is taken in by Ducard and Ra's al Ghul and trained in the ninja arts, only to part ways with his mentors when they ask him to kill another criminal and lead their League of Shadows in the destruction of Gotham. From these experiences, Bruce returns to the city with a more defined idea of his mission and how he will accomplish it. Through the development of the Batman persona, he begins to use fear and theatricality to terrorize his enemies, and he begins to save Gotham from the likes of Falcone, the Scarecrow, and even Ducard/Ra's himself, who is ultimately revealed as the criminal mastermind behind the plot to destroy the city. As the newly promoted Lieutenant Gordon tells him at the end of the film, Batman has "really started something: bent cops running scared; hope on the streets" (Nolan). But, ironically, *Batman Begins* is not the beginning, and, to better understand exactly how this Batman becomes a contemporary response to history, we need to look at the history of Batman.

The First Batman

Although Nolan's retelling of the myth also becomes a way of recharacterizing Batman from the increasingly glitzy look that he had in the nineties, the new film actually returns him to his post-Depression 1930s' roots from the comics. (Gotham, in fact, is just coming out of an economic depression in *Batman Begins*, and these financial circumstances help to account for the city's severe crime rate and the desperation of its inhabitants.) With the success of Superman in 1938, the editors at DC Comics were looking for a new hero to sell to the public and were, subsequently, approached by the dynamic duo of artist Bob Kane and writer Bill Finger with an idea for a character in a different vein from the high-flying "Man of Steel." Combining elements of the flying aliens from the *Flash Gordon* comic strips, the acrobatic exploits and the dual identity of Douglas Fairbanks in *The Mask of Zorro*,[3] and even the design of Da Vinci's winged ornithopter, Kane fleshed out the look of their hero. But, to have him "throw fear and respect into all the villains that he would encounter" (Steranko 44), Kane turned to a villain for inspiration. He added darker, gothic touches and background from the cinematic portrayal of mystery writer Mary Roberts Rinehart's character "The Bat," "a detective who [was] secretly a costumed killer" (Daniels 21).[4] Finger, in turn, complimented Kane's vision by drawing on the more severe characters that he found in popular pulp fiction. As Finger has explained, "Batman was originally written in the style of the pulps" (Daniels 25), and, in terms of both look and tone, he followed the menacing manner of "The Shadow," "a take-no-prisoners crime fighter" (Daniels 25) who was every bit as ruthless as the very criminals that he opposed, if not more so.[5]

Their creation first swung into action in *Detective Comics* in May of 1939, and, if he was somewhat crudely designed at first, this rawness only served to contribute to his macabre impact.[6] Considering his initial appearance, comic book artist and writer Jim Steranko points out that the early Batman "displayed a truly forbidding set of ears" (42) that made him seem all the more frightening and monstrous. Batman "conjured up visions of vampires with his black cloak, grim visage and white slit eyes," emerging "Dracula-like at night for fantastic nocturnal forays amidst moonlight settings" (43). Added to this image was the fact that there was no telling exactly how far he would go in his pursuit of "justice." As Bat-historian Les Daniels recalls, "In his first years," Batman was more of a vigilante, "casually killing criminals" (30). (Nolan's film deliberately draws line between Bruce Wayne's mission and vigilantism a and murder.[7]

Figure 7.1. The first appearance of Batman in *Detective Comics*

Bruce turns on Ra's al Ghul and the League of Shadows specifically over this issue.) If he was not throwing them off a roof or breaking their necks, then he was knocking them out a window and letting them fall to their deaths. And he almost never expressed any remorse for what he did or for their grisly ends. In fact, he was usually satisfied when it happened.

In the very first story, "The Case of the Chemical Syndicate," after punching the villain Alfred Stryker into a vat of acid, Batman considers his death "A fitting ending for his kind" (Kane, Finger, and Fox 9). Unsurprisingly, neither the criminals themselves nor the police really knew what to make of him. U.S. Senator and lifelong Batman fan Patrick Leahy, who actually appears (as himself) in 1997's *Batman and Robin*, remembers that, "[i]n the early days, the police were always trying to arrest him" (5). Some early storylines even have the police shooting at him as he drives away from a crime scene or jumps off a rooftop. Nevertheless, Bob Kane admittedly "liked this dark version best" (Daniels 30).

Figure 7.2. An early cover, showing the darker, more gothic Batman

Given the character's almost immediate popularity, Batman clearly fulfilled a number of fantasies within the context of the times. Although the nation was pulling out of the Depression and although Capone had been convicted of income tax evasion in the early thirties, crime, corruption, and personal violence continued to be very real threats for so many Americans. Gerard Jones notes that "vigilante justice" began to "[reassert] itself in small cities and towns" (93-94). The more high profile criminal figures of the day, according to Bill Boichel, became appealing and attractive in this regard, precisely because they "operat[ed] outside the law, on their own terms" (7). This aspect of their characters often fueled the actions of many pulp fiction heroes, who felt similarly compelled to find their own breed of justice beyond the legal system. Bruce Wayne enjoyed a wealthy lifestyle that was removed from Gotham City's bustling streets and that so many youths and their parents at the time, struggling to make ends meet, aspired to. Batman, however, was a by-product of the city's crime and corruption, an all-too human avenger who purposely dedicated himself to prowling those dark streets like the criminals that he hunted; he dispensed justice, in the same fashion, by operating outside of the law. Leahy agrees that "search warrants were not an issue when Batman crashed through the door" (5). And even more than that, Batman did not just want to punish the guilty; he wanted to terrorize and torment them. When Bruce Wayne begins to develop this persona in Finger and Kane's now legendary back story, which actually was not published until about six months after the Batman character first appeared, he deliberately chooses a face that will "strike terror into [the] hearts" of criminals (Daniels 35).[8] This was, perhaps, one kind of response that both the comic's creators and its readership had toward the villainies that they read about or witnessed in their own lives. (As he explains to Alfred in Nolan's film, Bruce Wayne similarly chooses "bats" as his "terrifying, incorruptible symbol" because bats "frighten" him, and he wants his enemies to share his "dread" (Nolan). Mark Cotta Vaz agrees: "To survive, the times demanded a righteous sense of Us versus Them" (11).

The back story, moreover, helped to explain the mania and the motivation behind Bruce Wayne's bizarre need to dress up like a bat and to prowl the dark streets of Gotham while simultaneously making him more sympathetic to the reader. On their way home from a movie, Thomas Wayne, his wife, and his son Bruce are held up by a criminal, who shoots and kills Wayne and his wife while the horrified, young boy watches. (This scene figures prominently in Burton's 1989 *Batman* as well as in Nolan's 2005 *Batman Begins*. After finding out about it, reporter Alexander Knox, in Burton's film, asks the telling question, "What do you suppose something like this does to a kid?" (Burton). As Danny Fingeroth notes, the murder of his parents at once leaves the young Bruce Wayne "alone and defenseless in the world, psychologically if not also physically" (64). In surviving this loss and coping with one of "our worst fears," he becomes truly "'relatable'" (65). He vows "to avenge [his parents] by spending the rest of his life warring on all criminals" (Daniels 25), and this vow and the pain and trauma of his loss motivate him to develop himself to his intellectual and physical peak and to carry out this "war" in the fearsome guise of Batman. In his analysis of the back story, Fingeroth argues that the central emotion for Bruce Wayne is "rage" (64);[9] it becomes the very heart of who and what he is and what obsessively drives him out into the night in search of revenge and justice for his loss.[10] In pointing out the essential differences between Batman and other heroes like Superman, Fingeroth refers to the extent to which these psychological scars play on him: "When Superman punches an adversary's face, [...] all he sees is the criminal's face [...]. When Batman punches a foe, he sees the face of the man who killed his parents and left him—both mercifully and cruelly—as a seven-year old wailing to the unheeding emptiness of the Gotham City night" (64). Regardless of how far Batman goes or what he does in his attempt to alleviate or exorcise his pain, virtually all of his actions become justifiable, or at the very least understandable, given the nature of his tragedy and how it continues to haunt him. (Clearly aware of this aspect of his character, Nolan plays up Bruce's connection to his father, the sympathetic physician who teaches his son about "picking himself up" from his falls just as he philanthropically works toward the improvement and the restoration of a financially depressed Gotham.[11]) In the end, then, Batman is very much a modern hero, human and vulnerable, with an extraordinary adult response to an extraordinary childhood trauma.

In order to attract new readers and in response to the growing industry in the late thirties and early forties, Batman's writers felt that their character needed to evolve even more from the stern, mysterious vigilante who appeared in those early issues. A little over a year after Batman was first introduced, Bob Kane suggested pairing him with Robin, the Boy Wonder, who, as penciller Jerry Robinson states, "was created out of Robin Hood's image" (Steranko 47) and was "someone the young readers could identify with more readily than this masked, mysterious figure" (Daniels 37). Like Bruce Wayne, Dick Grayson, Robin's alter-ego, also loses his parents, circus performers, to crime, as gangsters sabotage the ropes during their trapeze act. Seeing himself in the boy, Batman takes him in and makes him take an oath by candlelight to fight "against crime and corruption and to never swerve from the path of righteousness" (Kane, Finger, and Fox 127). Not only did Robin solve one of the major problems with the character for Bill Finger by giving Batman "a sidekick to talk to" (Gerard Jones 150), but Robin's "brighter personality also affected the mood of the comic" (Daniels 38). He brought a youthful enthusiasm and humor to the initial brooding, somber tones of the series, just as his yellow cape, red vest, and green gloves and boots colorfully contrasted with Batman's darker gray and blue. Batman could no longer be so grim or menacing because, as Steranko explains, he "had to be an example for the boy" (47). Instead, he was "Refined," in Will Brooker's words, "into a cheerful costumed lawman" whose stories now "became playful experiments" (99-100). Where he once scowled, now most of the comics showed him smiling as he fought with an enemy or foiled a crime. Vaz points out that his "moral code [now] prohibited killing" (11), and he did not obsess as much about the crime that created him or the pain that fueled his mission, perhaps because such thoughts would be inconsistent with Batman's new role or the comic's new attitude. Even after avenging the death of Robin's parents and bringing the criminals responsible to justice, Bruce Wayne and Dick Grayson, rather than dwelling on his loss or comparing their mutual tragedies, can only smile as they look forward to their next adventure together, which Dick enthusiastically predicts will "be a corker" (Kane, Finger, and Fox 136).[12] (In many ways, this change in the character becomes the source of future tension for Batman writers, artists, and filmmakers, as they are forced to choose between these two traditions and these two versions of the hero, between the relentless, raging "dark knight" tormented by childhood tragedy and the light-hearted surrogate father out to guide his impulsive young ward.) As sales increased through World War II and the late 1940s, Batman and Robin soon were solving their crimes on the radio[13] and in film[14] and battling a vast array of enemies, from the Joker to the Japanese.[15]

Batman vs. the "Diabolical" Dr. Wertham

Perhaps Batman's biggest threat, though, came in 1954, with the publication of *Seduction of the Innocent* by the psychiatrist Dr. Frederic Wertham. As Vaz explains, the American public was still caught up in the grip of a "postwar paranoia" (42) that Joe McCarthy had exploited through his congressional hearings, and their "fears, and the resulting period of repression, affected the arts as well" (44). Amidst this atmosphere, Wertham, convinced that comic books corrupted children, believed "that readers would imitate the crimes committed in [them]" (Daniels 84). From his own personal interviews with homosexuals and male prostitutes, he leveled specific charges against Batman and Robin and referred to "a subtle atmosphere of homoeroticism which pervade[d] [their] adventures" (Wertham 191). Inasmuch as their relationship and the lifestyle that they enjoyed in "stately Wayne Manor" amounted to the "wish dream of two homosexuals living together" (191), "the Batman type of story," Wertham theorized, "[could] stimulate children to homosexual fantasies, of the nature of which they [might] be unconscious" (192).[16] As a way of "ward[ing] off further charges of homosexuality" (13) and protecting themselves from public condemnation, the writers started to introduce more female love interests, according to Boichel, like Batwoman and her niece. Daniels adds that they also tried "to create a faux family atmosphere" (85) by bringing in characters like Bat-Girl, Bat-Hound, and Bat-Mite; through one "distressing metamorphosis" (Daniels 95) in 1962, Batman himself even transformed into the more family friendly "Bat-Baby."

As the decade continued, two significant events took place in the development of the character. First, in an effort to raise lagging sales, Batman was given a "new look" in the comics, with a yellow oval "around the bat emblem on the hero's chest" (Daniels 99), like the Bat-Signal,[17] and with plotlines, to complement this change in appearance, that revolved around more traditional villains and detective stories. And, second, of course, was the 1965-68 television show with Adam West and Burt Ward that worked as a campy send-up of the Kane and Finger creation and "revealed the man in the cape," as Andy Medhurst notes, "as a pompous fool, an embodiment of superceded ethics, and a closet queen" (162). With its colorful cast of sixties' celebrity guest stars and its onomatopoetic pop-art sound effects, the series became a kind of cultural benchmark, and, in evaluating the anxiety of its influence on the future of the franchise, Medhurst believes that "for some [...] there will never be another credible approach" (158). For a nation that was coming through Kennedy, Malcolm X, the Civil Rights Movement, Vietnam, Martin Luther King, and the growing counterculture, heroism and morality could no longer be so neatly or simply defined. In this context, Adam West's Batman, with his shiny blue cape and his gray tights, became, for lack of a better word, the ultimate "square," an unabashed straight man who could—"BAM, POW"—defend the law and sincerely deliver a few platitudes in half an hour, while the audience was left to deal with the more serious issues at home and abroad. If Batman and all that he stood for seemed absurd, then the series reveled in that absurdity and used it to keep viewers coming back to that "same Bat-time, same Bat-Channel."

Figure 7.3. Batman and Robin from the 1960s' television show

The history of Batman since the sixties has largely amounted to an attempt to rescue him from that absurdity and to reconnect him to his darker origins, a process that Medhurst refers to as "the painstaking reheterosexualization of Batman" (159). "[I]nfluenced by writers like Lovecraft and Poe" (Daniels 138), writer Denny O'Neil returned Batman to the night in the seventies and crafted more gothic tales with gruesome villains and bleaker landscapes.[18] If the previous Batman was "much closer to a family man, much closer to a nice guy," O'Neil's version was, as he admitted in one interview, "an obsessed loner" who was "a lot nastier than that" (Pearson and Uricchio 19). Daniels notes that "[p]art of O'Neil's agenda involved reemphasizing Bruce Wayne's childhood tragedy" (Kane, et al. 6), a reemphasis that would, in turn, revive his rage and revisit his fanatical commitment to punishing the criminal element. (Again, *Batman Begins* operates within this tradition.) As an example of just how far Batman had come from the early sixties and how this kind of agenda played out in the comics, in writer Steve Engelhardt's 1974 story "Night of the Stalker," a relentless Batman chases down a group of bank robbers after they kill a young boy's parents out on the street, a crime that immediately recalls the murder of Bruce Wayne's own parents those many years ago. After terrorizing and savagely beating the robbers into submission one at a time, he returns to Wayne Manor, only to break down into tears at the memory of his own tragedy and to become "that boy again" (Kane, et al. 94). According to Engelhardt's story, this regression takes place "for this single moment in infinity" (94). But, as Fingeroth has said, Batman relives that crime every time he "punches a foe" (64) and so, on some level, he must always regress (and never progress or resolve these issues) in order to tap into that child's fury that brings out "the bat" in him as an adult. (In Nolan's film, when Ducard asks Bruce what he fears after beating him into unconsciousness in Ra's al Ghul's mountain fortress, Bruce immediately flashes back to his childhood encounter with the bats in the cave and to his parents' murder, those twin traumas that give birth to the Batman persona.[19])

Perhaps the most significant turn in the character from there took place in 1986, when writer-artist Frank Miller (who had already re-energized the *Daredevil* series for Marvel Comics) provided readers with a violent, stark, futuristic look at Batman (with some rather apparent eighties' touches) in his mini-series *The Dark Knight Returns*. In the process, Miller revitalized both the franchise and the industry. Anticipating the general cultural attraction to these comic book myths, he proved that they could be designed for a more mature audience and told provocatively, addressing political questions and social concerns. Not only did Miller, as Robert Harvey suggests, break with tradition artistically by imposing his own "individual graphic styling" on well known characters—his Batman, for example, appears as a gritty, extremely muscular, physically imposing figure—but he also presented a hero who "teeter[s] on the edge of sanity" (148). As Miller himself explains in an afterward to *Batman: Year One*, his subsequent Batman project for DC, "For me, Batman was never funny" (134).

Figure 7.4. Batman after his final battle with the Joker in Miller's
The Dark Knight Returns

In *Dark Knight*, Batman has been retired for 10 years, but Bruce
Wayne still cannot deny the memory of his parents' murder or suppress
the call of the bat, "not with wine or vows or the weight of age" (25).
Though he is older, he dons his costume again to take on Two-Face and
the Joker, who have resurfaced to threaten the safety of a bleak Gotham
City, and to accept the challenge of an anarchic street gang known as the
Mutants. Though he can frequently rely on his superior technology to win
these battles, he often foregoes it for the thrill of physical combat, to prove
to himself and to his adversaries that he "still has it," and usually sustains
extensive physical injuries as a result. (The Mutant Leader nearly kills
him in their first fight, the Joker stabs him, and, in the last chapter,
Superman breaks his ribs.) In this second coming, he is aided by a new
female Robin, thirteen-year-old Carrie Kelley, who wears the same red,
green, and yellow costume as the original and whose characterization,
according to Daniels, may have been yet another "response to the
homophobia inspired by Dr. Wertham more than thirty years earlier"
(151).[20]

Miller, however, presents a Dark Knight who is coldly uncompromising and dangerously obsessive, particularly with regard to his sense of justice in this changing society. (Symbolically, even his costume reverts over the course of the series from the "new look" blue and gray with the yellow Bat-Signal to a darker black and gray with a black bat logo on his chest.) As Superman explains at one point, the government, in this version of the future, began to crack down on superheroes, in part, because Batman testified, in defense of their vigilante ways, that they were and had "to be criminals" (135). (This again refers to the "vigilante" aspect of the character that Nolan's film is quick to dismiss. Miller's Batman conversely embraces vigilantism as a necessary evil in the pursuit of his own moral imperative.) While the media, the police, and a Reagan government debate the propriety of his actions upon his return, he takes his war on crime to a whole new level. As he blinds the Joker in one eye with a batarang before nearly breaking his neck with his bare hands, even the Clown Prince must admit must admit that this new Batman is "out of [his] mind" (144). After Superman's attempt to divert a Soviet warhead creates a national blackout, Batman, on horseback, leads the remaining members of the Mutant gang through Gotham to maintain order. As he tells them before they set out, "Tonight, I am the law" (173); in the face of anarchy, he will impose his personal sense of justice on the city. When Superman is finally directed by the government to apprehend him at the end of the series, a shrewder Batman even orchestrates the Man of Steel's defeat, only to fake his own death and go underground to train his private army "to bring sense to a world plagued by worse than thieves and murderers" (199). Amidst the political, social, and cultural complexities of the world, Miller's Batman, then, not only operates outside of the legal system, but, in the end, abandons the system entirely, transcending his heroism for some larger revolutionary purpose.[21] With *The Dark Knight Returns*, Miller paved the way for future portrayals of Batman, like Nolan's, by daring to consider just how obsessed, self-righteous, and driven he might really be.

Working off of this more mature recasting, Miller followed *Dark Knight* up with *Batman: Year One* in 1987, which he wrote but did not draw and which conversely parallels Bruce Wayne's beginnings as a crime-fighter with Lieutenant James Gordon's graphic struggles with a corrupt police administration. (*Year One* also anticipates the cinematic rebooting of Batman and is probably the primary source for *Batman Begins*. A number of elements and segments from the film, including the final reference to the Joker, are based upon scenes from *Year One*. Miller himself even worked up a film treatment of *Year One* before Nolan's film.) Using dark, flat, subdued tones, the series presents a grimly realistic Gotham and a simply drawn yet sophisticated Batman, again dressed in black and gray without the "new look" Bat-Signal on his chest, who evokes some of the rawness of Kane's early work. Where *Dark Knight* incorporates the superhero world and supervillains from Batman's comic history into its storylines, *Year One* instead pits him against robbers, pimps, drug dealers, and police SWAT teams. Acting more like Bronson's Paul Kersey in *Death Wish*, Bruce Wayne, in his first attempt as a vigilante, dresses up like a war veteran and winds up fighting with a pimp and an underage prostitute in Gotham's crime-riddled East End, only to get shot by the police. In a revision of Finger and Kane's back story, Bruce, bleeding profusely from this botched encounter, again remembers the night of his parents' murder. Staring intently at the bust of his father in his study, he wonders, "What do I use ... to make them afraid?" (20), before the iconic bat "crash[es] through [his] window" (22) and inspires him to develop his new persona. Batman takes to the streets, terrorizing both criminals and corrupt officials alike. Realizing their common goal, Batman and Gordon soon forge a partnership, a partnership that is solidified when Bruce, out of costume, rescues Gordon's infant son from kidnappers. Again, if previous writers and artists had made Batman a work of almost childish fantasy, Miller returned the character to credibility by placing him at the heart of such a tense, realistic story in *Year One* and by placing him within what artist David Mazzucchelli calls "a world we recognize" (*Year One* 103).

"I'm Batman": the New Batman Films

Miller's *Dark Knight* conception and his cinematic vision of Batman (as well as Kane's original and Alan Moore's 1988 graphic novel *The Killing Joke*)[22] were also part of the inspiration behind Tim Burton's 1989 film, which marked the beginning of the new film series and essentially started the new wave of superhero films that continues to generate significant returns at the box office.[23] (In this regard, Burton's *Batman* becomes an intriguing postmodern amalgam, perhaps best illustrated by his black costume with long ears and the yellow and black Bat-Signal on his chest, part-Kane, part-Miller, part "new look" Batman, part "Phantom of the Opera"). Like the comics, the series started out darkly and gradually moved toward exaggeration, comedy, and perhaps even camp with Schumacher's *Batman and Robin*. *Batman*, however, set the bar by considering its subject matter grimly and gothically for the most part[24] and hinting at the awful, deep-seeded issues plaguing the man beneath the mask by recalling the tragic back story, just as O'Neil had done in the seventies.

As Burton and Michael Keaton portray him in the film, Batman is a brooding, psychologically scarred hero meting out justice in a bustling Gotham (yet another *pastiche*) that exists somewhere between post-Depression America and eighties' pop culture.[25] Batman itself essentially amounts to a conflict between two severely traumatized figures, as Keaton's Caped Crusader tries to save the city from Jack Nicholson's deranged Joker. (When Batman calls the Joker "psychotic," Vicki Vale quips, "Some people say the same thing about you" (Burton). The film links the characters even more dramatically by making Jack Napier, the Joker's alter-ego, the murderer of Bruce Wayne's parents and by showing Batman's role in the Joker's origin (an origin that is similar to the one in Moore's *The Killing Joke*), as Napier falls into a vat of chemicals during a botched heist. When he confronts the Joker on the cathedral rooftop at the end of the film, Batman/Bruce Wayne is finally able to express his rage and vows to kill his foe, only to have the Joker remind him of how Batman is responsible for what Napier has become. (Batman rejects the Joker's argument here, since, as he points out, Napier "made [him] first" (Burton), and his crime could be considered the true origin of all that comes thereafter.) Richard Reynolds explains that "[t]he great Batman villains all mirror some key point in Batman's character" (68). (Ducard/Ra's al Ghul certainly has a great deal to do with Batman's origin and with Bruce's sense of justice in Nolan's film, just as the Scarecrow parallels Batman's use of fear to terrorize his enemies.) Not only has the Joker's connection to Batman been established and solidified through his presence in the comics over time—even Nolan has to mention him at the end of his film—but, in the eighties, Miller and Moore both probed the sexual/psychological connection beneath their relationship. (In *The Killing Joke*, the Joker realizes that, like him, Batman once "had a bad day, and it drove [him] as crazy as everybody else" (Moore n.p.). In Burton's interpretation of these characters, Batman and the Joker create each other as much as they create themselves and, in the personas that are born from their tragedies, represent the fine line between obsessed hero and unhinged villain, the fine line that consistently defines them.

Figure 7.5. Michael Keaton as Batman

In Burton's 1992 follow-up, *Batman Returns*, the Penguin and Catwoman similarly refer to aspects of Batman himself. Like Bruce Wayne, Oswald Cobblepot is an orphan preoccupied with his past.[26] However, where Bruce's parents were murdered, Cobblepot was abandoned as an infant by his parents who, horrified by his appearance, left him to be raised by penguins in the sewers of Gotham. Seeking acceptance from the city above, he performs mock acts of heroism and, with the help of corrupt magnate Max Shreck, even runs for mayor. When Batman reveals his deception, however, Cobblepot rejects his given name for his Penguin identity and, in the spirit of Exodus, promises to kill the first-born of Gotham and destroy the city with his armed army of penguins, plots that Batman ultimately foils.

Like Batman, the Catwoman is also a persona created through crime, from Shreck's attempt to kill his secretary, Selina Kyle, after she stumbles upon his fraudulent power plant scheme. At the conclusion of the film,

Batman tries to pacify her murderous rage toward Shreck by revealing his secret identity and comparing how they are both psychologically "split right down the center" (Burton), but she instead chooses revenge and burns one of her nine lives by electrocuting both herself and the conniving tycoon. Though nearly all of the villains are destroyed—as the final scene suggests, the Catwoman is still out there—the issues that drive the main characters (in both films) are issues that they can never resolve or, at least, only resolve through their own destruction. Having come through and survived these experiences, Bruce Wayne may be a little wiser, but he, and for that matter, the Catwoman, are still compelled to don their costumes and to go out into the night to release their darker halves.

In his book *The Batman Filmography*, Mark S. Reinhart particularly takes issue with the portrayal of Batman in this film, charging that he is little more than "a cold-blooded killer" (172). Not only does he turn the Batmobile's afterburner on the Circus Gang fire-breather and set him ablaze, but he disposes of the strongman by stuffing a load of dynamite into his clothing and tossing him into a sewer. For Reinhart (and a number of other Batman fans),[27] these behaviors stand as "an insult to the character's 50-plus-year history" (172), although Burton's vision is perhaps not as radical or as heretical as he suggests. Aside from the fact that Kane's original does kill, Burton is probably not out to portray Batman as a killer here. The scenes that Reinhart refers to are perhaps more cartoonish than he describes. (Danny Elfman's playful score also seems to indicate this tone.) And they focus more on Batman's ingenuity than on homicidal rage or bloodshed and gore. From the fire-breather's attack, Burton leaves us to marvel at the Batmobile's 180 degree spin, and, while the vicious afterburner blast subdues Batman's foe, we cannot be sure that he is, in fact, dead. Burton does not show us the dead fire-breather, as he shows us Shreck's charred remains, to emphasize this point. When Batman confronts the strongman, moreover, the large, candy-striped device that he employs is more along the lines of the Roadrunner and the Coyote or Burton's own *Beetlejuice* than Hitchcock's *Psycho* or Scorsese's *Taxi Driver*. The Penguin even tries to frame Batman for the murder of the Ice Princess, which would be a strange thing to do if he was generally seen as a killer. And, at the end of the film, Batman specifically tells a distraught Catwoman, intent on killing Shreck, that they are not above the law and that the villainous executive should go to jail for his crimes, arguments that are at odds with the suggestion that Batman is a killer.[28] In either case, *Batman Returns* raises issues about the interpretation and portrayal of the hero—for the critics and the fans as well as the filmmakers—and how those aspects refer and respond to the ongoing history of the character.

While both of Burton's Batman films were financially successful[29] and, generally, well received,[30] the somber vision of *Batman Returns* was still too bleak for some, "especially," as Daniels notes, "for a movie bound to attract large numbers of children" (169). After Tim Burton stepped back from directing the third film (and signed on instead as producer), the studio turned to Joel Schumacher for *Batman Forever*, but this change also signaled a change in the tone and direction of the first two films, a change that ultimately cost the franchise Michael Keaton. Despite a $35 million offer, Keaton turned down the role (which subsequently went to Val Kilmer) specifically because he saw the series "becoming broader and lighter" (Vincent). Ironically, Keaton maintains that he wanted the third film to be "somewhat of a prequel so you know how [Batman] got there" (Wilson), which is what Nolan and Bale eventually did in the 2005 film.

Indeed, although the back story is present in 1995's *Batman Forever*, as Bruce Wayne remembers his first encounter with "the bat" after his parents' wake and works toward accepting his dual identity with Batman-fetish psychologist Chase Meridian, the film is more tongue-in-cheek and self-deprecating at points. Not only does Batman tell Alfred that he will "get drive-thru" at the beginning, but he later wonders if the sexually aggressive Chase is "trying to get under [his] cape" (Schumacher). (The film explores Batman's sexuality in more detail, from gratuitous shots of his costume to anatomical changes in the costume itself[31] to his "Dracula-like" midnight rendezvous with a fair-skinned, red-lipped Chase, wrapped in a silken white bedsheet, on her balcony.) Although Jim Carrey's Riddler and Tommy Lee Jones's Two-Face ham it up and do their best to kill the hero—they even blow up the Batcave—their characters are not as directly connected to Batman's, at least not in the thematic way that linked him to his villains in the other two films. According to Richard Reynolds, Two-Face is "[a]rguably the key Batman villain" (67), yet, in spite of the unique similarity between Two-Face's constant desire to allow chance to choose between his personalities and Batman's own identity issues, the film does not explore their connection as deeply or as dramatically as it could have.

With the introduction of Dick Grayson/Robin, Batman's parental role demands that he critique the very obsession that drives him. After rescuing a young woman from a menacing street gang, Dick is the one who admits that he "imagined that it was [Two-Face, who killed his family,] that [he] was fighting" (Schumacher), leaving Bruce to lecture him about how his willingness to kill will only lead him out "into the night to find" a multiplicity of faces and make revenge his "whole life" (Schumacher).   Where Two-Faces' "faces" are constantly at odds, Bruce/Batman, having resolved his "identity crisis," is able to live with his fragmented "postmodern" *psyche*, as he tells the Riddler after foiling his plans and saving both Chase and Robin from certain death, now as a matter of choice. In terms of the scope of the series, this acceptance and this self-awareness point to a kind of growth on the part of the character and a development in his role as hero.

In the end, *Batman Forever* tried to walk the line between dark drama and comic camp. In the same way that Batman's costume changes from the dark black of the Burton years to a "shiny dark gray-gun metal blue" (Reinhart 184), the film clearly showed, however, where the franchise was going. As with the comics, its lighter tone and the colorful addition of Robin, in metallic red, green, yellow, and black, anticipated a softening of both the character and the series for a more general audience.[32]

For all of the "therapeutic" progress that Batman might have made, the series clearly was losing steam, both critically and creatively, by the time that George Clooney donned the outfit in 1997's *Batman and Robin*. Though the combination of Arnold Schwarzenegger, Uma Thurman, and Clooney seemed like a good choice, the film's frequent lapses into campish absurdity made it difficult for viewers to take it seriously or to rank these performances and this portrayal of Batman alongside their predecessors. In his initial review of the film, *Washington Post* writer Desson Howe remarked that "Clooney—bless him—wouldn't know psychic baggage if he had to check it at the airport" ("Winged Defeat"). Daniels believes that "Batgirl's appearance suggested a degree of desperation" (187) on the part of the filmmakers. And, as Reinhart laments, the film, "*so* similar to *Batman Forever* that it [felt] about as imaginatively constructed as a child's 'paint by numbers' set," was "completely divorced from any sense of reality" (205), with gravity-defying car chases, absurd skyscraper jumps, and bizarre mid-air stunts.

This time, the heroes are called upon to stop Mr. Freeze from bringing a new ice age to Gotham and to stop Poison Ivy from repopulating the planet with her mutated plants. Alfred's thrill-seeking, computer savvy niece shows up as Batgirl, and the villains are sent off to Arkham Asylum at the end, but the darkness is all but gone here, replaced instead with colorful costumes and comic one-liners. (As Mr. Freeze exclaims after freezing the guards at the Gotham Museum, "The Iceman Cometh!" (Schumacher), and Batman later wonders why Batgirl did not choose a more "PC name," like "Bat-Person or Batwoman" (Schumacher). Where the first three films considered the rather bizarre nature of his lifestyle and examined his unique psychological issues in detail, *Batman and Robin* takes the presence of Batman as a given and essentially ignores the rage that drives him. (At best, Alfred and Bruce Wayne soberly philosophize about the meaning of Batman as "an attempt to control death itself" (Schumacher). Batman is no longer such an anomaly; he is the city's best line of defense. When Dr. Pamela Isley (Poison Ivy's alter-ego) warns the audience at the Gotham Observatory that they soon will have no protection from the plants and flowers of the world, a gossip columnist patronizingly chimes in, "In Gotham City, Batman and Robin protect us" (Schumacher). By the end of the film, Batman, in the process of saving the day, also becomes a kind of father figure, learning the difficult lesson that, sometimes, he must allow Robin and Batgirl to face danger and brave death on their own without his help.

In addition to recalling the 1960s' television series at times both in terms of its plot and tone, the film's emphasis on what screenwriter Akiva Goldsman calls Batman's attempt to create "a new family to replace the biological one he's lost" ("Creating the New Story") once more evoked the ghost of Frederic Wertham and the portrayal of a family-friendly Batman, a portrayal that added to its critical failure. (Describing the film as "the family values 'Batman,'" *Los Angeles Times* critic Kenneth Turan admitted that it was "a relief to have it over" (Rev. of *Batman and Robin*). Moreover, in an ironic turn, Schumacher's "anatomical" costumes, more blue and silver than black, and physical close-ups did not, for many, suggest a domestic hero, but instead became "associated," in Brooker's words, "with all the qualities many comic fans had learned to abhor— camp, gayness, the aesthetic of the TV show" (299).

These elements of the lighter Schumacher films, and of *Batman and Robin* specifically, thus made it difficult for audiences in the late 1990s to believe that such selfless heroes always stood ready to protect their cities from fanatical enemies, intent on their destruction. In the new millennium, little did they know how right they would be.

Batman Begins: Newness or Nostalgia?

Julian Darius reports in *Batman Begins and the Comics* that several different writers attempted a Batman reboot after Schumacher and before Nolan, attempts that perhaps speak to the cultural desire to (re)create a Batman who would more appropriately refer to contemporary circumstances and contexts. None of these projects, of course, was ever realized. In 1999, Tim McCanlies pitched a show to the WB network about a young Bruce Wayne's return to Gotham, but the network became "engaged in a turf war [with the Warner Bros. film studio] over the Batman franchise" (8), and the series fell through. (The WB went on to explore a similar concept dealing with a young Clark Kent, leading to the television hit *Smallville*.) Frank Miller also developed a film script based upon his *Batman: Year One* that "got as far as storyboards, completed in 2003" (14). As Darius explains, however, this graphic, violent vision of a Batman "snapping arms and kicking criminals when they're down" (13) was "closer to Travis Bickle in *Taxi Driver* than to previous versions of [the hero]" (9), a vision that may well have been too disturbing for the studio as well as for some Batman purists. Even the Wachowski brothers "drafted a proposal for a different film entitled *Batman: Year One*" (Darius 14) around this time, but they gave up on it so that they could concentrate on their *Matrix* sequels. From these failures, Warner Bros. turned to Nolan, who subsequently brought on writer David S. Goyer, for *Batman Begins* in 2003.

While Nolan's movie may arguably be, as Darius suggests, "the finest *Batman* film ever made" (1), this long history of the character begs the question if this or, for that matter, any Batman could ever be considered "new" or "original" or "cutting edge." In an increasingly complex world governed by spectacle and simulacra and without a master narrative or a knowable real, postmodern critics might be quick to say, "No." In his essay on "Fredric Jameson's Postmodern Marxism," Jonathan Clark argues that Burton's *Batman* exemplifies Jameson's concept of a nostalgic film in that "it does not represent one particular style or period but rather displays an array of many styles and periods to produce a nostalgic effect" ("Postmodern Marxism"). As Clark points out, this *pastiche* ultimately does not amount to anything new; instead, it refers to "the decline of 'genuine' historicity" ("Postmodern Marxism") and to what Jameson defines as our cultural inability to "[fashion] representations of our own current experience" (*Postmodernism* 21). If Clark and Jameson are right, then, essentially any *Batman* film runs the risk of being derivative and nostalgic, inasmuch as it must recall some aspect or element of the character's extensive cultural history. Nolan's *Batman Begins* is certainly just as guilty here. It unapologetically works off of Kane's original premise, Burton's update, Miller's vision in *Dark Knight* and *Year One*, O'Neil's "The Man Who Falls," and a variety of other comic sources to return Batman to the big screen. In Bale's first appearance in costume in the film, in fact, he even tells a horrified Falcone, "I'm Batman" (Nolan), a direct reference to Burton's first film, where Michael Keaton introduces himself to a thug in the same way. Following this argument, the film might be "cutting edge" only to the extent that it is the latest copy of a copy of a copy and yet another tragic attempt to take refuge in an illusory historical past, which, according to Jameson, "itself remains forever out of reach" ("Consumer Society" 118).

In *The Politics of Postmodernism*, however, Linda Hutcheon suggests that some of Jameson's conclusions about postmodern film are "of questionable validity," since it "is, if anything, obsessed with history and with how we can know the past today" (114). Steven Best and Douglas Kellner similarly consider such postmodern theoretical "claims concerning the end of history, society, the masses, and so on [as] laughable in the face of the resurgence of historical drama and upheaval" (296-7). Inasmuch as historical context has consistently been a factor in the portrayal of the hero, *Batman Begins* does draw upon the long history of Batman and on those contexts; however, rather than wallow in them wistfully to escape the present, it combines, reworks, and reinvents them to create a product of and a commentary on contemporary history, a commentary that begins with the casting of Christian Bale.

As with all of the other Batman films, casting becomes an issue in terms of what it says about the perception of the hero in the context of the times. Batman purists, for example, were extremely outspoken in their rejection of Michael Keaton when he was first announced for Tim Burton's film, particularly because they had a preconceived notion of who or what Batman was, a notion that Keaton, based upon his previous roles, simply did not seem to fit. As science fiction writer Harlan Ellison lamented, "Here's the only prominent superhero without special powers; here's one of the very best detectives who ever lived, and he's being played by a scrawny comedian in plastic armor" (Rodman 38).[33]

Figure 7.6. Christian Bale as Batman

Conversely, as Alan Jones reported in a 1989 issue of *Cinefantastique*, "[Bob] Kane had envisioned actor Jack Nicholson in the role of his Joker as far back as 1980, when he drew a likeness of the character over a still of the actor from *The Shining*" (Alan Jones) and strongly encouraged producers to get Nicholson for the new film. For Kane, Nicholson's performance as the unhinged and ultimately homicidal Jack Torrance perfectly captured the insane menace that he had in mind when he thought of Batman's devious adversary.[34] Ironically, when Nolan began to cast his film over a decade later, he, too, turned to an actor who had successfully played a psychotic killer, but, this time, he made him "the good guy."

Given Bale's all too convincing performance as Patrick Bateman in *American Psycho*, audiences who have seen both films cannot help but make the connection between the two characters, especially since they are similar in a number of ways, and this was, perhaps, precisely the point in the casting. Inasmuch as fear is one of the primary themes of the film and one of Batman's primary weapons, Nolan wants both Bruce and Batman to be somewhat "frightening" and "dangerous" here. Lurking in the darkness, this Batman certainly is, covered almost completely, nightmarishly in black (aside from his gold utility belt), with no "new look" Bat-Signal logo, no silver or gray contrasts, and none of Schumacher's whimsical anatomical modifications.[35] Through the Scarecrow's weaponized hallucinogenic, he even appears as an inhuman monster to the crooked Dr. Crane and the hysterical Gotham masses as well as to the audience. (Again, if the villains say something about Batman, he inspires just as much fear as the Scarecrow himself, if not more.) But Bale brings a unique sense of menace to both sides of the mask. From Patrick Bateman's bloody chopping and chainsawing in New York City, his Bruce Wayne deals with some of the same moral intangibles and wrestles with some of the same questions about the propriety of his actions. In the same way that Bateman conceives, "There is an idea of Patrick Bateman, some kind of abstraction, but there is no real me" (Harron), Bruce becomes Batman by devoting himself "to an idea" (Nolan), by essentially becoming a symbol or an abstraction, and the film ends with Rachel Dawes's insight that Bruce Wayne is the mask and that his "real face is that one that criminals now fear" (Nolan). We can never be quite sure of exactly what Bruce/Batman will do in the film or how far he will go to get the job done. Like Miller's dark knight, he, too, "teeters," to recall Harvey's words, "on the edge of sanity" (148). When Bruce Wayne shows up at a restaurant with two women, in a scene that could have been taken straight from *American Psycho*, we almost have to wonder if his dates will make it home safely or if someone will wind up eating a urine cake before the evening is over. (The presence of Rachel Dawes and Bruce's "dates" also addresses the question of Batman's "sexuality," that source of so much trouble for Wertham.) Although this Bruce/Batman generally draws a line between subduing his foes and killing them (another point of contention in the character's history), he is rather viciously determined to terrorize and psychologically torment them, (a fate that may well be worse than death), as when he picks apart Falcone's henchmen in the dark on the waterfront or suspends the corrupt police detective Flass several stories off the ground to grill him for information. If Kilmer's Batman sent the Riddler off to Arkham Asylum at the end of *Batman Forever*, Bale's could definitely keep him there. Moreover, unlike most of the other films where Batman deliberately explored his severe psychological issues, Bale's hero never does, but instead focuses single-mindedly on the act of becoming and on expressing those complex violent emotions stemming from his parents' murder. Even Alfred admits, at one point in the film, that he was tempted to "[call] the men in the white coats" when he first heard about Bruce's "grand plan for saving Gotham" (Nolan), and Bale's casting begs that we walk that fine line between heroism and insanity in the assessment of Batman's character in the film. As *Boston Globe* reviewer Ty Burr keenly notes, "From Patrick Bateman to Batman, Bale hints, is a very small step" (*"Batman Begins* Movie Review").[36]

In this regard, Nolan's re-casting of Batman speaks to the postmodern rebooting of pop culture icons, like Darth Vader, James Bond, or Hannibal Lecter, who have all recently had their back stories retold (and perhaps "rehistoricized") in more graphic, realistic ways, and to the increasing demand for "edgier" heroes who operate outside the limits of moral law and the justice system, and even sanity itself. *The Sopranos* examines the trials and tribulations of a mob family as opposed to the FBI agents trying to capture them. Deadwood is attractive to settlers, because there is "no law at all" there. Agent Jack Bauer on *24* must kill and torture on a weekly basis in the interests of national security. The most intriguing character in the X-Men films (and the comics) is Wolverine, a short-tempered killer with retractable metal claws. If Hannibal Lecter was once a villain, his cannibalistic behavior is essentially justified in *Hannibal Rising*, and Showtime's *Dexter* series follows a police detective who moonlights as a serial killer (or maybe it is the other way around).[37] Even the latest *Spider-Man* sequel focuses on Peter Parker as he explores his dark side through his new black costume, disfiguring Harry Osborn and trying to kill the Sandman for his uncle's murder. (With heroes like these, who needs villains?)

If our heroes say anything about us and our sense of contemporary history, then this new postmodern hero might function as an evolved expression of the modern fantasies that spawned them, the evolved expression of a world coming to grips with a more terrifying range of criminal activities and a more complicated moral spectrum. Where racketeering and street crimes once provided the inspiration for the superheroes of the world, we now wrestle with the ongoing possibility of suicide bombings, bioterrorism, and airline hijackings, in addition to those drug-related murders, hate crimes, sex offenses, and school shootings that have become a regular part of our network news broadcasts. In that pre-9/11 landscape, Mr. Freeze and Poison Ivy's desire to destroy Gotham was an act of cartoonish absurdity; Ducard's apocalyptic plans for Gotham and his attempt to unleash a chemical weapon that inspires fear certainly are not portrayed as comically, but instead must refer to that terrorism that has become our daily portion of reality. (In this regard, Nolan's Batman, in his "war on crime," is literally equipped like a soldier, wearing military grade body armor and driving a "Batmobile/tank/Tumbler" through the streets of Gotham.) Inasmuch as the character of Batman responds and is a response to the context of the times, the present psychological need for a hero who can encounter and counter our fears in kind, for a hero who can terrorize those who terrorize us, for this darker dark knight, becomes all the more urgent and understandable. One day, we may be horrified to find that we have, in some way, become the thing that we beheld. (In Miller's film treatment for *Year One*, Gordon goes so far as to call "Batman a 'terrorist'" (Darius 13), a label that is conspicuously absent from Nolan's film.) But in these years of restraint, as we try to apply reason and forethought to the acts of violence or the loss of life, both domestically and abroad, that we read about, to the alerts and cells and plots and possibilities, these heroes may provide some kind of relief by vicariously exploring the shadows in our repressed psyches and satisfying our desire to go beyond the law and to punish those villains that we will never see. They express our rage as well as our outrage. They do what we cannot and should not, but they do so, fiercely and violently, in that fictional world where the choices are more clear cut, so that we can cathartically purge what we might consciously or unconsciously imagine and work toward understanding and diplomacy in this postmodern world where they are not. To the extent that we can continue to foster more reasonable alternatives as a result of this cinematic release, these ends, then, justify the necessity of that ominous signal in the night sky and the more disturbing casting implications of *Batman Begins*.

Works Cited

"All-Time Worldwide Box Office." *Internet Movie Database* 18 July 2007
       <*http://www.imdb.com/boxoffice/alltimegross?region=world-wide*>.
Best, Steven and Douglas Kellner. *Postmodern Theory: Critical Interrogations*. New York: Guilford, 1991.
Boichel, Bill. "Batman: Commodity as Myth." *The Many Lives of the Batman*. Eds.

Pearson, Roberta E. and William Uricchio, New York: Routledge, 1991: 4-17.

Brooker, Will. *Batman Unmasked: Analyzing a Cultural Icon*. New York: Continuum, 2000.

Bur, Ty. *"Batman Begins* Movie Review." Rev. of *Batman Begins*, dir. Christopher Nolan. *Boston Globe* 14 June 2005. 29 March 2007 <*http://www.boston.com/movies/display?display=movie&id=6870*>.

Burton, Tim, dir. *Batman*. Perf. Michael Keaton, Kim Basinger, Jack Nicholson, Robert Wuhl. DVD. Warner Bros., 1989.

—. *Batman Returns*. Perf. Michael Keaton, Danny DeVito, Michelle Pfeiffer, Christopher Walken. DVD. Warner Bros., 1992.

Cieply, Michael. "Surprise! Spartans Assault Box Office." *New York Times* 12 March 2007, late ed.: E1.

Clark, Jonathan. "Fredric Jameson's Postmodern Marxism: A Politics of Aesthetic Representation." *Codgito: The MUN Student Journal of Philosophy* 4 (1996). 28 June 2007 <*http://www.mun.ca/phil/codgito/vol4/v4doc2.html*>.

Corliss, Richard. "The Caped Crusader Flies Again." *Time* 19 June 1989. 28 March 2007 <*http://www.time.com/time/printout/0,8816,957980,00.html*>.

"Creating the New Story." *Batman and Robin*. DVD Special Features. Dir. Joel Schumacher. Warner Bros., 1997.

Daniels, Les. *Batman: The Complete History*. San Francisco: Chronicle, 1999.

—. Introduction. Kane, et al. 4-7.

Darius, Julian. *Batman Begins and the Comics*. Honolulu: Sequart.com Books, 2005.

"Dex, Lies, and Videotape." *Dexter*. Dir. Nick Gomez. Perf. Michael C. Hall, Julie Benz, Jennifer Carpenter, Erik King, *Lauren Vélez, James Remar, Keith Carradine, Jaime Murray. Showtime. 4 November 2007. Engelhardt, Steve. "The Night of the Stalker." Kane, et al. 81-94.*

Fingeroth, Danny. *Superman on the Couch*. New York: Continuum, 2004.

FlaBat. "Re: Did Batman go too far?!!" *Batman: Yesterday, Today, and Beyond*. 24 February 2007. 5 November 2007 <*http://www.batmanytb.com/forum/viewthread.php?forum_id=17&thread_id=2181&pid=24939*>.

Fleming, Michael. "'Batman' Captures Director Nolan." *Variety*. 27 January 2003. Reed Business Information. 15 May 2007 <*http://www.variety.com/article/VR1117879566.html?categoryid=1236&cs=1*>.

Freccero, Carla. "Historical Violence, Censorship, and the Serial Killer: The Case of *American Psycho*. *Diacritics* 27.2 (1997): 44-58.

Harron, Mary. Dir. *American Psycho*. Perf. Christian Bale, Reese Witherspoon, Justin Theroux, Josh Lucas, Jared Leto. Universal, 2000.

Harvey, Robert C. *The Art of the Comic Book: An Aesthetic History*. Jackson: Mississippi UP, 1996.

Hinson, Hal. "*Batman*." Rev. of *Batman*, dir. Tim Burton. *Washington Post* 23 June 1989. 10 June 2007 <http://www.washingtonpost.com/wprv/style/longterm/movies/videos/batmanpg13hinson_a07fb8.htm>.

Howe, Desson. "'Batman': Winged Defeat." Rev. of *Batman and Robin*, dir. Joel Schumacher. *Washington Post* 20 June 1997. 1 April 2007 *<http://www.washingtonpost.com/wpsrv/style/longterm/movies/review97/batmanandrobinhowe.htm>*.

"It's Official: Bale is Batman!!!!" *Batman On Film*. 11 September 2003. 1998-present. *Batman On Film* and William E. Ramey. 15 May 2007 *<http://www.batman-on-film.com/b5newsarchives23.html>*.

Jameson, Fredric. "Postmodernism and Consumer Society." *The Anti-aesthetic: Essays on Postmodern Culture*. Ed. Hal Foster. Port Townsend, Washington: Bay Press, 1983: 111-125.

—. *Postmodernism, or, The Cultural Logic of Late Capitalism*. Durham: Duke UP, 1991.

Jones, Alan. "*Batman*." *Cinefantastique* November 1989: 48-62. Rpt. in *Batman Movie Online: The Definitive Batman Movie Resource*. 25 March 2007 *<http://www.batmanmovieonline.com/behindthescenes/articles/batmanproduction.htm>*.

Jones, Gerard. *Men of Tomorrow: Geeks, Gangsters, and the Birth of the Comic Book*. New York: Basic Books, 2004.

Kane, Bob, Bill Finger, and Gardner Fox. *The Batman Chronicles*. New York: DC Comics, 2005.

Kane, Bob, et al. *Batman: The Greatest Stories Ever Told*. New York: DC Comics, 2005.

Kellner, Douglas. *Media Culture: Cultural Studies, Identity and Politics Between the Modern and the Postmodern*. New York: Routledge, 1995.

Lalumière, Claude. Rev. of *The Dark Knight Strikes Again*, by Frank Miller. *Infinity Plus*. 12 April 2003. 18 June 2007 *<http://www.infinityplus.co.uk/fantasticfiction /darkknightagain.htm>*. Rpt. from *Montreal Gazette* 21 September 2002, late ed.: H6.

Leahy, Patrick. Foreword. *Batman: The Dark Knight Archives*. Vol. 1. By Bob Kane. New York: DC Comics, 1991: 4-7.

Leverenz, David. "The Last Real Man in America: From Natty Bumppo to Batman." *American Literary History* 3.4 1991: 753-781.

Medhurst, Andy. "Batman, Deviance and Camp." Pearson and Uricchio 149-163.

Miller, Frank. *Batman: The Dark Knight Returns*. New York: DC Comics, 2002.

—. *Batman: The Dark Knight Strikes Again*. New York: DC Comics, 2002.

Miller, Frank, writer, and David Mazzucchelli, artist. *Batman: Year One*. New York: DC Comics, 2005.

Moore, Alan, writer, and Brian Bolland, artist. *The Killing Joke*. New York: DC Comics, 1988.

Nolan, Christopher dir. *Batman Begins* (Two-Disc Special Edition). Perf. Christian Bale, Caine, Michael, Liam Neeson, Katie Holmes, Gary Oldman, Cillian Murphy. DVD. Warner Bros., 2005.

O'Neil, Denny, writer, and Dick Giordano, artist. "The Man Who Falls." *Batman Begins: The Movie and Other Tales of the Dark Knight*. New York: DC Comics, 2005. 71-87.

007-11. "Director of 'Memento' and 'Insomnia' Christo." "Reader's Talkback." *Ain't It Cool News*. 28 January 2003. 15 May 2007 <*http://www.aintitcool.com/talkback_display/14315#comment_574125*>.

Pearson, Roberta E. and William Uricchio. "Notes from the Batcave: An Interview with Dennis O'Neil." Pearson and Uricchio 18-32.

Reinhart, Mark S. *The Batman Filmography: Live-Action Features, 1943-1997*. Jefferson, North Carolina: McFarland, 2005.

Rexi. "Re: Was Batman a Killer in Burton Bat movies?" *SuperHeroHype Boards*. 6 August 2006. 1997-2007. Coming Soon Media. 5 November 2007 <*http://forums.superherohype.com/showthread.php?t=245711*>.

Reynolds, Richard. *Super Heroes: A Modern Mythology*. Jackson: Mississippi UP, 1992.

Robinson, Jerry. Foreword. *Batman Archives*. Vol. 3. By Bob Kane. New York: DC Comics, 1994: 5-7.

Rodman, Howard A. "They Shoot Comic Books, Don't They?" *American Film* May 1989: 34-39.

Schumacher, Joel. dir. *Batman and Robin*. Perf. George Clooney, Chris O'Donnell,

Silverstone, Alicia, Arnold Schwarzenegger, Uma Thurman, Michael Gough. DVD. Warner Bros., 1997.

—. *Batman Forever*. Perf. Val Kilmer, Nicole Kidman, Jim Carrey, Tommy Lee Jones, Chris O'Donnell, Michael Gough. DVD. Warner Bros., 1995.

Steranko, Jim. *The Steranko History of Comics*. Vol. 1. Reading, Pennsylvania: Supergraphics, 1970.

Travers, Peter. "*Batman Returns*." Rev. of *Batman Returns*, dir. Tim Burton. *Rolling Stone* 7 February 2001. July 15 2007 *<http://www.rollingstone.com/reviews/movie/5949279/review/5949280 /batman_returns>*.

"Trivia for *Maquinista, El* (2004)." *Internet Movie Database* 2 April 2007 *<http://www.imdb.com/title/tt0361862/trivia>*.

Turan, Kenneth. "*Batman and Robin*: Meanwhile, Back at the Batcave...." Rev. of *Batman and Robin*, dir. Joel Schumacher. *Los Angeles Times* 20 June 1997. 14 July 2007 *<http://www.calendarlive.com/movies/reviews/cl-movie970620- 5,0,5219709.story>*.

Hise, James Van. *Batmania*. Las Vegas: Pioneer, 1989.

Vaz, Mark Cotta. *Tales of the Dark Knight: Batman's First Fifty Years 1939-1989*. New York: DC Comics, 1989.

Vincent, Mal. "Film Left Keaton Talking to Himself." *Virginian-Pilot* 20 July 1996. 12 July 2007 *<http://scholar.lib.vt.edu/VA-news/VA-Pilot/issues/1996/ vp960720/07190053.htm>*.

VoteRoslin08. "Hell yeah!" "Reader's Talkback." *Ain't It Cool News*. 28 January 2003. 15 May 2007 *<http://www.aintitcool.com/talkback_display/14315#comment_574125>*.

Walters, Barbara. *The Barbara Walters Special: 25th Annual Oscar Edition—George Clooney, Patrick Dempsey, Matthew McConaughey, Mariah Carey*. ABC. WABC, New York, 1 March 2006.

Wares, Paul J. "A Retrospective of *Batman Returns*." *Batman on Film*. 20 April 2006. 2005. *Batman On Film*. 5 November 2007 <http://www.batmanonfilm.com/opinion_pjw_returnsretrospective.html>.

Waxman, Sharon. "'Spider-Man 3' Conquers Box Office and Bodes Well for Summer." *New York Times* 7 May 2007, late ed.: E1.

Wertham, Frederic. *Seduction of the Innocent*. New York: Rinehart, 1954.

Wilson, Staci. "Michael Keaton: The 'White Noise' Interview." *Horror.com*. 1 January 2005. 12 July 2007 *<http://www.horror.com/php/article-661-1.html>*.

Wright, Bradford W. *Comic Book Nation: The Transformation of Youth Culture in America*. Baltimore: Johns Hopkins UP, 2001.

Notes

[1] When Michael Fleming first announced the story on *Variety*'s website, he anticipated that Nolan would "undoubtedly bring the wildly inventive style that so quickly brought him to the directing A-list after 'Insomnia' and 'Memento'" (Fleming). Posters on boards like *Ain't It Cool News*'s "Readers Talkback" agreed that the choice of Nolan was inspired. "VoteRoslin08" noted that "[t]his guy has some REAL talent" (VoteRoslin08) and "007-11" added, "[C]onsider my interest piqued" (007-11).

[2] As the writers on the fansite *Batman On Film* exclaimed after the announcement of Bale's casting, "After five years of wishing and hoping, and ups and downs [,] [... w]e have finally won! We perhaps ARE getting the ultimate Bat-film!" ("It's Official").

[3] Frank Miller actually pays tribute to this influence in both *The Dark Knight Returns* and *Batman: Year One*, as Bruce Wayne's parents take him to see this movie before they are gunned down on the way home. Inasmuch as Poe's detective stories also figured into the creation of the character, Alfred talks about reading "The Purloined Letter" to a young Bruce Wayne and "explain[ing] the importance of Mr. Poe's contribution to detective fiction" (*The Dark Knight Returns* 188).

[4] Referring to the influence of this character on the development of Batman, Jim Steranko notes that, in some early Batman comics, "he began the habit of leaving his calling card attached to his defeated adversary in the style of [...] Rinehart's [villain]" (45).

[5] Batman works as a postmodern figure in this regard inasmuch as he himself is a "*pastiche*" of different cultural elements. In addition, Batman, like so many other comic book superheroes, has, perhaps, continued to speak to generations of readers and viewers because his perpetual "dual identity crisis" and his ultimate lack of a "unified self" anticipate and reflect the complexity of postmodern existence, where "identity becomes more and more unstable" (Kellner 233).

[6] In his professional assessment of these early stories, Steranko agrees: "Kane's art was primitive, [...] anatomy was stiff, unrealistic; the rendering weak. Still, the inadvertent betrayal of realism seemed to add rather than detract from the grim romanticism of the Batman formula" (44).

[7] Ducard dismisses Bruce's initial attempt to brand the League of Shadows as "vigilantes." "A vigilante," he asserts, "is just a man lost in the scramble for his own gratification. He can be destroyed or locked up" (Nolan). Ducard suggests that Bruce, by contrast, can "become something else entirely" by devoting himself "to an ideal"; he can become "a legend" (Nolan).

[8] In Frank Miller's *The Dark Knight Strikes Again*, after beating up Lex Luthor and scaring "the crap out of [him]," Batman even admits to enjoying this aspect of his work: "Striking terror [is the b]est part of the job" (110).

[9] Richard Reynolds agrees that "A Batman without anger is a Batman retired" (74).

[10] Frank Miller disputes Batman's interest in revenge and suggests that "he's much more noble than that. He wants the world to be a better place, where a young Bruce Wayne would not be a victim ... In a way, he's out to make himself

unnecessary. Batman is a hero who wishes he didn't have to exist" (*Batman: Year One* 101).

[11] Julian Darius points out that Nolan took this falling theme from a 1989 "Batman origin story written by Batman legend Denny O'Neil and illustrated by Dick Giordano" called "The Man Who Falls" (34).

[12] Fingeroth also comments that "Robin seems to have little of the bitter angst that fuels Batman" (65).

[13] Daniels notes that Batman "never got a [radio] program of his own" (64), but Batman and Robin periodically showed up as guest stars on *The Adventures of Superman*.

[14] Columbia released two Batman movie serials, but, according to Mark S. Reinhart, neither one was well done. The first, *Batman* (1943), "was filmed very quickly and cheaply" (15), although it did introduce the character of Bruce Wayne's butler Alfred, who went on to become an integral part of the Batman story, both in the comics and on film. The second, *Batman and Robin* (1949), was "every bit as poorly realized as its predecessor" and similarly "lacking in quality" (18).

[15] Vaz states that, during the World War II years, "Batman took to the patriotic calling with a surprising fervor" (33) and was used to sell bonds and to promote the war effort on the home front. Brooker disputes the extent of the character's involvement here, however, pointing out that *Batman* comics during this period largely paid "lip service to the war effort" (75) and that the stories themselves largely did not focus on the war or make Batman a part of it.

[16] A number of other critics and readers of the comic have argued for the validity of this interpretation. In his book *Batman Unmasked*, Brooker, for example, believes that this reading "is by no means as absurd as [Wertham's] critics want to suggest" (102). And, in response to Barbara Walters's question about playing a gay character in a 2006 interview, George Clooney quipped that he already had when he played Batman and that he deliberately "made him gay" (Walters).

[17] In *The Dark Knight Returns*, Miller's Batman suggests that this "new look" had a practical purpose and that he deliberately wore a reinforced "target on [his] chest" to draw enemy fire because he could not "armor [his] head" (51).

[18] As James Van Hise points out, O'Neil and artist Neal Adams, in re-imagining Batman in the seventies, recast the Joker as well: "[T]hey decided the character was, and always had been, gay. The original ruthlessness was not only returned to the character but so were veiled references to his sexual preferences" (11). Where the danger of Batman for Wertham was his subtle, heroic defense of homosexuality, he, in what may well have been the ultimate turnabout and the ultimate response to the Wertham controversy, was now committed to stopping a homicidal, unstable, homosexual arch-enemy.

[19] The Denny O'Neil story "The Man Who Falls" similarly flashes back from a present day Batman, about to foil a crime, to a young Bruce Wayne's fall into a cave on the Wayne estate, where he is attacked by bats, and to the death of his parents, who "fell" and "never got up again" (76).

[20] Again, in what may well have been an ironic reversal or perhaps yet another attempt to rescue Batman from Wertham, Miller, according to Daniels, also made

the Joker, a criminal, "the only gay person in sight" (151). Richard Reynolds similarly identifies a homoerotic element to their hostility in Miller's portrayal, nothing that, "[a]t the end of their fight to the death [,] the Joker and Batman are linked together visually in a near-sexual embrace" (103).

[21] Miller considered this purpose in more detail in his 2001-2002 sequel *The Dark Knight Strikes Again*, which picks up three years after the end of *The Dark Knight Returns*. Where Batman liberated himself in the first series, he goes on to liberate the rest of the superhero world in the second series from a corrupt government with a computer generated president. As Superman, Wonder Woman, and Captain Marvel finally see that Batman has been right all along, Lex Luthor and Brainiac are revealed as the real government leaders, who have been using their political power to imprison all other superheroes or to drive them into hiding. As revolutionary, Batman leads the charge to overthrow Luthor and Brainiac, to free the heroes from the system that has oppressed or imprisoned them, and to level the preexisting order. After a pitched battle with a genetically altered Dick Grayson, Batman even destroys the Batcave and is left to nurse an injured Carrie, now dressed as a more mature "Catgirl," back to health. The response to *The Dark Knight Strikes Again* was mixed, however; reviewers like Claude Lalumière found "its emphatic call for responsible civil disobedience [...] both stirring and heartfelt," but ultimately felt that "its careless execution [was] regrettable" (Rev. of *The Dark Knight Strikes Again*).

[22] Referring to the director's interview in the fanzine *Speakeasy*, Will Brooker reports that Burton "had read both [...] prior to filming" (289).

[23] In spite of so many negative reviews, Marvel's *Ghost Rider* "surprised distributors at Sony Pictures Entertainment with a $45 million [opening] weekend" in February 2007 (Cieply E1), and *Spider-Man 3* recently broke a number of opening weekend records, racking up "an estimated $148 million in domestic ticket sales [... and] an estimated $227 million in 105 foreign countries" (Waxman E1).

[24] Burton's work, in turn, became the inspiration for the stylized *noir* Batman cartoons, from *Batman: The Animated Series* to the more futuristic *Batman Beyond*.

[25] Burton's Gotham, in fact, frequently references the history in between these markers, a history that Batman as a character has lived through and evolved with. For example, the Joker is transformed by and, in turn, transforms "Axis Chemicals," a name, as David Leverenz notes, that is, "of course, not accidental" (766). Not only does it suggest the menace and malevolence of the Axis powers in World War II, but Leverenz argues that "Anton Furst's sets [...] evoke the awed helplessness induced by Nazi architecture" (766).

[26] Bruce Wayne's butler, Alfred, also sees a connection between the two. Questioning Bruce's suspicions toward the Penguin, Alfred wonders if Bruce is determined to "be the only lonely man-beast in town" (Burton).

[27] Paul J. Wares, who edits the *Batman on Film* fansite, also takes issue with Batman's actions in this film. While he admits that Keaton's portrayal is largely in keeping with his interpretation of the character, he "still [has] problems with Batman killing" (Wares). In a thread dealing with this question on the

SuperHeroHype Boards, poster "Rexi" refers to this Batman as "a sadistic murderer" (Rexi). And on the *Batman: Yesterday, Today, and Beyond* message boards, "FlaBat," like Reinhart, similarly believes that Burton's Batman is "a killer, which we all know is against his own personal code" (FlaBat).

[28] Even Wares has difficulty reconciling these lines with his view of Batman as a killer in the film and admits, in his "Retrospective," that they "completely [contradict] the character we've been watching for the last hour and forty-five minutes" (Wares).

[29] The *Internet Movie Database*, in fact, lists *Batman* in the top 100 and *Batman Returns* in the top 200 "All-Time Worldwide Box Office" sales (www.imdb.com/boxoffice/alltimegross ?region=world-wide).

[30] The *Washington Post*'s Hal Hinson, for example, told his readers that *Batman* was "as rich and satisfying a movie as [they were] likely to see all year" (Hinson), while *Rolling Stone*'s Peter Travers described *Batman Returns* as that "summer's most explosively entertaining movie" (Travers).

[31] As Reinhart explains, one of the primary controversies surrounding the film involved Schumacher's physical modifications to the costumes: "Longtime Batman fans [as well as Batman creator Bob Kane] were generally very perturbed by Schumacher's decision to put nipples on the [black] Batman costume" (183-184). Robin's costume also sported them, and, in spite of this negative reaction, Schumacher kept them on the Batman and Robin costumes in the next film.

[32] Reinhart maintains that *Batman Forever* was initially "a far deeper 'character study' of Batman than any previous big screen adaptation of the character to date," but that a number of key scenes were cut from the original script "in order to shorten the film and simplify its narrative" (183).

[33] In response to these attacks, Keaton joked that he was "a little nervous [...] about the scene where [he] fantasize[s] making love to Mary Magdalene" (Corliss).

[34] The creation of the Joker is a matter of some dispute. Steranko claims that the Joker was "the sole creation of Jerry Robinson" (47), although, according to Daniels, Bob Kane insisted "that he himself had already originated [the character] with writer Bill Finger" (40). In either case, both Robinson and Kane admitted that the character's unusual appearance was inspired by pictures of "actor Conrad Veidt in the makeup he wore to play the disfigured hero [in the 1928 film] *The Man Who Laughs*" (Daniels 40).

[35] Darius believes that one of Nolan's jobs was to "eras[e] the cinematic audience's memory of [Schumacher's] *Batman and Robin*" (151), a task that he accomplished, in part, by redesigning the costume.

[36] Reflecting on the derivation of the name "Patrick Bateman" in Ellis's novel, Carla Freccero wonders, in fact, if it directly refers to "Norman Bates? Batman?" (51).

[37] While both *Batman Begins* and Reinhart's reaction to *Batman Returns* reflect a sensitivity toward the portrayal of Batman as a killer, a recent episode of *Dexter* actually refers to Batman in this context. Commenting on the popularity of the "Bay Harbor Butcher" (a serial killer who only kills criminals) with the public, FBI agent Frank Lundy affirms, "Everybody in Miami thinks they've found their own personal Batman" ("Dex, Lies, and Videotape").

CHAPTER EIGHT

DELIRIOUS POSTMODERNISM: BAZ LUHRMANN'S MOULIN ROUGE!

ROBERT MORACE

That Baz Luhrmann's *Moulin Rouge!* (2001) is a postmodern text is obvious, and was to reviewers, who, for the most part, used the term postmodern indiscriminately and pejoratively to sum up all that they believed to be wrong with the film. For these reviewers, "postmodern" is a synonym for excessive, mocking, narcissistic, self-indulgent, self-involved, superficial, hyper-stylized, hyper-ironic, inhumane, etc. "Textbook postmodernism at its worst," complained Jose Arroyo in *Sight & Sound*; "a relentless *pastiche* of pop-cultural sounds and representations sutured into the service of a cliché." "Empty spectacle," lamented the *Houston Chronicle*'s Eric Harrison. The film's "roaring—some would say maddening—cinematic language," said the *New Yorker*'s John Lahr, "personifies the hellish interior space of contemporary life: what art critic John Berger, speaking of Bosch's vision of hell, calls the disparate, fragmentary present . . . a kind of spatial delirium. . . . The old musicals were about flow and the feel of humanity; 'Moulin Rouge' is about interruption and the feel of technology. What you get is sensation without joy." "The only real interest stirred by the plot is in recognition—picking out the occasional lift," warned the *New Republic*'s Stanley Kauffmann of a film that, according to *Slate*'s David Edelstein, "fails as a melodrama and is a disaster as a musical."

The Postmodern

Although it will never be a candidate for best-loved musical (that honor goes to *Singin' in the Rain*), the vehemence with which many reviewers responded to *Moulin Rouge!* will surprise those who recall that Luhrmann's film won two Academy Awards (for Best Art Direction and

Best Costumes) and was nominated for six others (Best Actress, Best Cinematography, Best Editing, Best Makeup, Best Picture and Best Sound.) The specific nature of the film's postmodernism and its singular and arguably unrepeatable accomplishment as a postmodern work deserve closer examination than the dismissive assumptions of Arroyo, Lahr and others allow, beginning with a brief descriptive (rather than evaluative) summary of postmodernism's key features. These include the "incredulity toward metanarratives" and "the blossoming of techniques and technologies" that Jean-François Lyotard first described and that have led us from the search for transcendent truth to the production of marketable forms of knowledge:

> The decline of [grand, or meta-] narrative can be seen as an effect of the blossoming of techniques and technologies since the Second World War which has shifted emphasis from the ends of action to its means; it can also be seen as an effect of the redeployment of advanced liberal capitalism after its retreat under the protection under Keynesianism during the period 1930-1960, a renewal that has eliminated the communist alternative and valorized individual enjoyment. (Lyotard 37-38)

Fredric Jameson has identified the more specific constitutive features and consequences of this paradigm shift: a "new depthlessness," new syntagmatic relationships, and new "emotional groundtone"; a weakened historical sense; the total flow of modern media; the spread of multinational capitalism; the primacy of the image, and the "pure and random play of signifiers in some heightened bricolage: metabooks which cannibalize other books, metatexts which collate bits of others texts" (Jameson 6, 96). The result in the case of *Moulin Rouge!* is a *mise-en-abîme* of *mise-en-scène*—"spectacular spectacular" (the title of the musical within the musical that is *Moulin Rouge!*)—in which the stern voice and visage of Christian's Scottish Calvinist father is supplanted by the succession and intersection of fragmented voices, images, signs, and spectacles, hurled about without end until "The End," itself a sign within this cinematic sign of the postmodern times.

The "wild eclecticism" (McFarlane) and intense physicality of images, voices, and other signifiers, seemingly emancipated from any Higher Purpose, recalls Susan Sontag's privileging of an erotics over a hermeneutics of art, Roland Barthes's deconstructive semiotics, Gilles DeLeuze and Felix Guitarri's rhizomatics and thousand plateaus, Jacques Lacan's overstimulated schizophrenic "reduced to an experience of pure material signifiers" (Jameson 26-27), Guy Debord's "society of the spectacle" and Jean Baudrillard's "ecstasy of communication" with its "general metastasis of value" (qtd. in Best and Kellner 136). In postmodern times as in postmodern art, "The world momentarily loses its depth and thereby threatens to become a glossy skin, a stereoscopic illusion, a rush of filmic images without density. But," Jameson goes on to ask, "is this now a terrifying or exhilarating experience?" (34).What terrifies, or exhilarates, is the postmodern space, or hyperspace, having exceeded the individual's ability to locate him- or herself within it. To understand *Moulin Rouge!* as a postmodern text, that is to say, as just such a delirious and disorienting space, as just such a "profoundly relational" "ecology" (Jameson 168, 174-175) or "rush of filmic images," requires recognizing and avoiding the traps into which many reviewers stumbled: either dismissing Luhrmann's film musical—or "musical cinema" as he prefers to call it (Germain)—as "noise" (Van Meter) or reading it nostalgically, measuring it against the supposed purity (and intelligibility) of the past (the Golden Age of film musicals.)

Stam's Theory of Adaptation

We can gain a better understanding of *Moulin Rouge!* as a postmodern text and of the kind of cognitive mapping (see Jameson 51-52 and 415) it both embodies and requires, by considering it from a seemingly unrelated angle. This is Robert Stam's essay "Beyond Fidelity," which provides an especially useful if not entirely new approach to film adaptations. Objecting to criticism of many film adaptations of literary novels as "profoundly moralistic" (a criticism that parallels reviews which faulted Luhrmann's alleged infidelity to "the musical"), Stam rejects "the chimera of fidelity" in favor of an approach that, instead of deriding film for its belatedness in relation to the novel, acknowledges and emphasizes film's far greater complexity of resources: word, image, sound. For example, characters in film are much more complexly rendered than in novels in so far as each character exists as "an uncanny amalgam of photogenie, body movement, acting style, and grain of voice, all amplified and molded by lighting, mise-en-scène, and music" (Stam 60) and often further affected and enriched by the actor's reputation and/or star status. Stam also emphasizes that film is not only a particularly synaesthetic art; it is an unusually synthetic one as well. It cannibalizes and incorporates not only other films but other media as well, far beyond the capacity of the novel, which Bakhtin defined as an anti-*genre* precisely because of its capacity for cannibalizing prior *genre*s. It is a tendency which, as we have already seen, culminates in postmodernism's "heightened bricolage."

Of course, *Moulin Rouge!* is not an adaptation, at least not in the conventional sense, least of all of an earlier novel (the situation to which Stam limits himself.) Nonetheless, *Moulin Rouge!* may be approached as an adaptation of a postmodern kind because it is a film that gives the impression of being an adaptation. It is a Baudrillardian simulacrum, that is, a copy without an original, "a real without origin or reality: a hyperreal," woven of its transtextual permutational relations and calling forth the typically postmodern "spectre raised by simulation": "that truth, reference and objective causes have ceased to exist" (Baudrillard, 168). What does exist is the intense intertextuality Bakhtin first described. Because "all texts are tissues of anonymous formulae, conscious or unconscious quotation, and conflation and inversion of other texts," adaptation, Stam contends, should be understood and evaluated "less as an attempted resuscitation of an original word than a turn in an ongoing dialogical process . . . of recycling, transformation, and transmutation, with no clear point of origin"—a condition which *Moulin Rouge!* furthers and foregrounds.

Understanding that "intertextuality can be conceived in a shallow or a deep manner," with the latter "rooted in social life and history," Stam adopts Gerard Genette's Bakhtin-inspired theory of transtextuality ("all that puts one text in relation, whether secret or manifest, with other texts") (Stam 64-65). Transtextuality comprises five more or less distinct kinds of intertextuality: quotation, allusion, plagiarism, generic markers, and relations between texts and paratexts (everything from titles and interviews to the kind of bonus materials found on DVDs). Stam then refines his theory of adaptation with a grammar of nine transformational operations, two of which—selection and reculturalization—are especially pertinent to a consideration of *Moulin Rouge!* as an adaptation in the form of a simulacrum. Selection, in *Moulin Rouge!*, refers not to scenes drawn from the source novel, the hypotext, but instead to those elements chosen from the vast intertextual range available to Luhrmann. In the case of *Moulin Rouge!*, for which there is no specific hypotext, reculturalization refers to differences in time and sensibility not only between the period during which the story is set (the *Belle Epoque*) and the period during which the film is produced and exhibited but between the latter and the Golden Age of film musicals (roughly 1930 to 1960) as well.

Intertextual Extravaganza

If *Moulin Rouge!* is, as Jonathan Van Meter claims in the *Independent on Sunday*, "a very hard-to-describe film"—"*Rocky Horror Picture Show* meets *Titanic*," "*The Wizard of Oz* meets *Apocalypse Now*"—then the reason derives from multiple sources. One is the density and range of intertextual reference. Another is what that density and range suggest about the film's status as simulated adaptation. The third is the film's embodying in extreme form the characteristically postmodern attitude of being "no longer . . . encumbered with the embarrassment of non-simultaneities and non-synchronicities" (Jameson 310). And the last is the fact that *Moulin Rouge!*'s intertextuality is "rooted in social life and history" (Stam 64). At some point, someone (or some committee) may try to compile a more or less complete list—preferably in the form of DVD—of the film's intertextual references. Here I will only call attention to the immense range of the film's intertextuality and the manner in which these references are deployed and combined. The decision to limit results from two practical issues and one theoretical consideration. The practical limitations involve both the finite space of this essay and the limits of this or any viewer's command of the various source texts to which *Moulin Rouge!* alludes.

Although many of these sources—the songs, most obviously—are easily identifiable, others (a particular look or shot for example, are not, especially in a film such as *Moulin Rouge!* in which Luhrmann, despite his being involved in every aspect of production and post-production, played the part of originator rather than elaborator (as gaffer Steve Mathis explains in Bosley). As a result, *Moulin Rouge!* is a collaborative effort to an extent unusual even for film, the most collaborative of all the arts. The theoretical consideration referred to above concerns a matter which at first glance will seem antithetical to a film adaptation of a source text, or, in the case of *Moulin Rouge!,* source texts of various kinds. This is the particular use I make of Bakhtin's understanding of the role of the reader, or in this case, the viewer, as co-creator, which I believe is very much in the spirit of *Moulin Rouge!* as a collaboration (this despite the complaints of hostile reviewers who faulted Luhrmann for being narcissistic and anal retentive.) According to Bakhtin, who is here referring to the relations between texts and readers in (or over) time, "Creative understanding does not renounce itself, its place in time, its own culture; *and it forgets nothing*" (Bakhtin 7; emphasis added.) In the case of *Moulin Rouge!,* creative understanding involves relations that are more spatial than temporal (recall the "new

syntagmatic relationships" that Jameson associates with postmodernism.)
Moulin Rouge! is intertextually exhaustive and encyclopedic not simply
because of all that it synechdochically and allusively includes but because
of all that it triggers in the viewer's mind (or cinematic imagination) so
that even a specific fleeting look, gesture or camera angle becomes a
Foucauldian node in a vast cinematic network which begins with the
filmmakers' (Luhrmann's and his co-creators') intentions and ends at the
farther reaches of the audience's collective cinematic memory.

The film's immense (and for this part of the discussion mainly
"authorial" intentional) intertextual range includes not only specific songs
(whole or in part), but song *genres*, styles and eras, covered, excerpted,
juxtaposed, sampled, recontextualized and recombined: Rogers and
Hammerstein and Kurt Cobain, cancan and hip hop, love songs and camp
carnival music, schmaltzy ballad and raunchy techno. The "Elephant Love
Medley" presents excerpts serially. Ziedler/Broadbent's recontextualized
rendering of Queen's "The Show Must Go On" works differently, echoing
42nd Street's "On with the Show" as well as the 1929 film on which it was
based, with visual echoes of *Evita* and *A Star Is Born*. Although it was
never a hit and therefore is not as readily identifiable to filmgoers as, say,
the Beatles' "All You Need Is Love," "On with the Show" resonates
differently—more obliquely and arguably more deeply—by creating a
parallel between Satine, dying of consumption, and Queen's Freddy
Mercury, dying of AIDS. Christina Aguilera, Lil' Kim, Mya, and Pink's
cover of Patti LaBelle's "Lady Marmalade" involves one kind of
collaboration, the two composited tango numbers quite another, and David
Bowie and Massive Attack's transatlantic cover of Nat King Cole's 1950s'
version of Eden Ahbez's "Nature Boy" yet a third, further complicated and
enriched by having Beck cover Bowie's "Diamond Dogs" elsewhere on
the film's soundtrack. "Hindi Sad Diamonds" comprises Anu Malik's
"Chamma Chamma" borrowed from the 1998 Bollywood action film
China Gate (1957 (a remake of *Seven Samurai* (1947) and *The
Magnificent Seven* "Diamonds Are a Girl's Best Friend" (heard earlier in
the film), and "The Hindi," an original composition by Steve Sharples.
Although it sounds like an old standard, "Come What May" is another
original composition, one which, because of Academy rules, could not be
nominated for Best Song because it had been written for Lurhmann's
previous film, *Romeo + Juliet* (1996), even though it not been used there.

Moulin Rouge!'s intertextual range also includes specific musi- cals,
most obviously in the film's first part, *The Sound of Music* (1965) and

Gentlemen Prefer Blonde (1953) as well as the full range of musical *genre*s and house styles, from the integrated musicals of Fred Astaire and Gene Kelly to the aggregate, or non-integrative, musicals of Busby Berkeley. On one hand, *Moulin Rouge!* is the most fully integrated film musical ever made because everything in it serves the love story. On the other hand, *Moulin Rouge!* is the apotheosis of the Berkeley aesthetic, with its emphasis on "heterogeneity over homogeneity, spectacle over story, excess over restraint, delay over progression" (Cohan 18) and its ambition "to spectacularize the entire film . . ." (Rubin 161). For in *Moulin Rouge!* "the entire film is the 'number'" (Macfarlane). Luhrmann's film also incor- porates recent variations on or mutations of the film musical (eg, music videos) while alluding to the pre- and early history of the film musical: in opera (Jacques Offenbach's *Orpheus in the Underworld*, Giacomo Puccini's *La Bohème*, and Giuseppe Verdi's *La Traviata*), stage drama, stage musical, revue, and circus, as well as the revival of the stage musical, *Les Miserables* in particular, even Bollywood with its distinctive narrative grammar (mixing comedy and tragedy, drama, song and dance, action and musical interlude) and, for the western audience, decidedly exotic yet strangely familiar materials. Luhrmann's *Moulin Rouge!* bears the same title and has a similar interest in color effects as John Huston's 1952 *Moulin Rouge* (one of sixteen "Moulin Rouge" titles listed on the Internet Movie Database and twenty-two Moulin Rouge based or themed films overall.) But Luhrmann's story line and some of the film's energy, color effects and exuberance as well as the shot of the fleeing Count quote Jean Renoir's *French Can Can* (1955).

Backstage film musicals such as *French Can Can* and *Singin' in the Rain* (1952) play an important part in *Moulin Rouge!* but so do non-musical backstage films such as Marcel Carné's *Les Enfants du Paradis* and the Marx Brothers' minimally musical *A Night at the Opera* (1935). The range of cinematic reference is astonishing: everything from *Black Orpheus* (1959) and *Black Narcissus* (1946) to *The Red Shoes* (1949) and *The Blue Angel* (1930) *Sunrise* (1927) to *Sunset Boulevard* (1927) chorus numbers to prop dancing, Federico Fellini to Vincente Minnelli (there is the same "fascinating mixture of *Kunst* and kitsch" in *Moulin Rouge!* that James Naremore finds in Minnelli's musicals [303]); silent film, sepia prints, frame tales and the quest archetype also play their parts, as does *Casablanca* (1942) whose airport searchlight becomes the windmill's rotating blades. *Moulin Rouge!* is rife with anachronisms but also with "authentic" period detail, some of it realistic in effect, some not, but all of it intertextually postmodern: nineteenth century symbols as nineteenth

century symbols (the caged bird, for example) and allusions as allusions
to, for example, Édouard Manet's *Olympia*, Toulouse-Lautrec's paintings
and posters, Edgar Degas' dark, fragmentary scenes backstage, in
performance or in rehearsal. Like *Moulin Rouge!*, the real Moulin Rouge
is itself a point of intersection where various classes, styles, cultures meet.
According to Christian it is a combination night club, dance hall and
bordello, according to the hyper-wised up Luhrmann, it is "a Can-Can
besotted version of Steve Rudell's discocrazed Studio 54 with Bangkok's
sex market meets Mardi Gras carnival" (Luhrmann qtd. in Litson).

The film's characters similarly serve as points of intersecting
intertextual reference, wearing allusions the way they wear their costumes
and make-up. (The costumes and make-up often are allusions.) Christian
is the young Scot played by a young Scot, Ewan McGregor, who had
played an Iggy Pop/Kurt Cobain-like rock star in *Velvet Goldmine*, the
lover in *The Pillow Book* who quite literally becomes a written text, and
the mainlining main character in music-rich *Trainspotting*. Christian is the
pilgrim who comes to Paris in search of love but who is subsequently
mistaken for a count while pretending to be an English writer. The
character is based on Orpheus but recalls other operatic figures—*La
Bohème*'s Rudolpho and *La Traviata*'s Alfredo—as well as musical stars
Dick Powell and Gene Kelly, hat on head, sweater draped around his
shoulders. Kidman's Satine is, like Christian, like so many of the musical
numbers, and "above all" (as the film likes to say) like the film itself,
another intertextual medley or amalgam. She is Eurydice to Christian's
Orpheus, the seamstress Mimi, who works in satins and silks, from *La
Bohème* (an adaptation of Henri Murger's *La Vie de la Bohème*), the
courtesan Violetta from *La Traviata* (and Alexandre Dumas' *La Dame aux
Camélias*), Marilyn Monroe, Madonna, Marlene Dietrich, Talcotte Carol
(in *Lola Montes*), and much more—Greta Garbo, Gloria Swanson,
Veronica Lake, Betty Grable, Judy Garland—including Nicole Kidman
herself as star and therefore as endless photographic and cinematic object
of the male gaze. As Graham Fuller has explained:

> When Satine descends on a swing above the slavering punters in the
> Moulin Rouge, she is dressed as Marlene Dietrich in *The Blue Angel*. The
> song she sings (in a raspy Rosalind Russell voice) is Marilyn Monroe's
> "Diamonds Are a Girl's Best Friend" *from Gentlemen Prefer Blondes*.
> But when Satine segues into "Material Girl," it's not simply Madonna who
> is inscribed, but Monroe again, since in her video for the song Madonna
> dressed as Monroe in her pink gown from the "Diamonds" number. That
> Kidman resembles Ann-Margaret playing Las Vegas in the scene adds to
> its complex allure.

The "complex allure" of Luhrmann's hyperactive intertextuality as well as the vertigo and sense of *déjà vu* it induces in the hyper-stimulated viewer characterizes not just this scene, which will end with Satine cast in yet another role, that of the consumptive tragic heroine of Nineteenth Century opera. It characterizes every scene, indeed virtually every one of *Moulin Rouge!*'s more than four thousand shots, from the most frenetically edited to slow-motion/freeze frame sequences which resemble slide shows of pictures at an impressionist exhibition. (Far from being the frantically paced film that so many reviewers condemned and that so many viewers misremember, *Moulin Rouge!* alternates hyper-active editing and slow-paced scenes much the way it alternates between its two main color effects, red and blue, and, in typical Bollywood style, between drama and farce.) Immediately after her high-wire swoon, Satine, a courtesan playing a music hall *artiste* aspiring to be "a real actress" modeled on Sarah Bernhardt, reappears dressed and coiffed like Rita Hayworth in *Gilda* but sounding as breathy as Monroe before going to her assignation in the Indian-themed boudoir with the count/English writer/Scottish naïf/pilgrim.

At one point, she hurls Christian across the room and onto the bed as we have seen done to other sexy women in other bedrooms in grand S&M style by Macgregor's/Christian's fellow Scot, Sean Connery, in so many James Bond movies (including *Diamonds Are Forever.*) But then, just before the courtesan/artiste morphs into the innocent, sweet-faced girl next door, Kidman/Satine reminds us of Shirley MacLaine, not so much the MacLaine of the musicals *Sweet Charity* and *Can-Can* (or the comedy *Irma La Douce*) but the MacLaine of *Being There* who performs for her comically naïve partner, Chauncey Gardiner, Chance the Gardner, who "just likes to watch." John Leguizamo's Toulouse-Lautrec, with his exaggerated lisp and short stature, reminds us less of José Ferrer's character in Huston's *Moulin Rouge* (or the real five-foot tall Toulouse-Lautrec at the real Moulin Rouge) than of the dwarfish as well as outlandish Toulouse-Lautrec of the popular imagination (with more than a touch of the art historian Sister Wendy Beckett, earnest, lisping host of the popular PBS art series, as Leguizamo has acknowledged ["Actor Inspired"]). Later, dressed as a sitar, Leguizamo's Toulouse will look like the hookah-smoking caterpillar from Disney's *Alice in Wonderland*, an appropriate, even logical change given his earlier function as White Rabbit and Kylie Minogue's Tinkerbell-like Green Fairy. That Polish-born, Australian-based actor Jacek Korman plays the narcoleptic Argentinan tango-dancing sitar player adds to the film's complex allure and postmodern, postnational complexity.

Not surprisingly, *Moulin Rouge!* includes many allusions to Luhrmann's earlier work: a 1994 production of Benjamin Britten's opera *A Midsummer Night's Dream*, set in a Maharajah's palace; his 1993 production of *La Bohème*, with its neon sign, L'Amour; his film adaptation of Shakespeare's *Romeo and Juliet*; and, less obviously but just as importantly Peter Brooks's decidedly postcolonial 1985 production of the Indian epic *Mahabharata*, on which Lurhmann assisted. But most references are, as the above examples indicate, much more accessible, parts as it were of the public domain: the pop-up book entry to Montmartre, Georges Méliès's moon, the Lumière Brothers' train, the cartoon-like effects, including sound effects ("whish whish"), a flamboyantly operatic style so campy that Cosmo Landesman has called *Moulin Rouge!* "the biggest, most opulent, ravishing and gloriously gay movie ever made—well, next to *Top Gun*, that is."

"Both a Synesthetic and a Synthetic Art"

As Stam explains, film is not only the most intertextual and cannibalistic of all the arts ("cinema carries this cannibalization to its paroxysm" [61]); it is also the most technological. (This is a point that is central to Stam's cutting edge theory of film adaptation and that is obscured by the tendency to think of films in terms of narrative, thereby subordinating technical and technological means to narrative ends.) Cinema exists as "both a synesthetic and a synthetic art, synesthetic in its capacity to engage various senses (sight and hearing) and synthetic in its capacity to absorb and synthesize antecedent arts" (61). Concerning the former, Stam writes:

> Each medium has its own specificity deriving from its respective materials of expression. The novel has a single material of expression, the written word, whereas the film has at least five tracks: moving photographic image, phonetic sound, music, noises, and written materials. In this sense, the cinema has not lesser, but rather greater resources for expression than the novel *and this is independent of what actual filmmakers have done with these resources* (Stam 59, emphasis added).

It is what its actual filmmakers have done with these resources that greatly contribute to the delirious postmodernism of *Moulin Rouge!* "*Mise-en-scène*, editing and sound, in all their sub-categories, constitute the language of cinema," Brian McFarlane notes, "and there is scarcely a moment in *Moulin Rouge!* when Luhrmann is not making them all work tirelessly." Thanks to the bonus material on the 2-disk *Moulin Rouge!*

DVD and, much more importantly, articles by Jo Liston in *Entertainment Design*, Rachael K. Bosley in *American Cinematographer* and Joe Fordham in *Cineflex*, we now know a great deal about some of the elaborate work which went on behind the scenes in the making of this postmodern backstage film musical. The articles and commentaries do more than explain how the filmmakers created the "heightened reality" effect which characterizes all of Luhrmann's "Red Curtain Trilogy" (*Strictly Ballroom* [1992] and *Romeo + Juliet* [1996] and *Moulin Rouge!*) in general; they help explain how *Moulin Rouge!* exploits cinema's potential as the most "synesthetic and synthetic" of the arts so fully, expertly and entertainingly (arguably more so than any other film has done and perhaps ever will do.) Artistic director Catherine Talcott explains *Moulin Rouge!*'s *mise-en-scène*—everything from sets to costumes—in Litson's "Roughing It." Don McAlpine discusses in great detail his work as *Moulin Rouge!*'s cinematographer in Bosley's "Bohemian Rhapsody": his (first time) use of the Panavision/Kodak Preview System, formatting (anamorphic except for scenes that would feature CGI, where Super 35 was used), various film stocks, lenses and lighting. Joe Fordham's "Paris by Numbers" gets off to a fast start in providing unparalleled insight into the film's 300-plus special effects shots.

The approach of combining miniatures, digital and live-action elements to realize background environments would spring from early work on the film's opening shot, which begins with a wide view of Paris, then pushes towards a street leading to the gates of Montmartre. . . . Talcott and her art department initiated the design of the opening shot by creating Photoshop collages of Paris based on period prints of the city. Using those, Chris Godfrey assembled a view of Paris, built in 2D layers, and animated a low-tech move into the image, producing what became 'the postcard effect." 'The idea was that we would first see a view of Paris, 1900, that would look aged,' Godfrey commented. 'Then we would start to move past these layers that looked like theatrical flats or a pop-up postcard—but with live action projected on them showing hundreds of people walking along the street, passing you in a 2D plane. Then 2D would become 21/2D—which is 3D squeezed in "z" depth—then slowly become 3D, then models, then live action." (16, 19)

Just as the filmmakers could create the illusion of depth (*as* illusion) in shots of exterior scenes of a film shot entirely on a soundstage by, for example, constructing models "in one-third, one-fifth and one-eighth scales, then backed by a painted cyclorama" (19), they could create a very different kind of depth intertextually. Broadly speaking, the scene of Christian's arrival in Paris at the Gare du Nord harks back to the beginnings of film in one of the Lumiére Brothers' earliest *actualités*, *L'arrivée d'un train en gare de La Ciotat* (*The Arrival of a Train at La Ciotat Station*, 1895); more specifically, the scene recalls both the beginning of F. W. Murnau's *Sunrise* (1927) (another film which begins with a postcard coming to life) and the segue from the Kit Kat club to the train station early in the film version of *Cabaret* (1972) in which another young writer arrives in a foreign as well as decadent city (Berlin.) (The fact that Bob Fosse's 1972 film is based on John Kander and Fred Ebb's 1966 musical, itself adapted from Christopher Isherwood's *Berlin Stories* (1946) and John Van Druten's 1951 stage version, *I Am a Camera*, thickens the intertextual stew.) And as Christian makes his way from the station to Montmartre, he passes through a more cheerful version of a street scene witnessed a few moments earlier, one which recalls the opening Boulevard of Crime scene of *Les Enfants du Paradis* (1945).

Thus, intertextual "quoting" affects every aspect of the film, from the blatantly obvious (the look and texture and jittery feel of old film stock, which, for the closing credits sequence, turns out is not a bit of computer simulation but a painstaking recreation) to the more subtly rendered effects of lighting, editing, costuming, set design, cinematography and CGI. As Todd McCarthy explains in *Variety*, "both cinematographer [Don McAlpine] and the f/x crew have gone far beyond the usual smooth CGI look of most modern films by combining elements in a satisfyingly rough, handhewn manner." Close-ups, for example, contribute to the film's overall effect. Some are rendered as freeze frames or near-freeze frames of period paintings, others simultaneously recall ads for not one but two Stanley Kubrick films: one of Malcolm MacDowell as Alex in *A Clockwork Orange* (1971) and the other of Kidman herself as the wife (the Tom Cruise character's wife!) in *Eyes Wide Shut*. Other close-ups are done as glamour shots taken not from a distance with a long lens, but shot with the actors three feet from a 40-50mm anamorphic lens, to create a sense of immediacy (Bosley), as well as of something more as the two-dimensional screen is used to create not just the illusion of a third dimension, but the hyperreality of a fourth.

Dream Time

Reviewers' efforts to pin down an art that at times amazed and often annoyed, in which the allusions are both singular and successive *and* layered and simultaneous, is itself noteworthy, especially given their penchant for describing the film's supposed shortcomings by means of similes and metaphors so different from, even opposed to the film's decidedly, at times ruthlessly synechdochic and metonymic style. "Hijacked from their moorings, they [snippets from songs] float aimlessly" (Mitchell). "A visual feast that leaves you famished"; "like a piano with its pedal removed, there's no sustain, just a moment-to-moment agitation that bursts over the screen and then dissolves, forgotten" (Quinn). "Luhrmann is like a hamster on a wheel" (Zacharek), the viewer is like someone "trapped in an elevator with a circus" (Ebert) or a victim of "assault and battery" (Edelstein), and the film itself, "drunk on its own daring" (Travers), is like "two hours of cranked-up movie trailers" (Guthmann) and "a head-on collision of the romantic and the grotesque" (Corliss). "A gorgeous folly" to some (Travers), "empty excess" to others (Edelstein), *Moulin Rouge!* is "self-reflexive, but not in any way that requires—or repays—much thought" (Harrison).

Moulin Rouge! may not provide much time for thinking, but it certainly offers ample reason to think. "Sooner or later everyone comes to Rick's" (*Casablanca*), and sooner or later everyone and everything seems to show up in a film in which more than the archetypes are holding a reunion (to borrow Umberto Eco's description of *Casablanca* in particular and cult films in general.) *Moulin Rouge!* explores and exploits all of film musical's many technical and aesthetic means, cultural contexts and related forms; in it boundaries blur and categories (including those with which scholars of film musicals are particularly obsessed) either intersect or dissolve altogether. But to what effect? *Moulin Rouge!*'s stylish postmodernism allows Lurhmann and his audience to indulge in "the *genre*'s nostalgic pleasures"—the hackneyed plots, depthless characters, corny passions and cornier songs and corniest of all, the bursting into song (Cohan, "Introduction" 1)—including the commercialized nostalgia of film anthologies such as *That's Entertainment* and *That's Dancing*. At the same time, *Moulin Rouge!* avoids being merely nostalgic (or merely commercial or merely self-indulgent—with Luhrmann playing of Dr. Seuss's Cat in the Hat, proudly and peremptorily proclaiming "Look at me, Look at me now".) But can *Moulin Rouge!* also escape the charge of using the past merely to create a typically postmodern sense of "pseudohistorical depth" (Jameson 20)?

For Lael Ewy the answer is simple: "At best, *Moulin Rouge!* is a lot of fun. At worst, it represents the erasure of history." But the answer to that

question depends on how we use the word "history." As Richard Dyer
points out, far from being escapist entertainment, film musicals respond to
history in a special way, through their form. And as Jane Feuer and
Talcott Rubin have noted, no form is as self-consciously aware of its
history and as adept at incorporating that history as the film musical. As
Feuer has persuasively argued, the MGM musical quotes earlier stage
forms because it aspires to be what, as a form of Twentieth Century mass
art, it is not and cannot be: folk art. The reason it does so, explains Feuer,
drawing on Claude Levi-Strauss's structuralist analysis myth and Albert F.
McLean's *American Vaudeville as Ritual*, has to do with "the function of
ritual and the ritual function of the musical. All ritual involves the
celebration of shared values and beliefs, and the ritual function of the
musical is to articulate and to reaffirm the place that entertainment
occupies in its audience's psychic lives. Self-reflexive musicals . . .
celebrate myths created by the *genre* as a whole" (Feuer, "The Self-
Reflexive Musical" 38). (And not just "the *genre* as a whole" in so far as
"the world of the musical [is], as Thomas Elsaesser says, "a kind of ideal
image of the [film] medium itself" [qtd. in Feuer, "The Self-Reflexive
Musical" 38].)

   Useful and influential as it has been, Feuer's approach does not, and
can not, quite explain *Moulin Rouge!* or its particular hold on our wised-
up, self-reflexive and highly self-conscious postmodern imagination. In
part this is because Feuer conceives of ritual (as Rick Altman also does) in
rather abstract, even formalist terms that cannot adequately account for
Moulin Rouge!'s dense intertextual texture. And it is also because the
self-reflexivity of backstage musicals, which Feuer rightly contends serves
"to perpetuate rather than to deconstruct the codes of this *genre*," hardly
applies to the far more extreme self-reflexivity of *Moulin Rouge!* (Rather,
the film musical's self-reflexivity seems to encourage a sense of
continuity, as in Stephen Hunter's claim that "in the movie musical, the
arrival of postmodernism could easily be missed because no *genre* is as
artificial as this one." True, but no musical is quite as artificial and quite as
artificial in quite so many ways as *Moulin Rouge!*.) We must also be wary
of making too much of *Moulin Rouge!* as an example of the deconstructive
metafictional musical identified by Jim Collins—films such as *All That
Jazz* (1979) and *Pennies from Heaven* (1981) that "explode codes and
conventions in an attempt to parody or critique the *genre*" (Collins 277).
In the case of *Moulin Rouge!* what we need to understand is the way in
which postmodern, deconstructive and metafictional means contribute to,
even create, the film's particular ritualistic effect.

Put simply, how can *Moulin Rouge!* be at once a "museum of cinema" (McFarlane), a "Dionysian theme park" (Jensen), "a ribbon of dream" (Orson Welles's description of all film) *and* a postmodern version of the Hollywood dream dump that Todd Hackett comes upon in Nathanael West's 1939 novel, *The Day of the Locust*? How can it mani- fest, in what we see and what we hear and in how we see and how we hear, the "archaeological dig through the history of the musical" that Luhrmann and his team undertook before filming began (Luhrmann, qtd. in Fuller and in "Baz Knows the Score"), the four years they spent "cracking" its code (Luhrmann, qtd. in Netherby), yet at the same time evoke the wonder of Luhrmann's primal, *Cinema Paradiso*-like encounter with the musical: seeing *Paint Your Wagon* (1969) while growing up "in the middle of nowhere in New South Wales" ("Baz Knows the Score") and Luhrmann's later encounter, just as he began conceiving his Red Curtain aesthetic (the stage version *Strictly Ballroom*), with Joseph Campbell's theory of a universal mythology (Andrew)?

The answer lies in the similarity between Luhrmann's *Moulin Rouge!* and Robert Coover's *The Public Burning* (1977), the only work that begins to match *Moulin Rouge!* in diversity, density and deployment of intertextual reference, as well as in pace, rhythm, extravagance, obsessiveness and effect. *The Public Burning* is a quintessentially post-modern novel and one of the chief examples of historiographic metafiction, the term Linda Hutcheon coined to rescue works such as *One Hundred Years of Solitude* and *Midnight's Children* from the charge of being mere metafictions lost in the funhouse of their own narcissistic self-reflexivity. Taking place over the three days leading up to the executions of Julius and Ethel Rosenberg in June 1953, Coover's 500-plus page novel creates "a mosaic of history," at once fantastical and strangely real. Coover recreates the times right down to the movies shown and the paranoia felt, all the while metafictionalizing the whole to expose the made-upness of history by depicting it as a 4-act drama *cum* 3-ring circus, with operatic intermezzos, Greek chorus and its very own clown, then Vice President Richard M. Nixon, whose narration of alternate chapters provides the kind of relief one finds in the love story segments from *Moulin Rouge!*'s often frenetic pace.

"Made up of thousands and thousands of tiny fragments that had to be painstakingly stitched together," *The Public Burning* "was like a gigantic impossible puzzle," Coover has said. "I was striving for a text that would seem to have been written by the whole nation through all its history, as though the sentences had been forming themselves all this time, accumulating toward this experience. I wanted thousands of echoes, all the sounds of the nation" (Coover, "An Interview" 75-76. This technique is especially evident in the *Public Burning*'s build-up towards a comically grotesque *grand guignol* showdown which forms the climax of the phantasmagoric Ed Sullivan-style variety show, presided over by Uncle Sam and culminating in the greatest show on earth: the public executions/exorcism of the Rosenbergs in New York's Times Square. In these chapters, the proliferating echoes are compressed and intensified to create what Roger Caillois calls "dream time." "This idea of a ritual bath of prehistoric or preconscious experience"—"the ritual return to the mythic roots of a group or people," Coover has explained—"was very attractive to me as I began developing the Rosenberg book, not merely for its contributions to the final section, but also because I realized that this was one of the great disruptive functions of art: to take the tribe back into dream time, pulling them in, letting them relive their preconscious life as formed for them by their tribe" (Coover, "An Interview," 74).

Adjusted for the difference between a decidedly national novel set during the Cold War but spanning all United States history (and researched and written by one person then living in England) and a highly collaborative musical set in *fin-de-siecle* Paris but made mainly in fin-de-millennium Australia in the image of the global economy and multi-national capitalism, Coover's remarks apply equally well to *Moulin Rouge!* (It is worth noting that in the short story collection *A Night at the Movies*, subtitled "You Must Remember This" and having a "Program" rather than a Table of Contents, Coover parodically takes on a multitude of films, film *genre*s, and film techniques, masterfully and hilariously deconstructing and recombining them.) Thinking of *Moulin Rouge!* in terms of dream time and as a historiographic metamusical explains a great deal about the film's nature and effect and why even several of Luhrmann's most critical reviewers found the film "ravishing" and "unforgettable."

It also helps explain why we are no more convinced by those who praise *Moulin Rouge!* on narrowly postmodern grounds as "a musical for the Napster age" (Bowman) than we are by those who damn it on the same grounds as an example of "textbook postmodernism." Thinking of *Moulin Rouge!* in terms of dream time and as a historiographic metamusical also helps us understand why we find similarly unconvincing Stacy Magedanz's taxonomic approach to the film's intertextuality and

Luhrmann's own explanations of *Moulin Rouge!* in terms of its Red Curtain aesthetic, its exaltation of story, and its recreating for the *fin-de-millennium* postmodern audience the feel of *fin-de-siecle* Moulin Rouge by creating a postmodern equivalent rather than a faithful and historically accurate facsimile.   (Luhrmann was closer to the mark when he said, concerning the film's underlying Orpheus myth, that *Moulin Rouge!* is "about growing up and coming to the point in your life when you realize that there are things bigger than yourself" [Fuller].) And it explains why *Moulin Rouge!* will not revive the film musical, not at least, as David Thomson thinks it will, by "showing a way ahead for that nearly moribund genre" (359), for as Uncle Sam explains in *The Public Burning*, we couldn't live this way all the time.

What *Moulin Rouge!* shows us is not the "way ahead." Rather, it shows us, as Stam's approach to adaptation helps us appreciate, all that film can do and metonymically, synechdochically, and above all intertextually, all that film has done and can do. Instead of looking ahead, *Moulin Rouge!* looks back, from a specifically postmodern point in time and with all the resources available to postmodern filmmakers, to a special time in film history, the Golden Age of film musicals, and to a historical period, the *Belle Epoque*, that has a special place in the cinematic imagination. *Moulin Rouge!* takes us back to the birth of the modern and of mass entertainment, to the city and the year in which Henry Adams found himself lying in the Gallery of Machines at the Great Exhibition, "his historical neck broken by the sudden irruption of forces wholly new" (Adams 382). *Moulin Rouge!* may not engage history as directly as Adams and Coover do, but this masterful celebration of film as the most collaborative, synaesthetic and synthethic of the arts engages history no less deeply. Utilizing the full range of technological and intertextual means available and made in the carnivalesque image of its namesake, *Moulin Rouge!* takes us back into dream time, letting us relive our preconscious life as formed for us by the tribe born of that "sudden irruption of forces wholly new," the force of cinema, "above all."

Works Cited

"Actor Inspired By Sister Wendy." *BBC News* 4 May 2001. *http://news.bbc.co.uk/1/hi/entertainment/ 1312989. stm*
Adams, Henry. *The Education of Henry Adams.* Sentry Edition. 1918; Boston: Houghton Mifflin, 1961.

Agresti, Aimee. "Yes She Can-Can." *Premiere* (American edition). February 2001: 68.

Altman, Rick. *The American Film Musical*. Indianapolis: Indiana UP, 1987.

—. "The American Film Musical as Dual-Focus Narrative." In Cohan 41-51.

—. "The Musical". In *The Oxford History of World Cinema*. Ed. Geoffrey Nowell-Smith. Oxford: Oxford UP, 1996: 294-303.

Andrew, Geoff. "Baz Luhrmann (1)." *Guardian* 7 September 2001. *http://www.guardian.co.uk/*Archive/Article/0,4273,4252667,00.html

Arroyo, Jose. "Moulin Rouge!" *Sight & Sound* September 2001. *http://www.bfi.org.uk/ sightandsound/ review/2000/*

Baudrillard, Jean. *Selected Writings*. Ed. Mark Poster. Stanford: Stanford UP, 1988.

"Baz Knows the Score." *The Observer* 19 August 2001. *http://film.guardian.co.uk/ interview / inter view pages/0,,539022,00. html*

Best, Steven and Douglas Kellner. *Postmodern Theory: Critical Interrogations*. New York: The Guilford P, 1991.

Bosley, Rachael K. "Bohemian Rhapsody." *American Cinematographer* 82 (June 2001): 38-51.

Bowman, James. Rev. of Moulin *Rouge! American Spectator* 34 (July/August 2001): 117-118.

Cohan, Steven. "Introduction: Musicals of the Studio Era," in Cohan, ed. *Hollywood Musicals* 1-16.

—. ed. *Hollywood Musicals: The Film Reader*. London & New York: Routledge, 2002.

Collins, James M. "The Musical." *Handbook of American Film Genres*. Ed. Wes D. Gehring. New York: Greenwood, 1988: 269-282.

Coover, Robert. "An Interview with Robert Coover." *Anything Can Happen: Interviews with American Writers*. Ed. Tom LeClair and Larry McCaffery. Urbana: U of Illinois P, 1983: 63-78.

—. *The Public Burning*. New York: Viking, 1977.

Corliss, Richard. "Face the Music: Hollywood at Last Awakes and Sings." *Time* 14 May 2001: 70.

Dyer, Richard. "Entertainment and Utopia." In Cohan, ed. 19-30.

Eco, Umberto. "Casablanca: Cult Movies and Intertextual Collage." In *Travels in Hyper Reality*. Trans. William Weaver. San Diego: Harcourt Brace Jovanovich, 1986: 197-211.

Edelstein, David. "Miracles Are Cheap." *Slate* 18 May 2001. *http:// www. slate.com/id/106186*

Ewy, Lael. "Moulin Rouge, the Erasure of History, and the Disneyfication of the Avant Garde." *EastWesterly Review http://www. Post modern-village. com/eastwest/issue7/7a-0003.html*

Feuer, Jane. *The Hollywood Musical.* 2nd ed. Bloomington: Indiana UP. 1993.

—. "The Self-Reflexive Musical and the Myth of Entertainment." In Cohan. 31-40.

Fordham, Joe. "Paris by the Numbers." *Cineflex* 86 July 2001: 16-20, 25-28, 119-122.

Fuller, Graham. "Strictly Red." *Sight & Sound* 11 June 2001: 14-16.

Germain, David. "Director Luhrmann Opens 'Red Curtain' For Latest Movie Musical." Associated Press 17 May 2001.

Guthman, Edward. "Red hot / 'Moulin Rouge' Reinvents Musical *Genre* with Audacious, Rapid-Fire Assault on the Senses." *San Francisco Chronicle* 1 June 2001: C1.

Harrison, Eric. "Superficial Spectacle: 'Moulin' Applies Lots of 'Rouge,' No Foundation." *Houston Chronicle* 1 June 2001: 1.

Hunter, Stephen. "'Moulin Rouge,' 'Knight's Tale': Making New Rules in Musicals; Stories from the past mix with music from the present as film's most unrealistic *genre* evolves." *Los Angeles Times* 1 June 2001: F13.

Hutcheon, Linda. *A Poetics of Postmodernism: History, Theory, Fiction.* London: Routledge, 1988.

Jameson, Fredric. *Postmodernism; or, The Cultural Logic of Late Capitalism.* Durham: Duke UP, 1991.

Kauffmann, Stanley. "Seeing Is Disbelieving." *The New Republic* 224 (11 June 2001): 28-29.

Lahr, John. "The Ringmaster." *New Yorker* 2 December 2001: 50-59.

Landesman, Cosmo. "Give 'Em the ew Razzle-Dazzle." *The Sunday Times* 9 September 2001: 10.

Litson, Jo. "Roughing It." *Entertainment Design* 35 (May 2001): 22-27.

Lyotard, Jean-Francois. *The Postmodern Condition: A Report on Knowledge.* Trans. Geoff Bennington and Brian Massumi. 1979; Minneapolis: U of Minnesota P, 1984.

McCarthy, Todd. "High-Kicking 'Rouge' Brings Razzle-Dazzle to Croisette." *Variety* 14-20 May 2001: 21, 28.

McFarlane, Brian. "The Movie as Museum." *Meanjin* 60 (2001): 212-218.

Magedanz, Stacy. "Allusion as Form: *The Waste Land* and *Moulin Rouge!*" *Orbis Litteraurm* 61, 2 (2005): 160-179.

Mikhail. Bakhtin, *Speech Genres & Other Late Essays*. Ed. Caryl
    Emerson and Michael Holquist. Trans. Vern W. McGee. Austin: U of
    Texas P, 1986.
Mitchell, Elvis. "Hey, Ginger and Fred, Glam Rocks." *New York Times* 12
    August 2001: 2: 23.
Moulin Rouge! Dir. Baz Luhrmann. Perf. Ewan McGregor, Nicole
    Kidman, Jim Broadbent, John Leguizamo, and Richard Roxburgh. 20th
    Century Fox, 2001.
Naremore, James. "Vincente Minnelli." In *The Oxford History of World
    Cinema*. Ed. Geoffrey Nowell-Smith. Oxford: Oxford UP, 1996. 302-
    303.
Netherby, Jennifer. "Helmer Does Legwork for Rouge Redux." *Variety* 1
    October 2001.
Quinn, Anthony. "Film: The Big Picture: A Visual Feast That Leaves You
    Famished." *The Independent* 7 September 2001. *http://findarticles.
    com/p/articles/mi_qn4158/is_20010907/ai_n14419715*
Rubin, Talcott. *Showstoppers: Busby Berkeley and the Tradition of the
    Spectacle*. New York: Columbia UP, 1993.
Stam, Robert. "The Dialogics of Adaptation." *Film Adaptation*. Ed. James
    Naremore. New Brunswick: Rutgers UP, 2000: 54-78.
Travers, Peter. "Moulin Rouge." *Rolling Stone*. 9 May 2001. *http://www.
    rollingstone.com/reviews/movie/5948391/review/5948392/moulin_
    rouge*
Van Meter, Jonathan. "Strictly Cancan." *Independent on Sunday* 18 March
    2001: Features 5-7.
Zacharek, Stephanie. "Moulin Rouge." Salon.com. 18 May 2001.
    *http://archive.salon.com/ent/movies/review/2001/05/18/moulin_ rouge/
    index.html*

CONTRIBUTORS

Stephen Brauer, Ph.D., is Associate Dean of First-Year Programs and Associate Professor of English at St. John Fisher College in Rochester, NY, where he teaches courses on U.S. literature and culture. He has published articles in American Quarterly, The CEA Critic, The Fitzgerald Review, and Working Papers on the Web, among others.

Donna M. Campbell, Ph.D., is Associate Professor of English at Washington State University. She is the author of *Resisting Regionalism: Gender and Naturalism in American Fiction, 1885-1915* (1997), and her articles have appeared in Studies in American Fiction, Legacy, and American Literary Realism. Recent publications include an essay on Edith Wharton in *Twisted from the Ordinary: Essays on American Literary Naturalism*, ed. Mary E. Papke (U of Tennessee Press, 2003), on Edna Ferber and Rose Wilder Lane in Middlebrow Moderns: *Popular Women Writers of the 1920s*, ed. Lisa Botshon and Meredith Goldsmith (Northeastern U P, 2003), and on the novel and film versions of James M. Cain's Mildred Pierce in The Novel and the American Left (U of Iowa Press, 2004). She writes the annual "Fiction: 1900-1930" chapter for American Literary Scholarship (Duke University Press).

Douglas L. Howard, Ph.D., is currently Assistant Academic Chair and an Associate Professor in the English Department at Suffolk County Community College in Selden, NY. His publications include articles, essays, and book chapters in *Literature and Theology, Poppolitics.com, The Chronicle of Higher Education, This Thing of Ours: Investigating The Sopranos, The Gothic Other: Racial and Social Constructions in the Literary Imagination* (co-editor and contributor), *Reading The Sopranos, Reading Deadwood, Reading 24*, and *Milton in Popular Culture*.

Anthony D. Hughes, Ph.D., is currently Professor of English at Hilbert College in Hamburg, NY where he teaches classes in Film Studies, Creative Writing, Poetry, and Literature. He also directs the College's Creative Studies Program which includes concentrations in Creative Writing and Film Studies. He completed his BA in English and his MA in Creative Writing, Poetry, from SUNY at Buffalo. He also received his

Ph.D. in English from SUNY at Buffalo where he studied Film Theory, Hawthorne, and Gender Studies. Over the past twenty years, he has presented numerous essays on education, writing, and film at local, regional, and national conferences and published poems in a wide variety of book anthologies, journals, and magazines. Most recently, he won runner up in the 2007 Bridport Poetry Prize in England for his poem, *Ephemeral*, and an Honorable Mention from the 2007 New Millennium poetry contest for his poem, *Bliss*. Dr. Hughes lives in Orchard Park, NY with his wife and son.

Miranda J. Hughes, Ph.D., has been an editor/writer for 20 years. Dr. Hughes received her BS from the University at Buffalo (State University of New York) and her Ph.D. from Weill Cornell Medical College (New York, NY) in Pharmacology. She currently works at the National Comprehensive Cancer Network (www.nccn.org) as an Oncology Scientist/Senior Medical Writer and lives in Wynnewood, Pennsylvania, with her husband and daughter. Her previous positions have included Annals of Internal Medicine, Journal of Infectious Diseases, and Turner White Communications.

Robert Morace, Ph.D., is Professor of English at Daemen College. His publications include *Irvine Welsh's 'Trainspotting'* (Continuum 2001), *The Dialogic Novels of Malcolm Bradbury and David Lodge* (Southern Illinois UP, 1989), *John Gardner: An Annotated Secondary Bibliography* (Garland, 1984), and *John Gardner: Critical Perspectives* (co-edited with Kathryn VanSpanckeren, Southern Illinois UP, 1982). His study of the Irvine Welsh phenomenon will be published by Palgrave Macmillan.

Lisa K. Nelson, Ph.D., is an Assistant Professor of English at Riverside Community College's Norco Campus (soon to be Norco College) to the East of Los Angeles. Her enthusiasm for the links between the academic and the political drew her back into academia after an early BFA in visual arts. She studied literature, gender, and representation at the University of Southern Maine. She received her MA from the University of California Riverside, where she studied gender, sexuality, literature, and popular culture. In both Maine and California, Dr. Nelson pursued avid interests in motorcycling and popular cultural analysis. Moving back East to New York, Dr. Nelson earned her Ph.D. at Columbia University, where an investigation of critical race studies enriched her former interests. Her dissertation, "Racing the Rebel; Romancing Rebellion", was an investigation of the conjunctions of discourses of race and masculinity at the sites of resistant bodies – rebels. The project is currently being proposed for publication, and Dr. Nelson is at work on her next project which examines the history of American leatherwear and its resonances with contested racial, national, and gender ideologies.

Thomas C. Renzi, Ph.D., is currently the Coordinator of Tutorial Services in the Academic Skills Center and has been an English instructor at Buffalo State University College since 1984. He followed an elaborately winding route to this present position. After receiving his BFA in music from the University at Buffalo (State University of New York), he played drums for various groups in Las Vegas and on the road before returning to University at Buffalo to earn his MA and Ph.D. in English. He has written several technical drum books and published three books dealing with one of his passions, film: *H.G. Wells: Six Scientific Romances Adapted for Film* (Scarecrow Press, 1992), *Jules Verne on Film* (McFarland, 1998), and *Cornell Woolrich, Pulp Noir, and the Noir Film* (McFarland, forthcoming.)

Barbara Tilley, Ph.D., is a Visiting Instructor in the English Department at the University of South Florida –Tampa where she teaches composition and takes the opportunity to expose young minds to the complexities of film, especially documentary film. Although her dissertation research at the University of Florida focused on Victorian images of men in the political New Woman novels of the British 1880s and 1890s, lately she has moved into the delicious realm of film and gender theory in the twentieth-century. Her current research focuses on the development and representation of the transgendered person in film.